Seton Lloyd

FOUNDATIONS IN THE DUST

THE STORY OF MESOPOTAMIAN EXPLORATION

with 80 illustrations

'. . . them that dwell in houses of clay
Whose foundation is in the dust,
Which are crushed before the moth!
Betwixt morning and evening they are destroyed.'

THE BOOK OF JOB

Thames and Hudson

Sources of the illustrations
The illustrations mentioned below are reproduced by courtesy of: British Museum, London, 3, 22, 30, 37, 40, 48, 50, 53, 54, 58, 63, 64; Hirmer Verlag, Munich, 56, 57, 65; Iraq Museum, Baghdad, 65; Professor Seton Lloyd, Frontispiece, 8, 9, 11, 14, 42, 66, 68, 71, 72, 74; Louvre, Paris, 32, 56, 57; Metropolitan Museum of Art, New York, 79; National Portrait Gallery, London, 31, 35; Professor David Oates, 77; Oriental Institute, Cambridge, 36; Oriental Institute, Chicago, 67; Staatliche Museen, Berlin DDR, 59, 60; State Antiquities and Heritage Organization, Baghdad, 69, 70, 73, 75, 76, 78; Wilfred Thesiger, 7; J. C. Thompson, 62; University of Newcastle-upon-Tyne, 18, 61.

Other sources are as follows: Alexander 1928, 5; Botta 1849, vol. I, 34; Buckingham 1827, vol. I, 15–17; vol. II, 10, 19, 20, 21, 23; Budge 1925, 26; Flandin and Coste, Voyage en Perse, Paris 1851, 27; Fundgruben des Orients, Vienna 1812, 12; Layard 1849a, vol. I, 41; vol. II, 43; Layard 1853a, vol. I, 13, 39, 44–7; vol. II, 38; Layard 1903, vol. I, 4; vol. II, 52; Loftus 1857, 49; Rassam 1897, 55; Rich 1836, vol. I, 24; vol. II, 25; Richardson 1840, 28, 29; Wigram 1914, 33. Ills. 1 and 2 were drawn by Hanni Bailey.

Frontispiece:
Layard in Bakhtiyari costume. A drawing by Ulrica Lloyd based on portraits in Layard's 'Early Adventures' and 'Autobiography and Letters'.

First published in 1947
Revised and enlarged edition © 1980 Thames and Hudson Ltd, London

Filmset in Great Britain by August Filmsetting, Reddish, Stockport
Printed in Spain

D.L. TO–676-80

Contents

Preface

The year in which this book was written coincided in time with the centenary of Sir Henry Layard's first great discoveries in the palace mounds of Assyria: a landmark in the exploration of Mesopotamian antiquity. With this in mind, my intention had been to recount the adventures of yet earlier travellers in that country, before turning to the long saga of archaeological research which Layard had unwittingly initiated. This fuller story could then be prolonged up to the middle years of the present century. For myself, endeavouring as I was at that time to make some further contribution in the same field, the instructive, and at times dramatic history of the enquiry itself had a peculiar fascination; and my familiarity over many years with the setting in which the action took place served to bring each episode into sharp perspective.

When the book first appeared in 1947 it was well received and further editions were printed; but from the late 1950s onwards it became hard to obtain. During more recent years the testimony of many friends and colleagues has suggested that my own continued affection for it might still be shared by others, and its frequent mention in favourable terms by critics of Mesopotamian literature has seemed finally to have confirmed this. My sincerest thanks are accordingly due to its new publishers for the action which they have taken to remedy this situation. Under its old title, it now reappears in an entirely new guise, complete with a final chapter bringing the archaeological narrative up to date, and generously garnished with illustrations.

The pictures are from various sources, but a high proportion originate in the records of early travellers and excavators: written (to quote Sir Leonard Woolley's introduction to my first edition) 'in the engaging full-blooded prose of their time and illustrated by cuts in which the artist-engraver's conventions cannot wholly suppress the sometimes crude liveliness of the amateur's sketch.' For their skilful reproduction, and much other help, my thanks are due to the staff of Thames and Hudson.

CHAPTER ONE

These came east

It is a curious fact that, owing to the almost universal ignorance of Arabic literature in the West during their time, our ancestors' knowledge of the geography of Mesopotamia and Western Asia generally was derived largely from the accounts of various European travellers. The writings, and for that matter the names, of the medieval Arab geographers were familiar only to a small minority of scholars, mostly Spanish. An English merchant, therefore, such as John Eldred,[1] who travelled to Baghdad in Queen Elizabeth's reign, had little reason to know any more about the country in advance than, for instance, Xenophon did when he reached the Euphrates two thousand years earlier, whereas a cultivated Frenchman such as L'Abbé de Beauchamp,[2] who became the Pope's Vicar-General in Babylonia in 1780, would at least have had Eldred's experience and that of a dozen or more like him to draw upon. He would certainly have had access to the accounts in Latin by the two famous rabbis, Benjamin of Tudela[3] and Pethahiah of Ratisbon,[4] of their visits to Jewish communities in the East in the twelfth century. He would have read the travels of the German physician, Leonhart Rauwolff, a contemporary of Eldred's, and those of his own three great compatriots, Tavernier,[5] Jean Otter,[6] and D'Anville,[7] while he could benefit from the works of earlier clerics such as the attractively named Vincenzo Maria di S. Caterina di Sienna,[8] Procurator-General of the Carmelite monks, and Emmanuel de St Albert, the Dominican.

Historically, one may suppose that, for an Englishman of that time, by far the most prolific source of information would have been Gibbon's *Decline and Fall of the Roman Empire*, which appeared between 1776 and 1788, but his knowledge of Babylon and Nineveh and of pre-classical Mesopotamia generally was in fact drawn largely from the Bible, and realities were confused with such semi-fabulous names as Nimrod, Sardanapallus and Semiramis, as indeed they were in Gibbon's own mind. Yet here again a scholar would be in no lack of stimulating material for thought among the writings of earlier European travellers, since scarcely one of those who reached Mesopotamia seems to have remained unconscious of his proximity to the traditional sites of Babylon and Nineveh or to

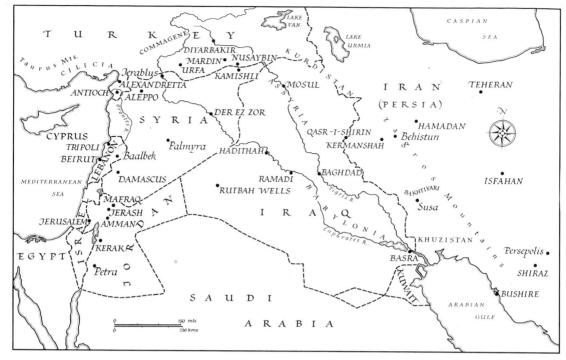

1 *The Near East, showing relevant place names.*

have refrained from adding his quota of comment and speculation
on their authenticity.

An Elizabethan merchant, to be sure, such as Eldred (concerning
whom it is interesting to remember that he sailed from London to
Tripoli *en route* for Aleppo in a ship called the *Tiger* – perhaps the
same whose master is mentioned by the witches in *Macbeth*) could
be excused some ignorance in the matter. And he in fact referred to
Baghdad, which he visited on several occasions, as 'New Babylon'
and confused the 'Olde City' of that name with 'Aqar Quf, which
he called 'the tower of Babel – almost as high as the stone work of
Paule's steeple in London'. Yet there can be little doubt that the
legends which had accumulated around the great mounds north of
Hillah were strong and plentiful. After all, the famous 'fortified
province' had only begun to lose its importance at the death of
Alexander the Great, and did not fall completely into ruin until the
first century AD, long after his successors had moved the capital to
Seleucia on the Tigris. As late as the tenth century the Arab writer
Ibn Haukal[9] speaks of it as 'a small village', yet Marco Polo passed
the mounds without comment.

The Italian nobleman, Pietro della Valle,[10] was perhaps the first to
take at all an intelligent interest in the real site of Babylon. In the
early seventeenth century he visited the Hillah mound and another
similar hill 'distant two leagues' from the first, which was evidently
Birs Nimrod, observing that one was in 'Mesopotamia' but the
other in 'Arabia'. He also took away with him 'some square bricks
on which were writing in certain unknown characters' and these,

2 *Mesopotamia and the principal sites mentioned in the text.*

together with copies of inscriptions which he had made at Perse-polis, were some of the first examples of cuneiform to reach Europe. De Beauchamp was, however, the first to make a proper examination of the trenches dug by the builders of Hillah in search of Babylonian bricks, and to examine the stories current among them of carved 'idols' and sculptured pictures, which seemed to him convincing enough.

The site of Nineveh fared similarly. The mounds across the river from Mosul were visited and commented on by almost all the early

European travellers, and here, as at Babylon, few could resist the quotation of some biblical prophecy of the city's destruction and desolation. Rabbi Benjamin observes in addition: 'Nineveh lies now in utter ruins, but numerous villages and small towns occupy its former space.'[11] Rauwolff confirms this, when in 1575 he writes, presumably of the Nebi Yunus mound: 'It was entirely honey-combed, being inhabited by poor people, whom I often saw crawling out and in in large numbers like ants in their heap.'[12] A few years later Sir Anthony Shirley also refers to Mosul itself (a city which, as it will presently be seen, has at various times been the subject of some passages of disparagement which rank very high in the history of 'hate literature') and calls it, in comparison to Nineveh, 'a small thing, rather to be a witnesse of the other's mightinesse and God's judgement, than of any fashion of magnificence in itselfe'.[13] So these and almost all other early visitors seemed satisfied with the identification of the site with Jonah's 'city of three days journey' (Jonah iii: 3). And in fact it always seems a little strange that there should have been any doubt about it, when, from the summit of the massive palace mound, one views the clear rectangle of city walls ('with four sides, but not equall or square', as della Valle remarked).

So the end of the eighteenth century is reached with Meso-potamia's great heritage of antiquities still safely bosomed in her mounds, and their history only the subject of conventional curiosity among Europeans. Yet there were great changes ahead and in England, even before the new century came in, the first symptom showed itself of a more than casual interest in the tales recently authenticated by scholars such as de Beauchamp. It was in fact an important turning-point when the East India Company ordered their Resident in Basra to obtain specimens of the inscribed bricks which the Abbé had seen at Babylon and to send them, carefully packed, to London. A little later there arrived in England a small case of antiquities, which for the moment represented all the known remains of Babylon and Assyria. They were the forerunners of the many hundreds of tons of antiquities which were to reach Europe during the following century.

It must be remembered that in the meantime Persia had also recently proved to be a fertile source of cuneiform inscriptions. In addition to cylinder seals and other small inscribed objects, the imposing ruins of Persepolis with its inscriptions and sculpture had begun to attract much attention, and the whole of the material derived from it had already been intelligently reviewed by the Danish scholar Karsten Niebuhr.[14] So in Denmark, as well as in France and Germany, scholars were already making a determined effort to find some formula for the decipherment of the wedge-shaped characters.

All these facts have a particular collective significance in relation to what followed, for it was with this background that Great Britain in the early years of the nineteenth century first established direct political relations with the Ottoman provinces constituting a unit known as Turkish Arabia. The first step towards this end had been taken in 1783, when the East India Company appointed a permanent non-British Agent in Baghdad. In 1798 his place was taken by a British Resident, who in 1802 received consular powers. Finally in 1910 Baghdad became the Political Agency in Turkish Arabia. Thus was initiated a most remarkable relationship between a Western power on the one hand and on the other an Asiatic country, the survival of whose identity as such resulted only from its traditional character and the inability of its conquerors to eradicate it. In the years which followed, this relationship was made all the more remarkable by the character of the individual Englishmen who were successively called upon to uphold it, and by the cultural orientation of their special interest in the country. Naturally the primary motive in the establishment of the Residency was a political one, connected with the interests of the Company and some exigencies of the Napoleonic War. Yet it is only necessary to recollect the names of such early Residents as Rich and Rawlinson in order to gauge the extent of their preoccupation with non-political matters. Also, grouped around these central figures in the Baghdad Residency were other Englishmen whom a variety of motives had brought to Mesopotamia. Scholar-explorers such as Buckingham and Ker Porter converged upon Rich's hospitable establishment, as Robert Mignan and Baillie-Fraser did upon that of his successor. Chesney's Euphrates Expedition brought Ainsworth and others; Loftus was attached to a boundary commission, while Layard, perhaps the greatest of them all, was prompted to exploration only by his own youthful initiative. Yet, whatever the motive which originally brought them to the country, they one and all remained captivated by the increasing fascination of its antiquities, and their purposeful application to archaeology made Assyriology a science.

It is hardly necessary to say that the names of all these Englishmen appear on the title pages of memoirs and accounts of their work and travels, in each of which there appears a fairly distinct picture of an individual with recognizable personality and characteristics. Furthermore, after their combined study and careful comparison one inevitably becomes aware of an elusive common denominator. It might at first naturally be assumed that this corresponded to some facet of national character or predilection, but later it becomes equally possible to associate it with the particular preoccupation of the whole group. Lincoln spoke of the American nation as 'dedicated to a proposition'. It is a phrase which could suitably be used of these pioneer archaeologists. Their 'proposition' was of course the elucidation of Mesopotamian history.

Nevertheless, in search of any further light which may be thrown on the character and circumstances of their work, it may be interesting here to examine some factors in the early lives of these individuals, which predisposed them towards their particular career. For this purpose we should perhaps give precedence to

Claudius James Rich, whose appointment to the Baghdad Residency in 1808 initiated our period of serious antiquarian research, and to his successor, Henry Rawlinson, and the great Austen Henry Layard.

RICH, RAWLINSON AND LAYARD: THE EARLY YEARS

According to his biographer,[15] Rich was the natural son of a certain Colonel James Cockburn, but little is known about his childhood, except that he spent a great part of it in Bristol. He was born in 1786, at a time when Bristol shared with Falmouth most of the shipping facilities for travellers bound eastwards; and one may read, for instance in the 'Journals' of Caroline or Barclay Fox,[16] how in both cities cultured Quaker families lent distinction to local society by their frequent entertainment of notable travellers. Indeed, it was their relative, Charles Fox, whose library of Persian and Arabic manuscripts first stimulated Rich's interest in eastern literature. At school Claudius had already shown the first signs of an almost uncanny talent for languages, and was at once fascinated by the smooth and decorative oriental script which he now saw for the first time. Fox, who was a considerable orientalist, took pleasure in his enthusiasm and, when the suggestion of tuition was made, willingly accepted so eager a pupil. In this way during the following years, in addition to the classics which he had learnt at school and 'several modern languages' which he had studied in his spare time, he acquired more than the elements of Turkish, Persian and Arabic. Simultaneously, from a local school teacher to whom he refers as 'my mathematical master', he learnt Hebrew, Syriac and a little Chinese. Such prodigies of intelligence naturally tax one's credulity and are in fact often liable to exaggeration. Yet, in partial extenuation of the biographer's claim, there is a charming episode a little later when young Claudius, walking on the downs above the city, encounters a gentleman who proves to be a shipwrecked Turk, and finds himself for the first time conversing fluently in a tongue which till now had been only grammar and exercises.

In Rich's case one may suppose that an interest in the East was a natural corollary to his knowledge of oriental languages. In any case at the age of seventeen he applied for and was granted a military cadetship in the East India Company. On presenting himself for enlistment, this was changed to an appointment more suitable to his peculiar talents, which appear from a passage in a contemporary number of *The Times* to have created something of a sensation. It reads: 'It was accidentally discovered by a Director that the young cadet was a perfect self-taught master of the Arabic, Persian and other Oriental languages, the truth of which was testified by the Company's Librarian, Mr Wilkins. This extraordinary circumstance . . . procured from the Directors at large a Bombay writership, which they immediately presented to the literary wonder!' But for the moment there was no vacancy in Bombay, so Rich

3 Claudius James Rich, born at Bristol in 1786, was appointed British Resident in Turkish Arabia at the age of twenty-one. While establishing the status and dignity of the Baghdad Residency, he was the first to initiate the serious study of Mesopotamian antiquity in his two 'Memoirs' on the ruins of Babylon.

found himself temporarily appointed secretary to the British Consul-General for the Mediterranean, whose headquarters were in Cairo, at a salary of £400 a year.

By a curious coincidence, some years after Rich's departure for the East, the cultured society of Bristol again provided a stimulating background for an impressionable boy, destined to become one of the greatest orientalists of his time. This was Henry Creswicke Rawlinson, who was born in Oxfordshire in 1810, but came to Bristol at an early age to recover from an eye disease under the care of his uncle, an eminent local surgeon. A detailed account of his life was written by his brother, Canon George Rawlinson, the historian and author of the *Five Great Oriental Monarchies*, who mentions[17] that his aunt was a prominent figure in the Bristol literary world at the time, and lists the names of distinguished writers, including Hannah More, with whom he would have been continually in contact in her house. After the Bristol period, which lasted until 1821, Henry Rawlinson's education ran on more conventional lines than Rich's. He was sent to a small school in Somerset and afterwards with a scholarship to Ealing, where he concentrated on classics. Yet its end was the same – a cadetship in the East India Company arranged for him in this case by an elderly relative in the Civil Service. Rawlinson therefore also quitted England for the East at the age of seventeen, but, unlike Rich, he had absolutely no knowledge of any Eastern language and was as ignorant as the average schoolboy of that time on the subject of oriental history.

A passage to India at the beginning of the last century meant four months on board ship, and it was during this voyage that Rawlinson made an important contact. Amongst his fellow-passengers was the Governor of Bombay, Sir John Malcolm, a soldier, diplomat and oriental scholar of considerable distinction, and also apparently an indefatigable raconteur. As Lord Roberts suggests in an introduction to Canon Rawlinson's biography of his brother: 'It was, without doubt, an enormous advantage to the lad of seventeen to be so closely associated with the "Historian of Persia", whose tales of his battles with the Mahrattas, and his experiences amongst the Persians, probably fired Rawlinson's youthful imagination, and gave that bent to his tastes which resulted in his subsequent choice of a career.' In fact on arrival in India he entered so wholeheartedly into the conventional life of a young subaltern that, during the years which followed, his youthful imagination might well have suffered an eclipse. Already horses had played a large part in his life at his home in Oxfordshire and his pride in his father's Derby winner[18] lasted throughout his life. So in 1832 we find Lieutenant Rawlinson with his regiment, the First Grenadiers, posted in Poona, offering 'to compete with any rival for a stake of £100, in running, jumping, quoits, racquets, billiards, pigeon-shooting, pig-sticking, steeple-chasing, chess and games of skill at cards', and actually winning an equally large wager by riding with a periodical change of horses from Poona to Panwell, a distance of seventy-two miles in under four hours. Writing of this period afterwards, he himself says: 'I had excellent health, was in the hey-day of youth, had tremendous spirits, was distinguished in all athletic amusements . . . and had the whole world before me.'

All this being so, it is more than remarkable that Rawlinson found much time for bookwork, that he in fact gained two interpreterships to his regiment in Indian languages and was able to apply himself vigorously to the study of Persian. Yet it was as much due to this as to his friendship with the Hon. G. Upton (who 'made interest for him' with his father, Lord Clare) that he eventually in 1835 found himself sent to Persia with a small body of officers of the Indian Army 'deputed to reorganize and discipline the Shah's troops, so as to restore them to that state of efficiency to which they had formerly attained under the supervision of British Officers'. This corresponded to the real beginning of Rawlinson's career. Twelve years after Claudius James Rich's death of *cholera morbus* in Shiraz, he was to take up the threads of epigraphic research, and for a time even to succeed to Rich's official position in Baghdad.

Rawlinson's later work in Mesopotamia was so bound up with the prodigious accomplishments in this field of Austen Henry Layard, that it is he whose early years next merit attention. Layard was born in Paris in 1817; but his travels in the East did not begin until he was twenty-two years old, by which time Rawlinson had been working in Persia for six years. Layard himself wrote the story of his earlier explorations many years afterwards when much of his life-work was already accomplished, and, as a concession to the curiosity of his friends, included some paragraphs about the circumstances of his early life and the impulses which directed him towards his subsequent career. His boyhood differed considerably from

4 *Austen Henry Layard as a child.
Born in Paris in 1817 and educated
elsewhere in Europe, he first studied
law in London, but at the age of
twenty-two abandoned this occupation
in favour of travel and exploration.*

those we have already examined in that his father's health, which
required continual changes of climate, resulted in most of his time
being spent in Switzerland and Italy. In Italy particularly, to use his
own words, he 'acquired a taste for the fine arts, and as much knowledge of them as a child could obtain who was constantly in the
society of artists and connoisseurs'. The results of this cosmopolitan
and probably somewhat desultory education became apparent
when, at the age of sixteen, he was sent back to London to study
law: for after spending six years in a solicitor's office and the
chambers of an 'eminent conveyancer', he 'determined for various
reasons to leave England and to seek a career elsewhere'. A glance at
the coloured engraving of a young man in Bakhtiyari costume
which forms a frontispiece to the *Early Adventurers*[19] is alone
sufficient to suggest that the 'various reasons' were adequate ones.

It is evident that long before this Layard's interest had begun to
turn towards the East. He describes how, as a boy, he used to pore
over the *Arabian Nights* and had read every available book of
oriental travels. In this connection he mentions both Rich's
memoirs on Babylon and the writings of Rawlinson's shipboard
acquaintance, Malcolm. He also refers specifically to a paper on
Susiana in the *Journal of the Geographical Society* by Rawlinson himself and the stories which he had heard of ruins and rock-cut
inscriptions in the Bakhtiyari highlands. His interest in these
matters appears to have become almost an obsession when, in 1839,
an opportunity for a journey to the East presented itself in the form
of an offer from a relative in Ceylon to find him employment there.
From the same source he received an introduction to another
young man of somewhat more than his own age, called Mitford, to
whom a similar offer had been made. Together they planned an

overland route to Ceylon which even today would be considered enterprising and to most people of that time would have seemed preposterous.[20] Central Europe, Dalmatia, Montenegro, Albania and Bulgaria to Constantinople was the first stage, and thence across Asia Minor, Syria, Palestine and the Mesopotamian Desert to Baghdad. 'From Baghdad', he says, 'we believed that we should be able to reach India through Persia and Afghanistan, and ultimately Colombo. . . .' Surprisingly enough the two young men were in no sense dissuaded from their project by the various experts whom they were able to consult in London. In particular Sir John MacNeill, a British diplomat recently returned from the Court of the Shah, felt that the journey across Central Asia might have some geographical value for official purposes. He also gave Layard some excellent advice on his manner of travelling. 'You must', he said, 'either travel as important personages, with a retinue of servants and an adequate escort, or alone, as poor men, with nothing to excite the cupidity of the people amongst whom you will have to mix.' The meagre total of Layard and Mitford's combined means left little doubt as to which course to adopt. Layard having prepared himself for the journey by acquiring some knowledge of Arabic and Persian, learning the elements of navigation from a retired sea-captain and of medicine from a doctor friend in London University, they left England on 8 July 1839.

Of the three principal figures who have now presented themselves, only Rich with his gift of tongues was especially equipped in advance for the career which he eventually chose. The remainder were impelled by an adventurous spirit and attracted to the East by its quality of romance and mystery – a mystery, be it said, which has today been so largely dissipated by increased accessibility as to need emphasizing. Six centuries had passed since the end of the last Crusade severed the connection between Europe and the Arab Empire. After the final fall of Acre, in Gibbon's words, 'a profound and melancholy silence prevailed along the coast which had so long resounded with the World's Debate'. For the Westerner, Arabian Asia had been shrouded ever since in this same silence and remained so until rediscovered as a subject of 'debate' by the world of the nineteenth century.

RICH'S FIRST TRAVELS

For Claudius Rich, leaving England in 1804, the immediate objective was Cairo, with Bombay looming remotely beyond – just how remotely he did not at the time realize. He was to meet his chief, Mr Lock, in Malta, and for this purpose obtained a berth on a supply ship carrying stores to Nelson's fleet in the Mediterranean. Almost at once he met with a major misfortune which, though entirely changing the character of his journey eastwards, also afforded him, as it turned out, an introduction to new fields of study and experience, for which he must afterwards have been continually grateful. Some miles off Barcelona the store-ship *Hindustan* caught fire and, having been run ashore on the Spanish coast, was completely burnt out. Rich, whom this disaster left with nothing but the clothes which he was wearing, was fortunately befriended by a Bristol merchant living in Barcelona and provided by him with the means of continuing his journey. In this way he reached Italy, but was detained there for three months pending Lock's return from a visit to Turkey. Many young men would have found in a stay of this length an opportunity for some profitable occupation. Rich, settled in Naples, applied himself passionately to the study of music and particularly of Italian opera. By the end of three months he had learnt to speak Italian fluently and given much study to its history and literature. He had also added to his social accomplishments a proficient performance both on the flute and the guitar.

In Malta another setback awaited him. He arrived there barely in time to be present at the deathbed of Lock, who had contracted a serious fever while travelling in the 'Plain of Troy'. So the Company suggested that he fill in the months before the arrival of a new Consul-General by visiting Constantinople in order to perfect his Turkish. His journey through the Aegean sounds a delightful one, since the small merchantman on which he was travelling stopped to trade at many of the larger islands. Rich would surely have appreciated the timeless world of the Greek archipelago, which a century later formed a background in T. E. Lawrence's mind for his brilliant translation of the *Odyssey*. He must also have enjoyed a quaint encounter on the deck of a Turkish boat with whose crew those of his own vessel were fraternizing. An imposing-looking Turk greeted him with a delighted '*Effendim, sizi taniyorim*' and was immediately recognized as his chance acquaintance of the Bristol Downs.

Once he had reached Turkey the Company seem to have been in no hurry for Rich to return and take up his official duties. There therefore follows a period of fifteen months during which he was able to wander most profitably through Asia Minor and adapt himself to the peculiar tempo of Turkish life. At Smyrna he even studied for a time in an academy for young gentlemen and made many friends. For the rest he travelled around Anatolia and as far south as Aleppo and Antioch on what his biographer surmises to have been some sort of confidential mission. The period does eventually end with his recall to Cairo, where the new Consul-General, Colonel Missett, had now arrived. Sailing from Smyrna, Rich took the opportunity of visiting Cyprus on the way.

Missett took an immediate liking to his new assistant and life in Cairo was very pleasant. In Egypt the parvenu dynasty of sometime Georgian slaves known as the Mamluks were still in the ascendancy, and Rich enjoyed the society of these strange, flamboyant figures. He now acquired an interest in horses and is said to have attained a complete mastery of Arabic – a statement which one is forced to accept in the absence of any supporting testimony from an Arab contemporary. It is not that there is any reason to doubt Rich's phenomenal ability to learn foreign languages, but as anyone of normal intelligence, who has conscientiously attempted to master this particular tongue in a limited time, will admit, it is not so much a form of speech as a complicated mental attitude. We may accordingly be excused a little envious incredulity. So often in the past one has heard of western orientalists, both of the present and past generations, credited with a perfect knowledge of Arabic, only to be disillusioned by the criticism of their surviving Arab acquaintances or by the testimony of one's own ears. It is perhaps a tribute to the subtle complexity of the language that the same cannot be said, for instance, of either Persian or Turkish. Be this as it may, we may safely assume that Rich's theoretical knowledge of Arabic, which had delighted Fox and impressed the 'Company's librarian' before he left England, had been so greatly strengthened in practice during his two years in the Near East that, when not dressed as a European, he would be mistaken (as, say, T. E. Lawrence usually was) for a member of some Arabic-speaking minority.

In fact, it is not impossible that this was one consideration which influenced Rich's choice of a disguise when he again set out on his travels. He was ordered at the end of 1806 to take up his original appointment in Bombay, and, of several possible routes to India, he chose the least direct one via Syria, Mesopotamia and the Persian Gulf, perhaps with the indirect purpose of revisiting acquaintances in Aleppo and elsewhere. He dressed as a Mamluk and, through the exact knowledge which he now had of the character and deportment which would be expected of him in that role, he was received with distinguished consideration wherever he went. From Aleppo his route carried him across the Euphrates and through the foothills of the Turkish mountains to Diyarbakir and Mardin. His first approach to Mesopotamia and Baghdad must thus have been down the Tigris – probably on one of the famous *kelek* rafts, an experience which will be referred to later as the special privilege of so many early visitors and so few of our own generation. In Basra he had his first contact with the Company's Resident, Mr Manesty, to whom he took a violent dislike. Manesty was an older man with a different background, and it is not difficult to imagine that a residence at the the head of the Gulf, prolonged over several summers, when the shade temperature rises to $130°F$ ($55°C$) would have produced in him that peculiar cynicism which responds so unsympathetically to youthful enthusiasm. However, it was for the moment a short encounter, for Rich at once found a vessel sailing for India and he arrived in Bombay in September 1807.

Before leaving England a letter of introduction had been written for Rich to Sir James Mackintosh, at that time Recorder of Bombay. Expressed in the rather pompous idiom of the period ('If it is consistent with your views to honour him with your countenance, he will not, I am certain, give you any reason to repent of your kind-

5 *Mary Rich, daughter of Sir James Mackintosh, Recorder of Bombay, married Rich at the age of eighteen, shortly before his appointment to the Baghdad Residency. She outlived her husband by several decades and was affectionately remembered by a niece who became her biographer.*

ness and condescension') this letter had considerable repercussions. Rich, who had already been corresponding with Sir James, went on his arrival in Bombay to stay at the Mackintosh house. Sir James had six children by two successive marriages, the eldest of whom was Mary, a girl of eighteen, and with her as well as her younger sister, Kitty, Rich now became extremely friendly. He later went to live with Sir James' young secretary, Erskine, but both continued to spend much of their time with the family and to enjoy their company. Rich taught Mary drawing and painting, and little poems on trivial subjects passed between them, Rich signing himself with quaint nicknames such as 'Orlando Furioso'. Later in the year, when Mary's father and stepmother returned from a short health cruise, Rich asked for Mary's hand. Almost simultaneously the Company decided that a permanent Resident with a knowledge of the customs and language of the Turks should be appointed to Baghdad and Rich, to his surprise and delight, received the appointment.

Mackintosh's reaction to both circumstances may best be judged from a surviving letter to a friend which is perhaps worth quoting in full. He says:

You may recollect, perhaps, to have read in the newspapers in 1803, that Mr Parry, the present Chairman, gave a writership here, to a young man of the name of Rich, merely on Mr Wilkins' report of his extraordinary proficiency in Eastern languages, without interest, and, I believe, without even personal knowledge. He came out as assistant to young Lock, who was appointed Consul at Alexandria; and, since his death has travelled over the greater part of Turkish Asia, in various directions, with the eye and pencil of an artist, and with the address and carriage of a

traveller among barbarians. He acquired such a mastery over the languages and manners of the East, that he personated a Georgian Turk for
several weeks at Damascus, amidst several thousand pilgrims, on their
way to Mecca, completely unsuspected by the most vigilant and fiercest
Mussulman bigotry. He was recommended to me by my friend Robert
Hull, and I had several letters from him. I invited him to my house; and
at his arrival on this island, on the 1st of September 1807, he came to us.
He far surpassed our expectations, and we soon considered his wonderful
oriental attainments as the least part of his merit. I found him a fair
classical scholar, and capable of speaking and writing French and Italian
like the best educated native; he joined every elegant accomplishment
and every manly exercise; and combined with them spirit, pleasantry
and feeling. His talents and attainments delighted me. . . . On my return
[from Malabar], I found that he was desirous to become my son-in-law.
He has no fortune, nor had he then even an appointment; but you will
not doubt that I willingly consented to his marriage with my eldest
daughter, in whom he had the sagacity to discover, and the virtue to
value, the plain sense, modesty, purity and good nature, which will, I
hope, make her a source of happiness to him during his life.

Soon after, the most urgent necessities of the public called for a Resident at Baghdad. He alone was universally acknowledged to be qualified
for the station. He was appointed; having thus twice before he was
twenty-four [*sic*], commanded promotion by mere merit. They were
married and are gone to Baghdad.[21]

So Sir James was quite immoderately pleased with the new
addition to his family. He had elsewhere described his eldest
daughter as being 'of homely exterior', and one can almost detect in
this letter a shade of curiosity as to the nature of her attraction for
Rich. Yet any doubt whatsoever as to Rich's good judgment in this
respect would have been most emphatically mistaken. Throughout
what remained of his short life Mary's unselfish and admirably
balanced character was to be a priceless asset, particularly during the
long months in Baghdad when no European visited the town
and they were entirely dependent on each other's company.
From her letters and the fragment of a journal published in the
Narrative, she emerges as a humorous and intelligent English girl,
submitting patiently to her frequent relegation by 'Mr Rich and the
gentlemen' to the disabilities imposed upon her sex in the East. She
outlived Claudius by more than half a century, and in her declining
years became, for her younger relatives 'Aunt Rich' – a quiet and
rather reticent old lady with a romantic past.

So Rich, now aged twenty-one, set out with his even younger
wife to take up his very responsible appointment in Baghdad.
The voyage to Basra (in convoy owing to the danger of French
privateers and pirates) took six weeks. On arrival they were received with proper ceremony by Manesty, but it was inevitable
from the first that the relationship between the old-established
merchant-consul with his twenty years' experience of Iraq and the
precocious young man who was now officially his superior
would not be an easy one. Manesty had just regularized his
relations with a locally-born lady by whom he already had a con-

siderable family, and he made the initial and perhaps excusable slip of saying that she would 'receive' Mrs Rich. This proposal received a polite refusal from Rich and a less restrained comment in a letter to Mackintosh ('. . . to expect that I would allow Mrs Rich to associate with a dirty drab'). Yet the outward demeanour of both men remained extremely decorous and their meeting resolved itself into a cautious sparring-match, with Manesty attempting to insist that Rich's dispatches to Bombay should be open to his perusal, and Rich firmly declining this or any other kind of dependence on the Basra Agency. Later, by the influence of Mackintosh in Bombay, Rich of course established his own precedence and was in fact eventually given the invidious duty of reporting confidentially on the conduct of his elder colleague. For the moment, however, he was too pre-occupied with preparations for his journey up the Tigris to Bagh-dad in the Residency yacht to be more than temporarily put out by his tiff with Manesty.

CHAPTER TWO

Land of the twin rivers

It seems desirable and even necessary at this point to introduce some sort of picture of the country which is to provide a setting for the greater part of the following chapters. This presents certain difficulties since, at the risk of becoming tedious to those who know it well, the picture must be clear enough to benefit those who do not. Moreover the land of Iraq has not the uncomplicated character of a health-resort, to be introduced to the public by an illustrated guide and a few gaudy posters. It may not, like an undistinguished vedette, be swung confidently on to the stage by a bowing impresario. In fact from among those who visit the country as passage-migrants surprisingly few are disposed to repeat the experience, and their hasty judgment is seldom easy to influence. Nevertheless it does often prove that, by providing information not only about the history of the people but about the geological background of the land itself, one can arouse sufficient interest to provide a basis for real appreciation.

A major clue, for instance, to the character of country and people alike is evidence of the varying degrees of success with which human ingenuity has countered disabilities of climate. For the great endowment of fertility, which nature gave Iraq with one hand, she partially neutralized with the other by withholding sufficient rainfall. One could therefore scarcely do better than start by describing how this came about.

The country which has come to be loosely associated with the historical term Mesopotamia is composed of lands made habitable by the middle or lower courses of the two great rivers, Tigris and Euphrates, with their tributaries. It consists of two sharply differentiated provinces, divided by an imaginary line which in fact corresponds to the limits of the Persian (now the Arabian) Gulf at an earlier stage in its geological development. Until late in the Palaeolithic era, the rivers seem to have reached the sea through separate estuaries, traces of which can today clearly be seen: that of the Tigris near Samarra and the Euphrates just below Hit. The creation of the southern province is therefore fairly easily explained. Whereas, for instance, in Egypt the Nile pushes out its delta into the open sea, the twin streams of Mesopotamia, depositing their burden of silt at the head of the Gulf, have caused its coastline to recede southwards, bringing into being a vast alluvial plain – 300 miles long and almost 100 miles wide – dead flat, without stone in any form and clearly most suitable for cultivation. It is limited to the east by the foothills of the Iranian mountains and, to the west, separated from the more elevated Shamiyah Desert by a broken line of low cliffs. Again, just as in Egypt one may stand at the abrupt edge of the high desert and look across the strange, verdant rift of the Nile Valley to another desert beyond, so for instance at Kufah in Iraq, from the parched and stony fringe of the Badiyah, one looks in spring north-eastwards over the tops of date-palms and sees deep-green cultivation as far as the eye can reach, and if the plain were not 100 miles wide, one would find that it terminated in the brown foothills of the Zagros mountains. Furthermore, if one is inclined to believe in a Mesopotamian Deluge such as that of which Woolley once claimed to have found traces at Ur-of-the-Chaldees, one is reminded that in the great mosque of Kufah there is a submerged shrine called As-Safinah ('The Ship'), where Moslems suppose the Ark to have rested. Its position on a cliff above the alluvial plain is undoubtedly a more convincing location than the summit of Mount Ararat, some hundreds of miles to the north.

Almost the whole of the alluvial plain is capable of being prodigiously fertile agricultural land; and a great part of it has clearly at one time or another been under cultivation. Evidence of this is the profuse network of ancient irrigation canals, now abandoned, whose spoil-banks, like parallel ranges of small hills, run far out into the plain beyond the scanty farmlands of the present day. For, unlike the Nile valley, Babylonia has no annual flooding of the rivers to depend on for irrigation and the winter rainfall is rarely sufficient to produce a crop. So it is left entirely to the labour and ingenuity of man to arrest the flow of the two great streams towards the sea and distribute their waters over the thirsting land. This has been accomplished with a degree of success and on a scale which varied from age to age in exact proportion to the political security and social stability of the country. It reached a peak of effectiveness in Babylonian times and another during the 'Abbasid Caliphate, but succumbed disastrously to the Mongol invasions in the thirteenth century. Agriculture in southern Iraq today remains a dim travesty of traditional accomplishment. In antiquity the actual method of irrigation varied according to geological circumstances, one of the most important of which was the diverse character of the two rivers. During the spring both reach a level a little above the surrounding plain and are consequently confined within *bunds*. But the bed of the Euphrates is considerably higher than that of the Tigris, so that from the moment that it issues out into the plain at the head of its prehistoric estuary a succession of parallel effluents are drawn off from its left bank and run eastwards to irrigate a wide area between the rivers, and eventually to empty their surplus into the Tigris. Nahr 'Issa, Nahr al Malak, and Shatt al Nil are such canals, famous under these or earlier names for some thousands of years. Together they create at this point, where the rivers draw most closely together, a major agricultural district. Further south the course of the Euphrates has varied greatly throughout the ages. Today it is divided by the modern Hindiyah barrage into two branches, from which again effluents are drawn off eastwards.

For the Tigris too some sort of barrage has always been necessary to divert any considerable volume of water over the surrounding country. So here again in ancient times, effluents were thrown off from both banks. One to the east, starting near Samarra, collected the waters of two tributaries, the Adhaim and Diyala, and carried them far out into the plain, rejoining the main river 150 miles further south. This was in its time the greatest canal of all, known as the Nahr Awan. Similarly at Kut, where the great steel-and-concrete barrage stands today, more primitive structures had from the earliest times split and resplit the waters of the Tigris into three different channels. One of these, the principal stream from the modern barrage and now known as Al Gharraf, is the first canal in the history of the world whose construction is recorded in a written document. It was dug in the third millenniun BC by a prince of Lagash to eliminate the continual friction between that state and its neighbour Umma on the subject of irrigation-water derived from the Euphrates.

Before the two rivers are finally united in the great channel of the Shatt al 'Arab, which carries their combined waters to the sea, they spread out temporarily into a vast area of marshland; a wilderness of waving reeds and a tangle of narrow waterways among the palm trees. Here, in a strange world of their own, the Marsh Arabs tend their water buffaloes from shallow-draft boats. In the intervals of cultivating rice they spear fish and net wildfowl for the town markets. Their life and circumstances closely resemble those of the earliest, prehistoric settlers in the delta, and the ornate, cathedral-like guest-houses of their sheikhs, built entirely of reeds and mud, approximate most closely to the earliest representations of proto-Sumerian temples in the fourth millennium BC.

6 The guest-houses ('mudhifs') of the Marsh Arabs are built exclusively of reeds and clay. Their design is reminiscent of proto-Sumerian architecture of the fourth millennium BC.

7 Sunset over the marshes of southern Mesopotamia, home of the elusive Marsh Arabs whose archaic life-style survives to this day.

In many maps of this area, the entire alluvial plain is deceptively coloured emerald green in contrast to the pale brown of the western desert and the deeper brown of the Iranian mountains. Any false impression this may give is immediately belied by a view of the country from the air. Apart from the southern marshes, only the main canals fan out into a checker board of rich cultivation. Pump-lifted water creates a green belt on either side of the rivers themselves, and some of the larger towns are surrounded with orchards and market gardens. For the rest the plain is *chol* – not desert in the accepted sense, but an interminable, flat expanse of dried mud, rarely encumbered with camel thorn or any kind of scrub, so that a car can proceed in any direction at high speed. The only obstacles are the ruined irrigation canals of the ancient cultivators and the mounds which represent their cities and villages. Once these are left behind one passes out into an empty quarter haunted by mirages and dancing horizons, strangely stimulating owing to an untrammelled quality curiously comparable to that of an Alpine landscape after a new fall of snow.

This first impression of emptiness is, however, an illusion which increasing familiarity renders ridiculous, for here is a world as populous with birds and small animals as a Scottish moor. Every tiny hillock gives shelter to hopping and burrowing creatures, affording them refuge from the jackals and lean, elegant foxes who come out in the evening. When winter rains are heavy the whole ground is afterwards covered with a fine sheen of grass and timid flowers. Then the Bedouin appear with their flocks from nowhere and the plain is dotted with black tents. Herds of gazelles, almost orange in colour, graze in the distance, out of reach of the dogs, and mile-long flocks of sand-grouse go flighting to their early morning watering-place, dark at first like a trail of brown

8 Birds and animals of the 'chôl' desert
in southern Mesopotamia, where
mounds mark the sites of ancient cities.

smoke in the sky, then wheeling amazingly in a glittering ripple of white breasts. Grey cranes circle slowly at a great height before alighting and migrating geese pass in ragged formation. Sometimes the rain itself, or water escaping from the tail of an irrigation canal, will form a shallow lake stretching to the horizon. This will be covered with a fine variety of waterfowl, from small active teal to ponderous pelicans and more rare flamingoes or white ibises; grey herons stand sentinel along the shore.

Iraq has been described by a French writer as '*le pays beige*'. Even in the villages the universal and neutral brown of the soil extends to the mud houses and the muddy reeds of which their roofs are made. The *chol* has this same unbleached quality, to which, after a long sojourn, the eye becomes so accustomed that a chance encounter with any other colour, however pale, acquires exaggerated importance. The dull russet and indigo of Bedouin attire become by contrast arrestingly brilliant, while suddenly to ride out into a patch of growing corn gives one almost the physical sensation of passing from sunshine into a green shade. Yet this can only happen in spring, and in fact our whole picture of the *chol* applies accurately only to the six months of spring and winter. Under the summer sun, with a shade temperature of 120–125°F (48–52°C), it is a region undoubtedly better avoided, and one must return to the cities, whose domes and minarets, glazed or gilded, shimmer in the heat-waves arising from a thousand brick houses; their flat roofs are lined with cowls to catch the slightest breeze and carry it into the cool, vaulted *sirdabs* amongst their foundations. For such is southern Iraq; a land where, without artificial contrivances, human life is barely tolerable for one half of the year and may only be supported through the recollection and confident anticipation of the other half.

Northern Iraq corresponds to the province of Assyria and again has a character of its own. Framed in a crescent of mountain country, it consists of the fertile valleys of the Tigris and its tributaries, with undulating uplands between. To the west is Al Jazirah – a desolate and uncultivable steppe, separated from the Syrian Desert only by the Euphrates and the narrow defile through which it flows. Climatically Assyria is distinguished from the southern provinces by a more plentiful rainfall in winter, which is sufficient to produce a crop without irrigation, and in a good spring the pasturelands are a credit to the Assyrian god of vegetation. There are no date-palms here, but fruit in abundance, while terraced cultivation in the foothills produces vines and tobacco. The villages too are terraced and their low roofs recede in horizontal arpeggios against a fine counterpoint of slim poplars. The mountain country, which differs little from eastern Turkey and the contingent districts of Iran, grows a little timber. The winter snows among the scrub oak are patterned with the pink feet of chukar partridge or trodden by pig and ibex. The Kurdish tribes who dwell there, as well as the Yezidis in the hills north of Mosul, will become familiar in later chapters. Both they and the country in which they live are best seen through the eyes of Rich and Layard.

In the nineteenth century there were half-a-dozen routes by which a European traveller could reach Baghdad, yet none of them, strangely enough, exactly corresponded to the approaches most generally used today. The metalled road crossing the Syrian Desert from Mafraq, and the Damascus earth track used by the principal transport companies before it, take a direct line which had no precedent before 1921; while the routes which the railway follows to Baghdad today, both from Aleppo and from Basra, would have been impracticable for caravans in the last century owing to the insecurity of the tribal areas through which they pass. One need, of course, hardly mention the air routes which give most modern travellers their first sight of Mesopotamia – in map form, with the bridges and minarets of the capital racing up out of the distance almost before the miniature market towns on the Euphrates have fallen behind. In Rich's time indeed the Company had found it essential to maintain a direct postal service with India, via Baghdad, and for this purpose had inaugurated their famous Dromedary Mail, which used a cross-desert route very nearly as direct as the present one, passing through Bir Melossa, somewhat to the north of Rutbah Wells. These riders, however, had a technique of their own. They rode alone, unarmed and carrying no money; but two other commodities, news and tobacco, made them welcome guests in the tents of those for whom rich caravans were fair game. For ordinary travellers the way was much more circuitous. Their route from Baghdad to Basra ran west of the Euphrates – not beside the river owing to the rapaciousness of the cultivating tribes – but out in the desert at a respectful distance. It swung westwards near Hadithah and followed approximately the direction of the modern pipeline to Palmyra, whence more frequented tracks led to Damascus or Aleppo.

Several of our early European visitors have described this journey in detail. Tavernier, for instance, travelled with a small caravan of 600 camels, Eldred with 4,000. They accomplished the journey from Aleppo to Baghdad in 25 to 36 days. Every night their camp was made like a tiny fortress against thieves – the camel-packs stacked in a circle and the camels themselves couched inside them. The travellers sat around communal cooking fires and a strict discipline was maintained by the official caravan leader. It is also interesting to find that carrier-pigeons were used to send back news of the caravan's whereabouts. Actually pigeons had been used for much the same purpose since the time of the Caliph Mahdi, who adopted this means of sending important dispatches. Later there was a highly organized pigeon-post from Baghdad to Alexandretta, with towers provided for relaying the birds every fifty miles or so. Such birds at this time were valued at from £300 to £500 apiece. Some of the famous Arab breeds like the 'Basrawi' and 'Iskanderun' types even reached England.

Aleppo was far the most common point of departure for Baghdad. Rich, for instance, we have already seen leaving that town on a longer and much more picturesque route, fording the Euphrates at Jerablus and striking north-east into the hills, to reach the Tigris at Diyarbakir. This route was followed twenty years later by Buckingham,[22] and early in the present century by Soane[23] and Gertrude Bell.[24] In every case it carried them through Urfah, and each duly noted the vanishing remnants of Roman Edessa and the sacred fish in the 'Pool of Abraham'. The sinister basalt walls of Diyarbakir to them were 'Black Amida' with its long record of sieges and massacres; from Diyarbakir the land-route led to Mardin on its cliff overlooking Mesopotamia, and so down into the plain to Nisibin and Mosul.

But a far more comfortable and leisurely means of transport for this last stage of the journey was by raft down the Tigris. These *keleks* have been used on the Tigris for at least three thousand years and in that time the technicalities of their construction and management have remained unchanged. They consist of a squadron of inflated goatskins, lashed to a wooden framework, on which the load is stacked, and they are steered by immensely long poplar sweeps tipped with cross-lathing. At the end of the journey the wood is sold and the deflated skins return on donkeys to their original point of departure. In 1907 Soane, whom Sir Arnold Wilson once described as 'an erratic genius', chose this means of travel from Diyarbakir to Mosul on his first visit to Kurdistan,

9 A 'kelek' raft of inflated skins, negotiating the Tigris in transit from Mosul to Baghdad: a form of transport used by several early travellers.

and in spite of adventures due to submerged rocks, bandits and the discomfort produced by heavy rain, he afterwards spoke highly of his experience:

There is an ease and comfort about it all that only the traveller fresh from the road can appreciate. The abundance of cool, clear water is the chief delight of the journey, contrasting with the ever-present trouble of the road, with its water often enough scarce, and always obtained only at the expense of considerable manual labour. The dust and filth, the long, wearying stages, the trouble of loading and unloading and of seeking food in obscure bazaars when one is dead tired, the awakening from a sleep all too short in the dark before dawn, all these are past, and all there is to do is to lie at full length upon the bales and give oneself up to the luxury of pure laziness and enjoyment of the view.

He adds:

The few Europeans who have adopted this pleasant method of travelling usually hired half the raft, erecting a booth or tent and carried a cook and servants, travelling tranquilly, with no more to do than admire the scenery and take snapshot photographs.

He himself had to be content with an improvised shelter of calico and a bed among the bales of dried apricots, which somewhat lost its attraction after a storm of rain. Yet his description of the remarkable scenery through which the river passes before entering Iraq below Jazirat ibn 'Omar is probably worth considerably more than the snapshot photographs of his contemporaries. In particular the gorge at Hassan Kaif is something which, strangely enough, one has never heard described elsewhere, though it sounds as if Soane were justified in calling it 'one of the most remarkable sights the Tigris has to offer'.[25] He says:

The right bank of the river rose in a vertical cliff to a great height, and was faced across the broad stream by a fellow cliff not so high, but honey-combed with cave-dwellings. . . . Most remarkable of all were the great piers of a once colossal bridge, that, springing from a lower point of the cliff, or rather from a spot upon its slope down to the foreshore, spans the space to the opposite cliff, bridging the Tigris further south than any stone bridge. Here the stream is broad and deep, and the mighty piers that tower above and shadow the passer-by in his humble *kelek*, speak volumes for the perseverance and talent of people past and gone, and, by comparison, the qualities of the Ottomans. And on both sides, on the left or east bank, where the cliff growing ever lower still hedges the river, and on the west where receding it leaves a fertile foreshore, the faces are pierced with cave-dwellings, rock forts that communicate with one another. Curious chambers, open at the river-side, mere eeries, looked down upon the stream, and it is only a near approach that reveals the mode of access, a passage diving into the rock. From the village above a staircase has been cut, zigzagging down the cliff face to where the river laps the solid rock wall. . . .

Starting from Aleppo other comparatively modern travellers, such as Gertrude Bell on her journey described in *Amurath to Amurath*, preferred the descent of the Euphrates and the route followed by so many invading armies in historical times. This again is the most interesting approach and today the fast motor road to Der ez Zor, and its continuation down the right bank of the river into Iraq, make the journey by car a simple one. Particularly striking is the evidence of a natural boundary at almost exactly the point where the modern frontier crosses the Euphrates. Here the cultivation, which, since the confluence of the Khabur tributary, has extended far out on either side of the river, abruptly ceases and the valley acquires an air of barren desolation with no village or foliage to be seen anywhere. By the time the Iraqi post at Husaibah is reached, the dust and gravel of the Jazirah on the left and of the Shamiyah Desert on the right have drawn in almost to the water. Then there is a ruined Parthian watch-tower on a low hill, the walls and ramparts of a Roman *castellum* and a prehistoric mound surmounted by the remains of what was probably an Assyrian military post, after which narrow strips of cultivation and eventually the first date-palms begin to reappear. One has indeed not only crossed the modern frontier of Iraq, but also the Roman *limes* and the age-old limits of Assyria.

From here to the cleft in the hills just above Ramâdi, which Xenophon called 'The Gates' and where in fact the river finally flows out into the alluvial plain, is a distance of about 120 miles. Along the whole of this way it runs through a fertile but extremely narrow valley, mostly confined by escarpments on either side. Here there are a succession of small but very ancient fortified cities: Anah, Tilbis and Hit, built originally on islands in midstream, and others such as Rawah, on the banks, protected by fortresses on the escarpment above. Anah, the largest settlement of all, has long ago overflowed from the island on to the right bank, but there finds the space between the river and the escarpment so restricted that today it straggles for several miles along the bank. One observes that both here and also at Tilbis the problem of burying the dead had at certain times in the past become formidable, for there was no room for graves on the island and the flat land beside it provided barely sufficient space for fruit and vegetable gardens. Sometimes the problem has been solved by hollowing out chambers in the soft stone of the cliff. Elsewhere the graveyards mount awkwardly up on to the high desert above.

The last stage of the journey to Baghdad by this route would normally be eastwards along the 'Issa canal and so past the ruins of 'Aqar Quf to the Tigris. Gertrude Bell, however, had crossed to the right bank of the Euphrates at Anah, and at Hit struck off southwards in search of a new desert-way to Al 'Ukhaidir.

Rich's second approach was, as we have seen, from the south, and Mary's first sight of Iraq was the Shatt al 'Arab. From Basra the journey to Baghdad continued by water up the Tigris, and even the comparative amenities of the Residency yacht can hardly have compensated for the tedium of its slow pace against the current and the monotony of what little landscape was visible beyond the banks. With the yacht tied up for the night, she had her first sight of Arab villagers who gathered to pay their respects and to satisfy their curiosity. The sheikh of the Muntafiq gave Claudius a dignified and impressive reception in his reed-built *mudhif*. In a letter home Mary described the tribesmen as 'dark, wild, and savage-looking', and gave an account of their dress, ending rather surprisingly with the words – 'but on going into battle they put on a shirt of mail and helmet in which they fasten two white ostrich feathers'.

Rich made his entry into Baghdad with a little discreet ostentation. He rode at the head of his sepoy guard who were also mounted, and behind came Mary in a mule-borne palankeen with a body-guard of Armenian servants. They were received at the Residency by Hine, the surgeon, who had for some time been Acting-Resident.

CHAPTER THREE

The Residency

In the early years of the last century the limits of the Ottoman Pashalik of Baghdad corresponded approximately to those of modern Iraq. In theory the Baghdad government was directly responsible to Istanbul, but in practice it exercised a degree of autonomy varying in direct relationship to the character of the contemporary Pasha and his capacity for ignoring the importunities of the Porte. At this time, in Istanbul and throughout the Empire, the declining virility of the Turkish ruling class had resulted in the rise to power of a slave dynasty, and here as in Egypt the monopoly of government had passed into the hands of Georgian Mamluks. So it was with the last four of the great Mamluk Pashas of Baghdad, Sulaiman-the-Little, Abdullah, Sa'id and Da'ud, that Rich was to find himself associated. The spectacular downfall of the dynasty at the end of Da'ud's reign he was unfortunately not destined to see.

The Arabs of Iraq meanwhile were now entering upon their seventh century of foreign oppression and their fortunes had reached a very low ebb indeed. Longrigg's description of the Pashalik at this time gives some impression of the groaning misgovernment to which the country was subjected. He says:

Of government in general, a true picture would indeed give prominence to the endemic tribal disobedience with which it was every year's task to deal – to robber-bands unsuppressed, travellers impoverished by way-side blackmail – to ruthless taxation of the few accessible, powerlessness to touch the rest. Towns and lands were still sold to be governed by this or that favourite slave or genial courtier, Aghas still bullied, troopers still raped and robbed. . . . The revenue of the Pashalik was collected by expedients of various age and origin, some survivals of feudal usage and some devised newly by the latest Pasha. His Customs, varying at his whim, were a source of gain less vexatious to trade and travel than the wayside tolls of every Shaikh and village headman; the farms of Sanjak, canal or tribal territory, brought to the Treasury but a fraction of what was squeezed from the ultimate payers, who suffered the more as they were weak and accessible. The poll-tax of Jew and Christian was collected with many abuses, by the highest bidder. Further sums accrued by taxes on goods in transit, by state monopoly in the commonest trades, by falsified exchange rates and corrupted coinage.[26]

A corollary to this open extortion was the very considerable state in which the Pasha himself lived and conducted the govern-

10 The Turkish Pasha of Baghdad with his entourage of officers and attendants, issuing from the Sarail on a state occasion: as seen by J. S. Buckingham during his stay at the Residency in 1816.

ment. In the Sarai the brilliant uniforms and good bearing of the Janissary Guards and Georgian attendants, the impression of finished luxury in furniture and appointments combined with the elaborate official ceremony were described by European visitors as 'a state perfectly that of a royal prince'. The Pasha's personal retainers, as in Istanbul, insisted upon their traditional titles of office – Masters of the Wardrobe, the Coffee, the Sweetmeats, the Harness, the Carpets, the Laving Water, the Drinking Water, the Pipe, the Standard, Riding Abroad, etc., etc. The Georgian bodyguard was, of course, a full-scale military force.

Yet all this outward pomp and ostentation availed nothing against the accumulating symptoms of a rotten administration. The medieval tyranny of foreign slaves had become an anachronism whose existence could not indefinitely be prolonged in a changing world. Most significant of all was the increasing contact of the Ottomans with Europe, and the intrusion of the European powers in the affairs of the Middle East. In Britain, Baghdad was regarded as a possible stage on Napoleon's road to the conquest of India, and this alone would have been sufficient to justify adequate representation at the Pasha's court. French attempts, so far unsuccessful, to anticipate this by establishing a paramount influence in local politics were an added incentive. Meanwhile the Pashas themselves had no reason for being averse to this new contact. They were becoming increasingly conscious of India as a great neighbour, a subject for measured diplomacy and a source of military supplies. In this way the omens were by no means unfavourable to Rich's arrival, and, as it proved, a better man for the post could hardly have been chosen.

Calling privately at the Sarai to present his credentials, Rich was received with great politeness, but was not impressed by the personality of the Pasha, whom he described afterwards as 'no great things'. In any case for the moment both he and Mary were preoccupied with the business of settling into their new house. The house used at that time as the British Residency faces the river between the two bridges and is today an hotel. For the author, remembering twenty years intermittent residence in Iraq, there is a temptation to take for granted many things about Baghdad which to Mary Rich must have seemed unfamiliar and even disconcerting. She writes:

This is a large and handsome house perfectly in the Turkish style. It consists of three different courts, one of which belongs to me – the harem, my place of confinement, and it is the most comfortable, retired part of the house. I have one large, handsome sitting-room which I have made the library and breakfast parlour, and where I always sit and receive my great visits. There are no less than six other small, comfortable rooms with a fine, large open gallery all round and an open courtyard. These apartments are perfectly separate from the other part of the house, which I never visit till the evening when business is over. The weather is now so warm we dine on the terrace, and in less than a month the heat will become so intolerable, that we shall be obliged to sleep in the open air, as no person in Baghdad could bear a close room in the hot months. The view I have of the renowned city is not the most beautiful. The streets are extremely narrow and the whole town is built of sun-baked bricks which gives it a very dirty appearance. There is nothing at all splendid about Baghdad. . . .[27]

In 1808 this was probably not an unfair appraisal of Rusafah, the medieval left-bank successor of Mansur's Round City. Baghdad indeed had not yet sunk to the extreme of ruinous decrepitude which resulted from the flood of 1830, and the town walls with their gates were still preserved in a reasonably intact condition. Yet over a century more was to elapse before the first *route carrossable,* now called Al Rashid Street, was cut through the maze of rotting houses and narrow alleyways from end to end of the town. Even today this street has a character dictated by climatic extremity, for the buildings on either side are built out over the footwalks to protect pedestrians from the sun, so that it runs between long colonnades of concrete pillars. For the same reason, in the narrower and more ancient alleyways the wooden upper storeys of the houses are corbelled out until they nearly meet, and their opposed windows make privacy practically unattainable. But these are the outer rooms used by the tenants for receiving their friends. The rooms used by the family have no outer windows and obtain their light from the court round which the house is built. In these days the reception rooms at least of such houses will be furnished in the western manner. Yet the few 'large and handsome houses, perfectly in the Turkish style', which still survive, have an undeniable graciousness. Balconies around their open courts are supported on carved wooden columns; downstairs rooms have finely-proportioned vaulting in cut brickwork and the ceilings of the principal saloons above are often ornamented with a delicate geometrical fretwork of wood, inlaid with a mosaic of mirror-

glass. Carved wooden grilles in the windows of the family apartments and wrought-ironwork from Mosul are not uncommon.

Mary was also right about the summer heat, which became an
increasing affliction to her and Rich during the years which
followed. One July day when Buckingham was a guest in their
house, he ascertained the shade temperature 'by the scales of two
excellent thermometers, carefully examined and compared' at a
2 p.m. maximum of 122°F (50°C) and a minimum at dawn of
112°F (44°C).[28] In 1820, after he had returned to Calcutta, he
received a letter from Rich in which he mentioned: 'So extra-
ordinarily bad was our last summer, so fearfully exceeding anything you experienced here (though *you* had a tolerable specimen
of our climate), that I had, at one time, intended to send you an
account of it for publication. . . .' Today scientific invention and
experience have gone a long way towards moderating the appalling
discomfort of life in such a climate. Air conditioning, electric fans,
refrigerators, fly-screens and insecticides are contributions of the
former, which have not yet entirely superseded more traditional
devices such as sunken rooms, tiled floors, porous water-coolers,
windows protected with watered camel-thorn and above all the
strict regime of a house opened completely to the night air, but
hermetically closed and darkened during the day. Offices open at
7 a.m. and close at 1 p.m. In the afternoon the city withdraws to its
sirdabs to sleep. Between 5 and 6 p.m. it reassembles on balconies,
in coffee shops and public gardens, and retires early to bed beneath
mosquito-nets on the roof-tops.

The Rich family on principle only left the house between 5 a.m.
and their 7 o'clock breakfast. The remainder of the day was spent
in the *sirdabs* until about 6 o'clock, when they emerged fully dressed
for dinner on the terrace. Here they spent the evening and apparently slept. Buckingham recalls:

From the terrace of Mr Rich's residence, which was divided into many
compartments, each having its separate passage of ascent and descent, and
forming, indeed, so many unroofed chambers, we could command at
the first opening of the morning, just such a view of Baghdad as is given
in the 'Diable Boiteux' of Madrid, showing us all the families of Baghdad,
with their sleeping apartment, unroofed, and those near our own abode
often in sufficiently interesting situations.[29]

Winter days were planned rather differently. Once the first rains
had laid the dust and the mud had dried, riding and even walking
became possible and most mornings were spent in this way. Mary
rode a donkey and was compelled for the purpose to adopt local
costume – a black veil, and the *charchaf*, an all-enveloping blue
checked sheet from which only her feet emerged in yellow half-
boots. Much of Rich's business was done in the afternoon and dinner
was at 4 o'clock. For this meal he appeared on all occasions fully
dressed, and Mary's views on the subject appear in a letter to her
sister in Bombay:

I know your idea is that there is no occasion to dress for dinner when there is no company; but let me tell you this is the way to treat your husband very cavalierly – to think that as no one dines with you, your dirty morning gown will do. If I did not come down as well-dressed as I should be in Bombay at a party of fifteen or twenty persons, Mr Rich would be extremely angry![30]

Poor Mary! After spending a good part of the day in complete seclusion, or wrestling with language difficulties amongst her servants and callers, the elaborate preparation for the moment when she emerged into the public part of the house to sip 'a kind of sherry' from Shiraz before dining alone with her husband must have been a comparatively pleasant part of her daily routine. As time went on, her demands on Bombay for clothes became more frequent and her wardrobe more elaborate:

24 shifts, petticoats, nightshifts, caps, and morning gowns; 24 shirts of cambric; fine lino for evening gowns, or fine muslin worked purposely. A few pocket handkerchiefs of palmacotta muslin; 1 dozen pair long sleeves, plain and muslin; one dozen short gloves and some nail brushes. I have just received 20 pair shoes from Calcutta, but please order me another dozen all kid and English made. The colours I like are black, purple, olive and doree.

And later:

two oilskin umbrellas from the China warehouse, and four or five pair stays, boned in front and laced behind, also morning gowns, high in the neck, in nainsook or fine cord muslin, and two coloured gowns.

Claudius himself seems to have been equally fastidious:

12 pair Irish *linnen trowsers* particularly high in the waist, very full and large in the legs. 2 dozen pair white nankeen pantaloons with tyes at the ankles, to come extremely high also in the waist. $\frac{1}{2}$ dozen shirts, which must be made of cambric muslin and *not of longcloth*: He cannot wear coarse shirts, and his trowsers *must* only be of Irish linen.[31]

The hours after dinner at the Residency were occupied with books and music, and sometimes Mary read aloud while Claudius drew or painted. Books came in packages from one of Mary's uncles who was proprietor of the *Morning Post*, but Bombay had to supply a variety of other needs. 'Please send a chess-board and men, and also a new flute for Claudius. Can you procure us a Wedgwood's copying machine, if there is such a thing in Bombay . . .'

From their first year in Baghdad onwards the Riches developed the habit of spending some weeks in spring and autumn in a camp on the banks of the Tigris at Ghararah about five miles below Baghdad. This made a welcome break in the formal routine of life at the Residency just before and after the hottest part of the year. It is not difficult to imagine how greatly Mary at least must have always looked forward to this release from the city during the period when the climate of Iraq disarmingly reverts to being one of the pleasantest in the world. For Ghararah could of old be very beautiful. Where the last houses were left behind, the river swung westwards and returned, making a narrow-necked loop which (until the planning development of recent years) was entirely filled

11 The author's own house at South Gate in Baghdad in the late 1940s: a Turkish building of the 'yala' type constructed mainly of wood. This front courtyard had a terrace overhanging the Tigris – the 'diwan', with its heavily enriched ceiling, being in the rear. The earliest British Residency is known to have been of precisely similar appearance.

with orchards and palm-groves. It was here, in this quiet oasis of deep foliage and tranquil rustic life, that a century later Gertrude Bell discovered the solace of her friend Haji Naji's garden. The ideal setting which it provided for an early-morning ride or an evening picnic, its nightingales and cathedrals of fruit-blossom in spring-time, subsequently earned for it among British residents the nostalgic if somewhat banal name of 'Devonshire'.

In local politics, meanwhile, Claudius had been 'showing the flag' to some purpose. His command of languages and experience of Turkish and Arab psychology gave him self-confidence in dealing with local notables, while his personal charm made a direct approach practicable. His fearless integrity and passion for justice at first puzzled his associates, but did not finally fail to impress them. Within months of arriving in Baghdad his reputation exceeded that of any foreigner in the Pashalik and French prestige was effectively eclipsed. With the Pasha himself, however, there was bound from the beginning to be friction. The comparative success with which he had browbeaten Rich's predecessors, Manesty and Harford Jones, suggested no reason for giving the new Resident any special consideration. Rich, on the other hand, had a conviction that in dealing with an Oriental, and especially a Turk, little was to be gained by temporizing or submission. 'Nothing', he once wrote to his father-in-law, 'but the most decisive conduct will do; any other will increase the insolence of his disposition.' Criticizing previous British policy in the Ottoman dominions, he said:

I am far from being an advocate of force and violence, but the weak line of conduct we have pursued is eminently prejudicial to our honour and interests, and will, I fear, be long felt by our representatives in the Ottoman Dominions. For I am certain that the Turks consider our lenity and forbearance as arising solely from fear and inability.[32]

In taking a strong line now, Rich relied for support at first on Bombay, unwisely as it proved, and afterwards, when a British Ambassador to the Porte was appointed, with greater confidence, on Istanbul.

There is no need to follow the stages in the development of Claudius' quarrel with the Pasha. During the summer of 1809 the latter had become abusive, insolent and threatening, and things came to a head in October while the Riches were in camp at Ghararah. The Pasha, hearing they were about to return to the Residency, refused them admission to the city and threatened their servants with the bastinado if they continued to serve them. All through the exchanges which followed Rich seems to have been in his element, for he wrote to Mackintosh: 'The Residency at Baghdad has become a desirable post to me owing to all its difficulties'.[33] Unfortunately the arguments which led to the eventual intimidation of Little Sulaiman are unknown to us, but by the end of the year Rich had succeeded in completely turning the tables. His family party were escorted back to the city by the Pasha's own bodyguard of 300 Georgians and he himself given a ceremonial audience in which his title of Resident with all its prerogatives was publicly acknowledged in the most unequivocal terms.

Considering Rich's age and the fact that he had brought about this triumph entirely by his own exertions, it is perhaps understandable that he should have now proceeded to increase the ostentation of his entourage in a manner compatible with his newly established prestige. At the Residency the sepoy guard of thirty men under a *subahdar* had already become an institution and remained so for nearly a century after his death. But in addition to these he now formed a troop of European hussars from discharged soldiers of various nationalities whom he collected in Baghdad. A European farrier also appeared on his staff (since he did not approve of the Turkish method of shoeing), and, for Mary's convenience, a *maître d'hôtel*. As might be expected, these and other increased liabilities were not easily comprehensible to a basically commercial establishment like the East India Company, and Rich was in continual financial difficulties owing to their parsimony. He complains above all that no definite salary and allowances were fixed for him before leaving Bombay. His own ideas as to the scale of permissible expenditure were fairly definite:

Could I obtain allowances of 3000 rupees per mensem for expenses of the Residency and 1500 or even 1000 as salary, I would be well contented. The allowances would enable me to live handsomely as a public representative ought to do; while my salary would be secured to me without the possibility of my breaking in upon it, and would be accumulating in the Agent's hands! To keep up the present establishment, I cannot possibly manage with less than 2,500. The Company's allowances are inadequate.[34]

The Company's allowances, in fact, remained inadequate all through his stay in Baghdad. He had enemies in Bombay and it will be seen later that he was at times treated extremely shabbily.

Yet if the British Government could have been brought to realize the unique position of authority and respect attained by this individual Englishman, and the widespread influence of his reputation throughout the whole of Turkish Arabia, they must needs have considered his services to be cheap at any price. In Baghdad, by 1811, the Pasha himself had incurred the serious displeasure of the Porte and was in a position to request Rich's intervention on his behalf. He was too late, however, for a *firman* deposing him had been followed up by a direct incitement to the tribes and provincial governors to take the law into their own hands. Raiding parties reached the very gates of Baghdad and the city was in an unreliable mood.

The Riches had withdrawn to their camp at Ghararah where, in the middle of so much disturbance, they were suddenly visited by General Sir John Malcolm, returning from a diplomatic mission to the Court of the Shah. He received a great welcome from his hosts and was indeed the first of a long series of distinguished guests who afterwards wrote in superlative terms of the Riches' hospitality. 'We pass our time very pleasantly here,' he observed. 'We have races every morning, games of chess after breakfast and in the evening swim in the Tigris and play bowls.' And before he departed: 'I shall leave Baghdad with very warm feelings towards the Residency. Mr Rich is a young man of extraordinary attainments, and his fair lady a most decided favourite of mine.' Two episodes during his visit must have impressed him with Rich's confident authority in Baghdad. First, when a Residency official was robbed on the road, Rich took his hussars and, with Malcolm's officers, galloped ten miles out into the desert to subdue the raiding party and recover the money. Secondly, when one of the Pasha's ministers appeared with his retinue in full retreat before a punitive force, Rich gave him sanctuary and afterwards successfully interceded for his life. The Pasha himself, however, had by now already been killed.

At the end of 1811 the Riches had a visit which afterwards became a landmark in their early life in Baghdad. This was from Mary's fifteen-year-old sister, Kitty Mackintosh. Her parents had returned to England on leave and Sir Gore Ouseley, the new British minister to Persia, had agreed to chaperone Kitty as far as Bushire. There, Mary had arranged to meet her, and Claudius, combining business with pleasure, accompanied her as far as Basra, in very high spirits at leaving Baghdad. Meanwhile the Ouseleys had left Kitty in the hands of a Mrs Bruce at Bushire and, in the way young girls have, she had got herself engaged to a young naval officer whom she had met on the boat. Mary was considerably shocked that Kitty's fiancé, who was described as 'impecunious though a baronet', should not have first addressed himself to her father. Yet later, when informed, Sir James made no bones about agreeing to this simple solution of Kitty's future, and she became Lady Wiseman. For the moment, however, Wiseman remained on duty and Kitty joined the Riches on the return journey up the Tigris in their yacht.

From Claudius and Mary's almost hysterical enjoyment of this visit one may perhaps gauge the austerity of their normal life, soured as it was by financial difficulties and unending political intrigues. The waggish and whimsical phrases of contemporary frivolity sound strangely now, but suggest much-needed relaxation. Mary writes:

Kitty and Claudius are making such a noise, they are fighting, sparring and kissing from morning to night, and consider me a common enemy, because I sometimes venture to call them to order. Kitty so adores him that I have called her 'the little sycophant'. I flatter myself that Claudius is as fascinating now as ever he was in Bombay. I tell him he is an impudent Irishman and requires to be a little taken down![35]

Nevertheless, in their spare time they also united to improve her education. She read history with Mary, while Claudius was teaching her music and drawing, also helping her with Italian and French.

Kitty's visit also provided an opportunity for Rich's first excursion to Babylon. From his arrival in Baghdad he had interested himself in archaeology and laid the foundation of what afterwards became a considerable collection of antiquities and manuscripts. An examination of the site of Babylon was an enterprise which he had long promised himself, and in the closing weeks of 1811 he completed the arrangements. The journey, which today is an easy two hours motoring, took two days. As a result of Rich's importance and the new Pasha's fear for his safety, the party became something of a cavalcade, the escort, as Rich himself records,[36] consisting of 'my own troops of Hussars, with a galloper gun, a havildar, and twelve sepoys; about seventy baggage mules, a mehmandar from the Pasha, and a man from the Sheikh of the Jirbah Arabs. . . .' Mary travelled in a palankeen,★ Kitty rode her new pony which Claudius had bought and broken for her, but a second palankeen was provided in case she got tired. The journey, as Kitty afterwards described it, is 'tedious travelling' at the best of times, and even Rich found little to record except periodical *khans* (caravanserais) and the principal irrigation canals. The party was met outside Hillah by a deputation which included the Governor's private band 'of double drums and zoormas, or Turkish hautboys'.

★This was the *takhterawan*, or mule-born litter, now extinct in Iraq. The only surviving examples which the writer has ever seen were at the monastery called Der Za'feran, near Mardin, where two were preserved in the chapel crypt. But these were ceremonial affairs, heavily upholstered and ornamented.

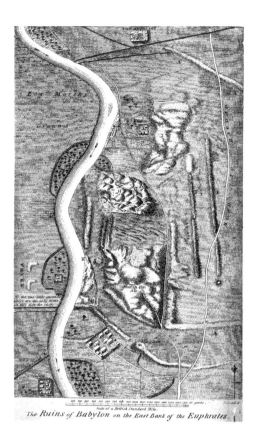

12 Rich's plan of the site of ancient Babylon. Drawn by Captain Abraham Lockett under Rich's instruction during his first visit to the site in December 1811, the plan corresponds to a remarkable extent with the modern one, based on Koldewey's excavations.

The *Ruins of Babylon* on the East Bank of the *Euphrates*.

During the ten days or so which followed, Rich accomplished a more intelligent and thorough examination of the ruins of Babylon than any that had till then been made, visiting, sketching and even approximately surveying the entire group of mounds on the left bank of the Euphrates, 'Amran 'Ali, Al Qasr and Babil, which we now know to represent the temples and palaces of the Inner City. He watched gangs of Arabs from Hillah excavating Babylonian baked bricks for building purposes and had no difficulty with their help in obtaining good specimens of brick-inscriptions. At Babil he employed workmen of his own to investigate the underground cavities which appeared among the ruins of the Summer Palace, and there was great excitement when they encountered 'a skeleton in a coffin'. He watched while 'piece by piece they pulled out the coffin and the bones' (not a very conventional procedure by modern archaeological standards). The famous stone lion was as usual disinterred from the sand drifts for his benefit, and he ended his tour with an expedition to Birs Nimrod, where, like most modern visitors, he was amazed at the vitrified masses of brickwork crowning the ruins of the great tower. The whole of his investigations he afterwards made the subject of a memoir which was first published in the Viennese journal *Mines de l'Orient*.

There would be no point here in enumerating Rich's theories, speculations and deductions. Thirteen years meticulous excavation by German scientists at the beginning of the present century have eclipsed their interest, without obscuring the fact that the Germans themselves owed much to Rich's original initiative. For it was undoubtedly the interest aroused by the publication of Rich's *Memoir* in 1812 which gave the initial impulse to Mesopotamian archaeology. Together with its sequel it even inspired the parenthetical lines in Byron's *Don Juan* (Canto V, 62): 'Though Claudius Rich, Esquire, some bricks has got, and written lately two memoirs upon't.'

Soon after the Riches' return to Baghdad, Sir William Wiseman arrived and he and Kitty were married. When she eventually left with her husband for Bombay she had just turned sixteen. After their departure, life at the Residency resumed its now familiar routine. Sulaiman Pasha's successor, Abdullah, had been treacherously murdered by the Muntafiq and his place had been taken by Sulaiman's son, Sa'id, whose life Rich had contrived to save from the vengeance of Abdullah. The result was a satisfactorily cordial relationship with the Sarai. At the same time Sir James Mackintosh, after arriving in London, had pleaded with the Directors of the Company for a more sympathetic treatment of his son-in-law, and dispatches from Bombay were becoming correspondingly less unreasonable. Any satisfaction, however, which Mary might have felt on these two counts was minimized by her anxiety about Claudius' health. Reaction to the heat of successive summers, culminating in a serious attack of fever, had reduced him to a state of lethargic depression most unfamiliar in one of his temperament and baffling even to Mr Hine. Finally, the only reasonable remedy seemed to be a holiday in Europe, so Rich applied for and was granted three months' leave. He and Mary left Baghdad in October 1813, travelling at first by barouche and later riding with the *tatar* couriers. Mary 'for greater comfort and safety was dressed as a *tatar* youth'.

CHAPTER FOUR

Buckingham

The Riches' departure for Europe and their prolonged absence from Baghdad seems here to afford an occasion for another considerable digression. So we may leave them for the moment toiling through the mountain passes of Asia Minor towards Istanbul, and follow a new cross-thread in the tapestry of Mesopotamian exploration: the eastward journey of another traveller whose goal was the Residency at Baghdad.

Before leaving for Europe the Riches had heard with much curiosity of the doings of Lady Hester Stanhope. This remarkable middle-aged Englishwoman, careering about Syria dressed as a Mamluk and 'with a considerable suite of gentlemen', at first seemed a little shocking to Claudius' orientalized sense of propriety, yet he afterwards found her a stimulating correspondent. Staying in Lady Hester's house at the beginning of 1816 was James Silk Buckingham, whose name has occurred in an earlier chapter. He seems likely at this time to have received through his hostess the introduction to Rich, which eventually brought him to the Residency on his way to India. The description of his journey, which he afterwards published,[37] is dedicated to Lady Hester, whom he considered 'one of the brightest ornaments of her sex and station'.

Buckingham was then thirty years of age. His character is today particularly satisfying to contemplate because it typifies a whole generation of Englishmen without whose memory posterity would be a great deal the poorer. His personality as well as his writings received much publicity some years later, as a result of his ultimate success in a truly monumental action for slander, which lasted nearly four years and cost several people, including himself, more than they could afford.

The story is certainly a remarkable one and the eventual outcome of the case was at the time evidently considered of some consequence, since the attention of the House of Commons was drawn to the obvious reflection which it implied upon the integrity of the Indian Government. From Buckingham's own point of view it had absorbed almost the whole of his income and energy over so long a period that his final vindication afterwards became the central fact of his life, and he may well be excused the twenty-two pages devoted to it in his last travel book.

According to his own account, it all began in the year 1816 at Jerusalem, where he made the acquaintance of a young man of his own age called Bankes. The two of them decided temporarily to join forces, and together they made a short journey to the ruined cities east of the Jordan. Both enjoyed it, and Bankes proposed adding his own sketches and comments to the more elaborate notes which Buckingham had made, for the purpose of afterwards publishing a joint memoir. On their return they parted; but during the following months Bankes several times wrote to Buckingham suggesting further journeys together to Palmyra, Baalbek and so forth.* These did not prove practicable, and in fact the two men did not meet again until five months later, when Buckingham was about to leave Aleppo for India. Up to this point their relations had been entirely cordial and, on leaving, Buckingham received from his friend a letter of introduction to the Governor of Bombay. The only circumstance which to him should have appeared a little peculiar was that Bankes asked him to return all his own letters. As it was, because he had no reason to suspect any ulterior motive behind the request, he at once complied.

On reaching India, circumstances induced Buckingham to remain there instead of returning to England; so any question of collaboration with Bankes in a publication was ruled out. Nevertheless, various prominent people in Bombay who saw Buckingham's own notes on his travels in Transjordan and elsewhere urged that they should be published, and the manuscript was dispatched to Murray, the London publisher. Bankes, now in Egypt, seeing the newspaper announcement of the article, 'appears to have been filled with the most ungovernable rage, or jealousy', and persuaded his father in London to stop its publication on the grounds that Buckingham was an ignorant charlatan who had pirated his own notes. At the same time he wrote a letter to the Governor of Bombay requesting that Buckingham be discountenanced and proscribed in India.

Murray, rather surprisingly, agreed to withhold publication of the article, but Buckingham approached Longman & Co., and was able to produce such undisputed proof of its authenticity that Longman published it. Bankes' reaction to its appearance in print was an anonymous article in the *Quarterly Review* containing an even more violent attack on Buckingham's character. This article, when it reached India, was made a pretext by Buckingham's

---

*He also visited Lady Hester Stanhope at Mar Elias, and her biographer describes him as follows: 'William Bankes, the future member for Cambridge University, arrived with a portfolio of sketches under his arm, a renegade Albanian soldier as his servant, and a gold-fitted dressing-case laden with perfumes. He was the kind of conceited, self-opinionated young man with whom Her Ladyship had very little patience' (Haslip (1934)). The 'renegade Albanian' seems likely to be a rather unfair description of Giovanni Finati, whose biography Bankes subsequently edited.

enemies for calling upon the Government to expel him from the country, and the Government being plainly disposed to comply, 'the floodgates of calumny were opened, and every species of atrocity attempted towards me by the favoured minions of power'. Figuratively squaring his shoulders and thrusting out his chin, Buckingham continues: 'I sought my remedy where an Englishman should be always proud to meet his opponents, and where I have never yet shrunk from mine, in a British court of justice.'[38]

His case as a plaintiff had in fact been considerably strengthened by a curious coincidence. While Bankes was no doubt priding himself on his own ingenuity in depriving Buckingham of all the letters which would have provided him with evidence of the good terms on which they had parted in Aleppo, Buckingham had the good fortune to find a single one of them still adhering by its sealing wax to the lid of an old portmanteau. So that, although the Indian Government descended to the considerable injustice of preventing him from prosecuting his case in person, by expediting his removal from the country, a verdict was given in his favour partly on the evidence of this letter, and his calumniators very heavily censured. Since, however, he was not aware of this until some weeks after his arrival in England, he had time to institute three separate actions, first against the *Quarterly Review*, and secondly against Messrs Bankes Senior and Junior.

The first two of Buckingham's opponents, having no judicial leg to stand on, climbed down with some alacrity and made no difficulties about paying costs. Bankes Junior, however, seems to have been an astonishingly tenacious personality. He resorted to every known subterfuge for prolonging the proceedings and complicating the issue. Testimonies were required from residents in India who proved to have returned in the meanwhile to England, leaving the documents behind. Living witnesses were summoned in person from Syria and Egypt without any clear idea of what their testimony was to prove. Thus in 1826, when the case came up for a final trial, over three years had elapsed since the first institution of proceedings, and both parties were practically impoverished.

The case had by now aroused widespread curiosity among the public and the court was crowded with literary and other personalities. They heard Mr Bankes 'at length compelled to adduce his evidence before a jury of his countrymen, whose verdict, after the most patient hearing of all that could be said in his defence, stamps his character in terms, of which the record will remain as long as the Court of King's Bench shall exist'. The verdict was £400 damages for Mr Buckingham – not a very large sum after being deprived of all his property in India.

Buckingham's journey from Aleppo to Baghdad was, as we have seen, performed alone 'without the pleasure, and advantage of a European friend, companion, interpreter, servant or attendant of any sort'. For obvious reasons of convenience 'the dress, manners,

13 View of a typical 'beehive' village in northern Syria (from Layard 1853), looking much as it would have done to Buckingham and still does today. Square compartments in the houses are roofed with domes of mud brick, to avoid the expense of timber.

and language of the country, were adopted and continued throughout the whole of the way'. It took almost two months. One pictures him as a more than robust and heavily bearded bachelor, by no means above an occasional curious (though strictly scientific) glance at the appearance and habits of the oriental ladies whom he met on his way. His costume for the journey, in which he doubtless eventually presented himself at the Riches' breakfast-table, 'consisted of the blue cloth sherwal, jubba, and benish, of the Arab costume; a large overhanging tarboosh, or red cap, falling over the neck and shoulders behind; a white muslin turban, and red silk sash'. His arms were 'a Damascus sabre, a Turkish musket, small carbine, and pistols, with ammunition for each'. And he adds,

the conveniences borne on my own horse were a pipe and tobacco-bag, a metal drinking cup, a pocket-compass, memorandum-books, and ink-stand, on one side of a pair of small khoordj, or Eastern travelling bags; and on the other, the maraboot, or chain-fastenings and irons for securing the horse, by spiking him at night to the earth, on plains where there are no shrubs or trees. A small Turkey carpet, which was to serve for bed, for table and for prayers, and a woollen cloak for a coverlid during the cold nights. . . .

Wishing to leave Aleppo in May, Buckingham found that the great regular caravan travelling to Baghdad across the Syrian Desert would not start until September. But finding a certain Haji – a Moslawi merchant, proclaimed by the British consul, Mr Barker, to be a person of great respectability – who was engaged in forming a smaller caravan (450 camels and about 100 asses and mules, etc.) to travel on the more circuitous route by Mardin and Mosul, he arranged to join it. For a small consideration his baggage was to travel among the ordinary merchandise, while he with his horse and trappings only was to ride with the Haji and be treated in every way as one of his family. This brought him into close contact with the Haji's son who, as Buckingham was to discover at an early stage in the journey, had not inherited any great measure of his father's respectability.

The caravan moved due east from Aleppo approximately on the line of the modern railway. Buckingham noticed the 'beehive' villages, still such a familiar feature of northern Syria, where every house is divided into square compartments, each covered by a dome of mud brick. A caravan, like a train, has the disadvantage that one cannot halt at will to investigate things seen from the road. So Buckingham was denied the pleasant experience of being entertained in one of these 'domed' villages. He would have found their architecture resourceful and surprisingly attractive and the interiors of the houses very clean and orderly. The domes are built on a simple corbelling principle and the square units which they cover are often grouped together with arches between to form a room of different proportion. Their purpose, of course, is to avoid using roofing-beams, which are scarce and expensive. In most large houses only the principal living-room has a flat roof and here a great archway is built across the centre in order to halve the span of the beams and reduce the size necessary. The aesthetic effect is very pleasant, especially as the greater part of the walls in these living-rooms are covered with an elaborate fretwork of relief ornament consisting of tiny ridges made with finger and thumb before the mud plaster is dry. The 'beehive' houses thus reverse the principle which obtains in most western buildings, where only a room of major importance is covered by a dome.

The 'beehive' villages, which are the homes of Arab cultivators, were soon left behind and their place taken by encampments of Turkomans. Buckingham noticed that their women were 'remarkably clean and perfectly unveiled', and, partly because he was approaching the neighbourhood of Harran, Abraham's second home, he was reminded that the Hebrew women of the Old Testament also uncovered their faces. He recalls the story in Genesis (xxxviii) of Judah and his daughter-in-law, and how Tamar 'covered herself with a veil' in order to be taken for a prostitute. Once the caravan was attacked by a party of mounted tribesmen, but they were driven off by a lot of haphazard musketry and the victory celebrated with the waste of a great deal more ammunition. But for the most part, for the purpose of his journal he had to be content with fairly trivial observations, such as that about a donkey which had survived an attack by a hyena though losing 'at least an English pound of flesh from each thigh. (He remembers hearing of Abyssinians 'cutting steaks from a live ox, sewing up the wound, and driving the beast on her journey'.) He also exaggerates a little, describing a pintailed sandgrouse as having a long thin feather projecting 'at least a foot and a half' from its tail.

As might be expected, the first *embêtement* which Buckingham encountered was over money. In Aleppo he had with him an excellent servant found for him by Lady Stanhope, but as there seemed little point in taking him further from his home he decided instead to obtain such service as he needed from members of the caravan. He accordingly arranged for a sum of money to be paid to the Haji through Mr Barker and divided equally between his cook, groom and one of his camel-drivers so as to assure their attention.

Buckingham had been used to saddling and unsaddling his own horse, rubbing him down and generally doing for himself; so for the first few days he hardly noticed the lack of any assistance from the Haji's servants, but when he observed that this state of affairs resulted in some disrespect from his fellow-travellers he decided to bring the matter up. The servants denied all knowledge of any payment and the young Haji, when approached, indignantly refuted the suggestion that either he or his father had received any money for this purpose from Mr Barker. So before reaching the Euphrates crossing at Bir, Buckingham sent a courier back to Aleppo to investigate. (It should be said that this was made possible by the fact that the caravan travelled extremely slowly, the habit of those on horseback being to ride to the head of the procession and then sit drinking coffee by the wayside until the tail had passed.)

On his return the courier did not catch up with the caravan until it had reached Urfa. But he brought with him confirmation of the payment to the young Haji and a sharp rebuke to the old one. Though the latter showed every sign of being extremely angry with the boy, Buckingham could not help reflecting on this 'sad picture of Eastern integrity' since at twenty-four this young man was 'of an age when the heart is generally most inclined to revolt at anything that is base or mean. . . .' He also quotes the Arab proverb: 'If thy neighbour has been once to Mecca, suspect him; if twice, carefully avoid him; but if three times, make haste to remove from near his habitation!'

URFA

It is Buckingham's description of his stay at Urfa (ancient Edessa)[39] which first gives one some measure of his genuine relish in the Eastern manner of living. Yet before recounting Buckingham's side of the picture, it may be of interest here to present for comparison some aspect of the author's own experience of his first short stay in Urfa in 1938, the memory of which has not been dimmed by longer and more recent sojourns there.

It should be said at once that, following Buckingham's example, on this occasion also the principle was conformed to of adopting the contemporary 'dress, manners, and language of the country', inasmuch as one travelled with a Turkish companion who knew no English, carrying a manageable suitcase and wearing an elderly lounge-suit with a soft hat. After travelling much of the night on a lorry, one arrived in the small hours of the morning at a hotel where, unlike Buckingham's picturesque *khan*, the rooms contained four to eight beds. Since it would have been unusual for anyone to occupy one of them after 8 a.m., a full quota of sleep had to be postponed. The greater part of the daylight was spent in accumulating notes and sketches of the town and its historical buildings, but with the best-arranged day of this sort there are certain hours, such as that directly after lunch, when relaxation is natural; also the process of lobbying in the local seat of government for permission to proceed to one's next destination involves many hours of waiting for interviews. It is at these times that, with hotels providing no daytime accommodation, one becomes conscious of one's western shortcomings. To the locally born, of course, no such problem presents itself, since his hours of leisure, whatever proportion of the day they may constitute, are spent in the coffee-shop, and there he has no temptation to make himself conspicuous by reading a book. For the Westerner on such occasions, increasing familiarity with the wooden chair and fly-blown oil-cloth justifies a more anxious anticipation of evening hours enlivened with a little *raki*. Here at at least he finds himself on common ground with those about him.

Yet, in retrospect, the discovery in oneself of such minor ineptitudes in no way impaired the clear picture which one rapidly acquired of the town's individuality. It lies in a saddle between two hills looking southwards towards the plain and is itself an oasis, in that it owes its existence to a great fountain which the Greeks called Callirrhoe. Its clear waters flow in open stone channels through the streets, forming wide ornamental pools in the public gardens and filling stone tanks in the courtyards of the principal buildings. Where there are no buildings the waters irrigate groves of white mulberries and much other fruit. Many of the buildings which Buckingham visited are still standing, but the city-wall has entirely disappeared, its neat ashlar masonry having doubtless proved too great a temptation to modern builders. From the ruined castle on the hill above, two isolated Corinthian columns thrust up skywards, and in the evening their shadows still creep strangely across the town. In the past Tamerlane raised trophies upon their summits. Today their bases are set in concrete to avoid the great disaster which, according to local tradition, will accompany their fall.

Buckingham's caravan halted outside the city-gate at a sort of 'transit-*khan*' used by merchants who did not wish to bring their goods into the city. Here the camels were unloaded and left in charge of a servant. Meanwhile the Haji, not wishing to create ill-feeling by accepting any one of the numerous invitations which he now received from friends in the town, took accommodation for his party in a large caravanserai called the *Khan-el-Goomrook*. Buckingham was delighted by this building, with the privacy of its small, clean rooms ranged around a paved courtyard, and the torrent of clear water which traversed it diagonally. He also remarked that 'this same stream was made contributary, also, to another convenient purpose; all the cloaca being supplied from it with a branch running under them, while it fed a little fountain in each, for the filling of a small square cistern, close by the left hand of the person sitting. . . .' On the upper floor a gallery gave access to a further range of rooms occupied by weavers of fabrics and block-printers.

That evening the Haji's party enjoyed the first of a long series of entertainments. This was a dinner given by a rich local Sayyid at his finely appointed house. In his description of the guest-room

Buckingham mentions 'carpeted divans', a familiar oriental amenity only remarkable for being so entirely uncongenial to western taste. But his account of the meal itself sounds really attractive, partly owing to the mention of a plentiful supply of ice brought down from the mountains.

The drinks included 'iced milk and lebben; a fine iced sherbet, made with honey, cinnamon-water, and spices; and the iced juice of pomegranates of the last year, diluted with water of roses'. Afterwards water-pipes were smoked on the roof, from which there was a fine panoramic view of the entire city. On returning to the *khan*, they found another party awaiting them, given by the humbler dependants of the caravan in return for the Haji's hospitality on the road. An elementary orchestra had been improvised and two Christian pilgrims, returning from Jerusalem, were dancing in a manner which shocked Buckingham but at the same time obviously aroused his curiosity, since he cites many references both classical and modern to such dances being known in other parts of the world. The footnote on the subject grows in proportion to the text until all but two lines are displaced, and there is a great use of italics for phrases like *'certain ideas'* and *'something not to be spoken of'*.[40]

A general returning of calls on the following day enabled Buckingham to see something of the town. He describes the famous Pool of Abraham very much as it appears today. He refers to the great carp swimming in the beautifully transparent water and mentions how visitors, as an act of diversion, 'purchase vegetable leaves and scatter them on the surface, by which the fish are collected literally in heaps'. The Pool is a shallow stone tank about 200 yards long, with flowering shrubs on one side and along the other a flight of steps, above which a screen of pillars and carved tracery gives glimpses of the courtyard of the mosque beyond. At the far end, overlooking the water, there is a charming colonnaded loggia, where, during Buckingham's visit, the Haji and his friends sat with their pipes for many pleasant hours. It was here that he listened with astonishment to a perfectly serious dissertation by an elderly Moslem on the sacred character of the fish and the failure of any known form of cooking to make them edible. At a Christian party on the previous evening he had much enjoyed a small plate of fried carp with his 'Rakhee'!

Buckingham's companions must have come in for a great deal more walking than they were accustomed to, for he seems to have insisted on exploring the town from end to end. Occasionally he was favoured with unexpected vignettes of domestic life which he duly noted in his diary. The larger lakes were often full of bathing boys, and once he came suddenly upon a party of females occupied in the same way. He was disappointed that his companions 'turned instantly aside, and obliged me to follow them, though we might have enjoyed this picture of natural beauty unobserved, and without disturbing for a moment the supposed seclusion of those who had chosen this retreat'.

14 *The Pool of Abraham ('Halil Rahman Gölü') at Urfa, with the mosque in the background. The pool still contains the 'sacred' carp mentioned by Buckingham.*

So the days at Urfa passed by with visits and entertainments, and soon the caravan was due to reform and move onwards towards Mardin. Before he left the *khan*, Buckingham paid a long visit to the workshops of the block-printers in the upper storey. He saw how the small block bearing a section of the pattern was bound to the palm of the left hand and impressed by a blow of the right fist. Noticing the clumsiness and slowness of the procedure, he explained to the printers some of the improved methods common in Europe. 'Their admiration was very powerfully excited, and the director of the establishment made me the offer of a very handsome remuneration if I would remain a few weeks at Orfah to superintend such improvements as the mechanics of the town might make, under my direction.' Charmed by the whole atmosphere of the town, Buckingham almost considered accepting the offer.

MARDIN AND BEYOND

The journey to Mardin was mainly remarkable for·the rapacious exactions of the principal Arab tribe through whose territory the way lay. At the temporary headquarters of their sheikh the caravan was submitted, almost without complaint from the intimidated merchants, to what really amounted to wholesale and arbitrary looting. Buckingham, having made himself conspicuous by not fawning to these bandits in the conventional manner, had to pay a sum of a thousand piastres, or thirty pounds, in blackmail to avoid losing the contents of his saddlebags. His valuable Damascus sword he had concealed against the small of his back, but faced with the

15 An attack by mounted Turkomans on the Arab encampment where Buckingham's caravan was already being looted.

difficulty of mounting his horse, was compelled to declare it and make further payment. During this transaction the looters suddenly found themselves being looted by a marauding band of Turkomans, and a complicated fight followed, in which Buckingham joined with some relish, 'coming into grappling contact with three individuals in succession, neither of whom escaped unhurt from the struggle'. This kind of tribal extortion continued to be the principal deterrent to regular trade between the Ottoman provinces well into the present century.

Mardin stands on the most southerly spur of the Turkish mountains, looking out over Mesopotamia. From this elevation the plain appears interminable, without contour, and featureless save for the little peaks of Jebel Sinjar away to the east. It is an extravagantly beautiful town. Tradition says of its inhabitants that 'they never see a bird flying above them', which of course refers to its dramatic situation. The rocky summit of the hill forms a great boat-shaped platform upon which, in early Moslem times, a considerable fortress once stood. Buckingham and others have left engravings showing a powerful line of towered walls against the skyline, but today only two or three ruined pavilions remain among a litter of fallen stones. Several hundred feet beneath, the town is terraced into the flank of the hill, and beyond the outermost line of houses there is a further drop of over a thousand feet to the plain level. The houses are built of a sort of honey-coloured limestone. This must be plentiful and easy to work, since there has grown up at some fairly recent period an almost unique tradition of craftsmanship in stone-cutting. In every building down to the meanest hovel, doorways, windows and all other prominent features are enriched with finely carved ornament – Byzantine, or, more nearly, Romanesque in character. Actually none of this work can be more than a century old, since Buckingham expressly remarks on the poor appearance of the houses, and seems only to have seen ornament in a single mosque. Like the present writer, however, he must have first approached the

16 A caravan at the approach to Mardin, whose terraced buildings and ancient castle overlook the distant plains of Mesopotamia to the south.

town from the west, a little before sunset, coming over the shoulder of the hill and being confronted with an almost orange glow on the stonework of the houses against a marine blue haze over the plain. He has left a quaint drawing of the scene as it appeared to him.

Here again at Mardin it was unnecessary for the caravan to climb up to the town itself, so the goods and baggage animals remained in a village called Soor at the foot of the hill, probably near the modern railway station. Buckingham had an introduction to the Syrian Patriarch of Mardin, and finding that he resided not in the city itself, but in a monastery called Der Za'feran a few miles to the east, parted from the Haji and made his way thither. Many of the pilgrims from Jerusalem travelling with his own caravan were there ahead of him and a big party was already in progress. He noted afterwards that 'not less than twenty jars of arrack were drank by as many persons – all of them, too, before the meal as a stimulant, and not a single cup after it'. Der Za'feran was at that time the centre of a flourishing Christian community. In the 1930s it was still maintained by a Bishop and half-a-dozen monks, but much of the building had fallen into decay and the village which Buckingham mentions outside the walls was in ruins. There was a cruciform chapel with a great deal of beautiful Byzantine carving and a much depleted library, which, however, still boasted of an enormous Syriac testament, dating from the middle of the twelfth century and with fine illustrations. Buckingham was shown this book and suspected it to be one seen by Tavernier in 1644.[41] He also attended morning service in the chapel, at which, like everyone else, he remained standing about four hours 'without even the indulgence of the crutches in use among the Christians of the Greek Communion'.

On moving up to Mardin, Buckingham found the usual uncertainty as to when the caravan would be able to leave for Mosul, and was driven by an impatience, familiar to all those who have experienced this kind of journey, to make a false step. He had authority from Barker in Aleppo to travel with any *tatar* or official courier going in the same direction, so he determined to ride northwards to Diyarbakir, the principal halting-place between Istanbul and Baghdad, in the hope of attaching himself to one. This afforded him an opportunity which he would otherwise have missed of seeing Diyarbakir, but as luck would have it, no courier was expected for some time, and when, having lost his Kurdish guide, he took the risk of hurrying back to Mardin alone, he found that the Haji's caravan in the meanwhile had already left.

Buckingham plainly did not enjoy his stay in Diyarbakir, owing to the disappointment which he encountered at the *tatar* head-quarters and the abduction of his guide by an angry creditor. His nicest moment was probably the first sight of the city which he obtained suddenly on approaching from the Mardin road. He says:

It was on the moment of our coming on the brow of the slope, which here formed the southern bank of the river [Tigris], and gave us the view of the stream flowing by, that we caught the first sight of Diarbekir, which burst upon us all at once, and presented a picture of so much interest, that I voluntarily checked the bridle of my horse to dwell upon the scene; while my companions, to whom it was a familiar one, dashed across the river without heeding it for a moment. . . .

This is indeed an unforgettable sight, for the long line of jet-black fortifications seem to crouch above the Tigris gorge, guarding the approach to the mountains beyond. Buckingham has again done full justice to it with a sketch, in the foreground of which his companions are to be seen galloping full-tilt into the river.

Back in Mardin, Buckingham reckoned the probable speed of the caravan on its journey down into the plain, and calculated that by leaving immediately he could overtake it at Nusaybin. He accordingly attached himself to a horse-dealer, who appeared to have the same intention, and found himself travelling in company with 'about fifty spirited and unsaddled horses'. Minor disadvan-

17 Buckingham crossing the Tigris at the approach to Diyarbakir.

18 A photograph taken by Gertrude Bell of the walls of Diyarbakir (Amida), which date in part from the Persian wars of the Roman Emperors. It was said of the city: 'Black the walls and black the dogs and black the hearts of Black Amid.'

tages of the arrangement became clear at the first halt, where he spent 'a night of imperfect repose, being hourly disturbed by the breaking loose of the horses and their fighting with each other. . . .' The following day, however, his luck changed. He was suddenly overtaken by a pair of *tatars* from Istanbul carrying mail to Rich in Baghdad. They had arrived in Diyarbakir on the same day as he left for Mardin. Furthermore he had been right about the caravan, which they found halted at Nusaybin, and again undergoing the hateful process of assessment for tribute by yet another tribal chief. The new arrivals at once attracted the unwelcome attention of the sheikh, and Buckingham was forced to part with the last remnants of his ready cash.

Nusaybin today is a Turkish village on the frontier neighbouring a somewhat larger Syrian market town called Kamishli. Here a curious corner of Syria known as the *Bec de Canard* runs eastwards to the Tigris, so that the present railway crosses two frontiers between Nusaybin and Mosul. Almost nothing is left of Nusaybin, the Roman fortress-city of Nisibis which for a brief period became capital of Iraq (Septimius Severus made it his headquarters when 'Parthia' became a Roman province); even the ruined classical temple and other columned buildings which Buckingham drew are now no longer visible. Between the Turkish frontier and the strange isolated mountain range of Sinjar is a wide expanse of fertile upland country, slightly undulating, which in Buckingham's time was apparently mainly occupied by Yezidis and Kurdish tribes.

He gives a fairly accurate description of the caravan's course south-eastwards from Nusaybin towards the eastern foothills of Sinjar;[42] yet on his map the Jebel Sinjar itself has slipped westwards onto the wrong side of the Jaghjagh river, and he shows the dotted course of a new and peculiar waterway, branching off from the latter and running south-eastwards to empty into the Tigris. The banks of this stream he probably intended to be the location of a curious episode which he describes on the road to Mosul.

Apparently in the Sinjar plain itself the danger from marauding bands of Yezidis was so acute that the lesser evil of a paid tribal escort had to be resorted to. Thus from a point near the modern Iraqi frontier the caravan was joined by a troop of eighty armed horsemen. This stage of the journey was to be at night, so the previous day was spent encamped at a place called by Buckingham 'Romoila' (probably Rumeilan – the Little Sandhills, near Tell Kotchek station). The whole of the Haji's guest-tent was occupied by the escort, and, it now being the first week in July, beneath the cloak which Buckingham rigged up as a shelter from the sun, his 'excellent thermometer' gave a score of 126°F (52°C). The night-march was begun with the horses and camels already thirsty, and by midnight the former were suffering considerably. It was at this point that in pitch darkness they came suddenly upon a deep stream flowing swiftly between rushes, but with a high cliff-like bank. Buckingham pictures most vividly the chaos which ensued, with the horses, unable to reach the water, plunging in with their riders or loads and some of them being swept away by the current. He himself had immense difficulty in controlling his mount, but was providentially assisted by a powerful Indian *fakir* travelling with the caravan, who restrained the rearing and snorting animal while he himself let down a large drinking cup on a string and drew up repeated draughts of cold water. The camels meanwhile pro-ceeded leisurely along the bank to a more convenient watering-place. This was Buckingham's first introduction to Iraq. On 6 July the caravan arrived in Mosul, but having no intention of prolong-ing his stay in that town, after a formal call on the Pasha and a brief visit to the mounds of Nineveh, he set out with the two *tatars*, Jonas and Ali, on the final stage of his journey.

19 Travelling off-track at night and short of water Buckingham's caravan reaches a river with steep banks (perhaps a tributary of the Khabur) and chaos ensues.

CHAPTER FIVE

Rich's last years

While in Mosul Buckingham heard that two months previously the Riches had spent some weeks there on their way back from Europe. Their leave from Baghdad, which had gradually prolonged itself on account of Claudius' ill health, had lasted just over two and a half years, and from their own point of view had been the greatest possible success. Claudius was a great deal better. He himself had not in the end reached London, but a prolonged stay in Vienna, Paris and other European capitals had provided an invigorating change of atmosphere and sufficient mental stimulation to equip him for a further period of work in Baghdad. Regarded from any point of view, it had been the kind of leave of which today nobody could complain.

Leaving Baghdad in the autumn of 1813 there is no doubt that Claudius had been an extremely sick man. Partly perhaps on account of this fact and of his anxiety to reach Europe, he had forced the pace a good deal during the whole of the journey to Istanbul, and except for a few days' stay at Mardin, where he was held up by a bout of fever, the party had ridden almost at *tatar* speed. Mary seems to have stood up to the journey remarkably well, only weakening on two occasions. The first was just short of Nusaybin, after riding 100 miles with only five hours' rest, when the party of a hundred people had to halt on her account. A little shelter was made for her with felts and spears and after two hours' sleep she was able to carry on. The second occasion was several days later on the road from Mardin to Diyarbakir. She says:

At one spot we had to round a huge cliff that hung over a precipitous ravine, which narrowed to one or two feet in width, broken and crumbling at the edge. Most of the escort and Claudius passed over, but I was too frightened and felt I could not attempt it. Claudius was quite stern and told me I must be brave, otherwise I should have to be left behind. Such severe words had their effect and, letting my horse pick its own way, I clambered round the bluff, to find Claudius waiting anxiously to see what I should do. He looked quite pale and I felt ashamed, as in our company was an unfortunate little girl, a slave who had been lately captured, about six years old, who, mounted on a horse with a halter, surmounted all difficulties without a murmur or the least assistance.[43]

20 A mountain road in Kurdistan depicted by Buckingham, not unlike those described by Mary Rich on her husband's overland journey to Istanbul in 1813.

Coming down on to the shore of the Sea of Marmara at Izmit some weeks later, the Riches were met by a dragoman of the British Embassy in Istanbul, bearing an invitation to stay with the Ambassador, Sir Robert Lister. The last hours of their journey along the coast road to Scutari and across the Straits were made less comfortable by a violent snowstorm, and arriving exhausted at the Embassy they persuaded the dragoman to smuggle them in through a back door, so as to have time to recover their composure a little before meeting their host and hostess.

But now for the time being their troubles were over. They had before them the delightful experience, after five years of comparative exile, of renewing acquaintance with the cultivated and elegant life of Europe. The Listers were kindly, pleasant people, and the cosmopolitan society of Istanbul served as a stepping-stone to the splendours in store for them at Budapest, and Vienna. Mary had been nineteen when she left Bombay, and her dress-allowance on a very modest scale. Choosing a 'gala' dress for her first ball in five years must have been something of a thrill.

They had planned to continue their journey overland, but it was April before Claudius was well enough to undertake the long coach ride through the Balkans. It took them through Bulgaria to Bucharest; then to Szeged on the modern Yugoslav frontier, across the Hungarian *puszta* to Budapest and so to Vienna. Here they remained some weeks and entered with great enjoyment into the musical-comedy world of the Hapsburg capital. At Schönbrunn they saw the Emperor return in state from a visit to Paris and drove back to find the city celebrating – almost the entire population dancing in *dirndls* and *lederhosen*. Later they were presented at court by the British minister. Mary was extremely proud of her husband, who wore a magnificent hussar uniform of french grey and silver.

While in Vienna the Riches heard that Sir James Mackintosh was to be in Basle at the end of September, so they travelled on through

Bavaria to meet him, and a great family reunion took place. After a few days Mary went off with her father to Lucerne on a short pleasure-trip, while Claudius went on ahead to Paris. The leave granted him by the Company had expired while he was in Vienna, but anticipating a favourable reply to his request for an extension on grounds of health, he had made no arrangements for his return to Baghdad. On reaching Paris he received his first mail from India, which included a rebuke from his employers for overstaying his leave and an intimation that his allowances were to be very considerably cut. By the time Mary rejoined him, however, he was enjoying Paris and had already met and dined with the Duke of Wellington, who at that time shared the illusion that the Napoleonic Wars were at an end. Irascible old colonial officials in Bombay must have begun to seem fairly remote. He now, however, took the precaution of sending Mary over to London, so that she might 'make interest' for him with certain cabinet ministers to whom she would have access through her father. This expedient (a familiar one to anyone who like Rich has lived long in Baghdad) was entirely successful. Mary spent a pleasant four months at the Mackintosh house in Great George Street, returning in May 1815, by which time pressure had been brought to bear. A very senior director of the Company had been impressed into Claudius' cause, and instructions had been sent to Bombay that he should return at leisure to the Baghdad Residency, and the cuts in his increment be modified. Sir Evan Nepean had by that time effected his dismissal, but was compelled to reinstate him.

With improved health Rich's horror of returning to Baghdad was diminishing, and it was now really time to make arrangements for the journey. A route was planned through northern Italy to the Adriatic and so by boat to Istanbul. As this allowed for a stay of several weeks in both Milan and Venice, no one could deny by the time he embarked that he had had an adequate share of European amenities. His six months in Paris had been largely spent in the distinguished company of people such as Madame de Staël, driving his own pair of horses in the Bois in the afternoon, and in the evenings visiting the opera. He also saw the return of Napoleon from Elba. In Milan there was more music. For the first time he heard Paganini play, and wrote in his journal a long, astonished commentary on his virtuosity. His final three weeks in Venice were the climax of his holiday. The familiar clichés used by his biographer to describe this ('the captivating romance of the Queen of the Adriatic'; 'the Piazza palpitating with life'; 'the beauty of the scene, with the wondrous succession of tints of an Italian sunset'; 'the silvery light of the moon, accompanied by the song of the gondoliers') are really superfluous. Claudius had always loved Italy, and with Baghdad looming ahead, Venice seemed the apex of European culture. On 29 June he met the Duchess of Devonshire, who informed him of Napoleon's defeat at Waterloo. A week later he and Mary once more set out on their travels.

There was a minor consolation at Trieste, where before embarking they were joined by a young German called Bellino, whom they had met in Vienna.[44] Rich had greatly liked him and, finding him a would-be orientalist, had engaged him as secretary at a salary of £80 per annum. This was the beginning of a long and very pleasant relationship, which ended only with Bellino's sad death of fever in 1820.

The voyage by sea down the Adriatic, past Crete and through the Aegean was mostly familiar ground for Claudius, but at this point it becomes clear that his journey was being deliberately prolonged. Rather than disembark at one of the Levant ports, from which he could easily have reached Aleppo, he preferred first to revisit Istanbul, where he remained for two months before repeating the arduous journey across Anatolia. The fact was that Claudius was still a little unsure of his relationship with the Company in Bombay and disinclined to reach Baghdad before his position was definitely regularized.

By the time he arrived in Mosul there was still no news, and he was kept uncomfortably hanging about there for over a month. Finally in March Hine arrived from Baghdad with the anxiously awaited dispatch, which told him that he was to return to Baghdad as Resident with his allowances not impossibly reduced. So the party embarked for the final stage of their journey on a large *kelek*, and on a spring evening a week later they saw the last rays of the sun gilding the domes of Kadhimain, and drew in beneath the pillared balconies of Rusafah.

BUCKINGHAM IN BAGHDAD

By the time Buckingham arrived in Baghdad the Riches had been back over four months and life at the Residency had resumed its normal course. His journey from Mosul had been a great deal less comfortable than theirs. From the outset, the noisy and conceited *tatar*, called Jonas, had been a great trial – lagging behind in Mosul when they set out in order to snatch a few last hours with one of the numerous wives he boasted of along the route, bad tempered and abusive when he caught up with them at the crossing of the Greater Zab. The way to Baghdad led by Erbil to Kirkuk and so onward through the Jebel Hamrin. At Kifri, where a change of horses should have been found, only one was available, and Jonas stormed off into the town to look for more. Buckingham and the younger *tatar*, Ali, assuming that if his bullying was of no avail there was a long wait ahead, retired quietly to bed, but on awaking next morning an ominous silence in the *khan* led to the discovery that Jonas had in the night mounted the only horse and left for Baghdad without them.

Several days elapsed before they found a friendly merchant taking a small caravan to the capital and persuaded him to provide them with mounts. Even then Buckingham's troubles were not over. At Kara Tepe ('Tuppe'), where the party halted to rest in the courtyard of a mosque, he somehow succeeded in offending the merchant, and when they came to remount, found that his horse had been given to someone else, and that in its place was an already heavily-loaded mule. As there was no alternative, he perched himself uncomfortably on the summit of the load and the caravan proceeded. After halting at Delhi 'Abbas, a start was made again in the hottest part of the afternoon and Buckingham, who had been seated 'with a jug of water in one hand and a fan in the other', found himself subjected to the indignity of himself reloading the refractory mule without even anyone to hold the halter. Fortunately, as he says, 'a proud determination not to sink under it [the indignity], bore me through all my labour', and after a while he succeeded. He was now streaming with sweat, so before starting he stripped and saturated all his clothes in cold water, including the skull-cap which he wore on his shaved head.

What happened next may perhaps be related at some length and in Buckingham's own words, since the amiable restraint of his style, contrasting as it does with the venom and irony of most modern travel-writers under similar provocation, is most characteristic of his whole generation:

It was just as we had crossed one of the canals, and while suffering intensely from thirst, that I asked a Dervish, who was drinking from the hollow shell of a cocoa-nut at the stream, to give me a draught of water from his vessel; but this man, though devoted by his office to the exercise of hospitality and charitable offices to all mankind, and though he had but the moment before returned me the salutation of the faithful, added insolence to his refusal, and pricking my mule with a sharp instrument, caused the poor beast, already sinking under his double burden of a lading and a rider, to rear and kick, and ultimately to throw me off, with a part of the lading upon me. The agility of the Dervish, who was young and active, enabled him to escape the punishment which I should otherwise have inflicted upon him, for this breach of his own precepts to others; but as I was now dismounted, I began to reload the articles that had fallen off, after which, I repaired to the stream, to allay both my thirst and my anger at the same time. On endeavouring to remount, which was a task of no small difficulty, as the lading of the beast was wide and high, and there were neither stirrups, nor a stone, or the smallest eminence of any kind near us, the whole of the poor creatures burthen came tumbling on the ground. . . . To increase the evil, as I let go the hold of the halter, in order to use both hands in securing the packages, the mule made off at a full gallop, frisking and flinging its head in the air, pawing with its forelegs, and kicking with its hind ones, as if in derision at my dilemma, and triumph for its own happy riddance and escape. As the rest of the party had by this time got far a-head, I waited in this miserable plight for two full hours, by the wayside, literally guarding the merchandise with one eye, and keeping a look-out with the other on the movements of my truant mule, who regaled himself on the shrubs near; besides being in continual apprehension of having the whole property (which was not my own) taken possession of by robbers, who are never wanting to follow up the stragglers of a caravan, and plunder all they can lay their hands on. At length, some peasants of the country coming by, very charitably assisted me to catch my mule, and even helped me to reload it, when, with their assistance, for it could not otherwise have been done, I re-mounted, and continued my way. . . .

Though I was now perfectly alone, and liable therefore to insult and pillage from any handful of men who might cross my path, I went on with a light heart at the prospect of my trouble soon to be at end, and had filled my pipe on the mule's back to smoke away my cares, and to make its enjoyment compensate for the want of a companion. As I aban-doned the halter of the beast, by throwing it for a moment across his neck, while I struck a light, which requires the use of both hands, and while I was in the act of drawing my first whiff, the refractory brute, probably from imagining the pricking of the Dervish to be near him again, first cocked his ears forward, then stood fixed and immovable and at length, after three or four repeated flingings of his hindlegs in the air, again unseated me, and now, in the confusion of this totally unexpected result, the baggage and the animal itself came tumbling after and upon me, and nearly crushed me to death by their fall. I was a long while before I could extricate myself from this state, for even the beast was in some way tangled by its own girths and bandages, and could not rise from the ground. When I had with difficulty regained my legs, I found the bur-then, from the firmness with which it was last braced on, to be all secure; and by my assistance, and a vigorous effort of its own, the mule rose again with all its lading fast as before. All my efforts to mount were, however, quite ineffectual; the packages, being large and comparatively light, making an elevation of three or four feet above the animal's back. My poor mule had had his share of disasters, as well as myself; and he seemed determined, by all the freaks and tricks in his power to perform, to show that he would not hazard any more. I was obliged therefore, bruised and tired and irritated as I was, to trudge the rest of my way on foot, holding the halter of my charge firmly in my hand, to prevent his escape, and much more disposed to give him the stripes of the Parisian ass-driver, as related by Sterne, than to feed him on the macaroons of the sentimental traveller.[45]

For Buckingham the journey's end was now almost in sight, but even so his troubles were not over. The minarets of Baghdad appeared on the horizon with the first light of dawn and it was still early morning when he arrived, dragging his mule, at one of the city gates – probably the *Bab al Wastani*. Here he was stopped by Turkish customs officials, and having admitted that neither the mule nor its load were his own, was not allowed to proceed until the owner appeared. While he was waiting humbly beside the gate, 'seated cross-legged on the dusty ground', an elaborately dressed cavalcade cantered past into the city amidst the respectful saluta-tions of the crowd. This was the Pasha himself, returning from a morning ride, and at the end of the procession came two well-mounted individuals, whom he immediately realized from their speaking English to be Hine and Bellino. Feeling the humiliation of his position he refrained from making himself known.

But now his patience was exhausted. 'Being', he says, 'able to bear with it no longer, I drew my pistol from my girdle, and daring anyone at the peril of his life to molest me, I led off my mule in triumph, amid the execrations of the guards, for my insolence, but cheered by the shouts and applause of the rabble, for my defiance of a class on whom they look with the hatred of an oppressed race towards their tyrants.' Before presenting himself at the Residency, there was one more score to settle. When he appeared eventually at the Riches' breakfast-table, he brought with him the *tatar*, Jonas, for well-deserved chastisement.

It is not to be wondered at that, after so many tribulations, Buckingham found the Riches' establishment greatly to his taste. On Rich's own part, the arrival of any British guest at the Residency was something of an occasion, while one of Buckingham's calibre could be sure of the most cordial welcome. But for the moment the visitor's immediate requirements were obvious, and after a few words with his host he was conducted by a servant to the bath, where he no doubt effected a substantial *changement de décor*, discarding the Moghrabi merchant's paraphernalia and reappearing at last, save for the bizarre circumstance of his shaved head, in the guise of an English Esquire. As he says, after much enjoyment there (at the bath), he then 'returned to pass a day of unusual happiness in the intelligent and amiable society of Mr and Mrs Rich and the other members of their family'.

No praise could be high enough for the hospitality which he now enjoyed. 'The change from all that could be disagreeable, in the way of living, to so much comfort, and, indeed luxury, as I found in the house of Mr and Mrs Rich, added to the still higher charm of the intelligent society with which I had become surrounded there, was sufficient to repay me for all the vexations I had suffered on my way.' He even confessed 'I continued to enjoy these pleasures uninterruptedly for several days, before I felt even a desire to gratify that curiosity which is so generally impatient on entering a large and celebrated city'.

In the weeks which followed he did in fact satisfy this curiosity with extreme thoroughness, and recorded the results of his investigations in a long and most detailed description of the city, which for many years continued to be accepted as an authoritative document. He also visited the more famous ancient sites accessible from the capital – 'Aqar Quf, the ruined *ziggurat* tower of the Kassite city Dur Kurigalzu, which, like most early travellers, he took to be a mausoleum; Babylon and Birs Nimrod, whither he rode with Bellino, wearing Bedouin costume and posing as his dragoman, and later Ctesiphon. Actually his stay with the Riches was destined to continue a great deal longer than he had expected, for immediately on returning from his journey to Babylon he was taken with a fever, which developed into a severe illness. This was in August, and in spite of the attentions of Hine and Mary's careful nursing his recovery was retarded by a spell of appallingly hot weather (between 119° and 122°F (48° and 50°C) for over a fortnight).

Buckingham might obviously have chosen worse places to be ill in. He says himself 'the tedium of my confinement was considerably relieved by the number and variety of excellent books, which

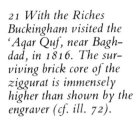

21 With the Riches Buckingham visited the 'Aqar Quf, near Baghdad, in 1816. The surviving brick core of the ziggurat is immensely higher than shown by the engraver (cf. ill. 72).

Mr Rich's library contained, and which were accompanied also by the most unreserved communication from the gentleman himself of everything calculated to increase the interest of my journey eastward'. He goes on to mention Rich's extensive and valuable collection of antiquities, among which he noted 'cylinders, amulets, idols and intaglios of the most curious kind'. Yet in his mind the association of their character is usually with objects he has seen in Egypt, making one realize the complete unfamiliarity at the time of Mesopotamian art. He did not, however, exaggerate the value of the collection, for after Claudius' death it was bought from Mary by the British Museum for £7,000.[46]

Towards the end of August, Buckingham assured himself, by means of an experimental ride to Ctesiphon, that his health had almost sufficiently recovered to continue his journey to India. But, there being for the moment no news of a vessel leaving Basra, he had a few days' grace in which to make some further observations of social life in Baghdad. During the early days of his stay he had experienced some difficulty in understanding the local brand of Arabic, which even today remains a fairly distinctive dialect. 'I had', he says, 'sufficient evidence myself of the Arabic being very bad, taking that of Cairo, of Mecca, and of the Yemen as standards of purity in pronunciation; for scarcely anything more harsh in sound, or more barbarous in construction, and the use of foreign words, can be conceived, than the dialect of Baghdad. Turkish, Persian, Koord and even Indian expressions, disfigure their sentences; and such Arabic words as are used are scarcely to be recognized on a first hearing, from the corrupted manner in which they are spoken.'[47] But since this circumstance perhaps enabled him more easily to pass for an Egyptian Moslem, he afterwards enjoyed mixing in every kind of social and religious circle in the town.

Some final observations he was now able to make without leaving the house. The routine of the Residency interested him – Rich's morning *diwan*, 'which was regularly attended by all the officers of his own establishment, and by the heads of the chief departments of government in the city . . . everything was conducted with great decorum, and nothing could be more evident than the high degree of respect for the Resident with which these interviews inspired the visitors';[48] the long hours of refuge in the *sirdabs*, and his bed beneath a 'mosquito muslin' on the highest part of the housetop with nothing above us but the starry canopy of heaven'. From this point of vantage his unblushing curiosity enabled him to examine 'without being once perceived, or even suspected to be a witness . . . the early-morning habits of some neighbouring families'. He gives a quaint and most detailed description of a Moslem lady humbly assisting with her husband's toilet, and turning finally to her own prayers only when she has him established comfortably on his cushions with his morning pipe. This brings him by devious ways to discussing the habit of tattooing, and the book ends on a now familiar note:

There are artists in Baghdad, whose profession it is to decorate the forms of ladies with the newest patterns of wreaths, zones and girdles, for the bosom or the waist; and as this operation must occupy a considerable time, and many 'sittings', as an English portrait-painter would express it, they must possess abundant opportunities of studying in perfection the beauties of the female form, in a manner not less satisfactory, perhaps, than that which is pursued in the Royal Academies of Sculpture and Painting in Europe.

KER PORTER, KURDISTAN AND A RESIDENCY SIEGE

The Riches spent four more years in Baghdad, the first three of which were comparatively uneventful. Claudius devoted himself with increasing interest to the study of archaeology, and added rapidly to his collection of ancient manuscripts and coins. His memoir on the ruins of Babylon, published in 1815, had now run into a fourth edition, but his arguments had come in for some criticism from a certain Major Rennell, an orientalist and historical geographer. In 1817 he accordingly paid a second visit to Hillah with Bellino and carefully rechecked his theories and topography. His second set of memoirs, subsequently published (1818), virtually exhausted the possibilities of inference without excavation.

Later in the same year his work in the archaeological field was greatly stimulated by a six-week visit from Sir Robert Ker Porter. Hilprecht says of Porter:

From childhood loving and practising the arts, he had become a famous painter of international reputation, whose eminent talents, striking personality and final marriage with a Russian princess had secured for him a social standing which enabled him, by his pen and brush, to reach circles hitherto but little influenced by the books of ordinary travellers and the scientific and often dry investigations of men of the type of Otter, Niebuhr, Beauchamp and Rich. In his popularization of a subject which so far had stirred the minds of only a limited class of people, and in

22 The wealthy traveller and artist, Sir Robert Ker Porter, in Russian uniform: a portrait by George Harlow dated 1808, ten years before his visit to the Riches in Baghdad.

appealing, by his religious sentiment, the manner of his style, and the accurate representation of what he had observed, not less to men of science and religion than to the aristocratic circles of Europe, on whose interest and financial support the resurrection of Assyria and Babylonia chiefly depended, lies the significance of Ker Porter as a Babylonian explorer.[49]

He had been spending some months in Persia, visiting and recording ancient monuments, and the ponderous volume in which he describes the journey[50] is decorated with the most spirited and excellent engravings made from his sketches, including those of the famous 'boar-hunt' and 'stag-hunt' at Tak-i-Bustan. Travelling down to Baghdad from Kermanshah, he found himself held up at Kizil Robat by two of his party becoming seriously ill with fever and himself, owing to a miscalculation, embarrassed for ready money. A courier was sent ahead to the Residency, and in a commendably short time returned with an impressive personage, who, introducing himself as Rich's *cawass*, delivered to Sir Robert a purse containing several thousand piastres. It is a remarkable reflection on Rich's reputation that, after the courier had left, the proprietor of the *khan* in which Porter was staying, having learnt the purpose of the courier's errand, at once himself offered the loan of a very large sum of money, requiring only a verbal assurance that it should be repaid to a friend in Baghdad.

Like Buckingham during his stay in Baghdad, Porter in Bellino's company visited four of the most accessible Babylonian sites: Babylon, Birs Nimrod (where he saw 'three majestic lions taking the air upon the heights of the pyramid'), Al 'Oheimir (the ruins of

Kish) and 'Aqar Quf. Of the last named he has not only left four admirable sketch-elevations, which constitute the most useful record for gauging the continued denudation of the ruin, but he arrived nearer than any previous visitor to the correct explanation of the building's original purpose.[51] 'I should suppose,' he says, 'the mass we now see to be no more than the base of some loftier super-structure, probably designed for the double use of a temple and an observatory; a style of sacred edifice common with the Chaldeans, and likely to form the principal object in every city and town devoted to the idolatry of Belus and the worship of the stars.'

Ker Porter, like everyone else, was charmed with Rich's company and hospitality, to which he afterwards paid a notable tribute, holding him up as a model for all British representatives in remote countries. Of his reception he wrote: 'Personally I was a stranger to Mr Rich; yet the most eloquent language cannot describe the friendly warmth with which both himself and his accomplished wife bade me welcome; nor can I express, in any words, my sense of their subsequent kindness.'[52]

Early in 1820 Rich made a short trip with Bellino to Qasr-i-Shirin and what he saw of the fringes of the Kurdish country greatly aroused his interest in the Kurds. Having in any case intended to spend the hot summer months of that year away from Baghdad, he now began to plan a more elaborate official visit to Sulaimaniyah and Kurdistan, and by the end of April was ready to leave. His writings on the subject of this journey are all embodied in the two volumes called *Narrative of a Residence in Koordistan*, which Mary edited after his death and published in London in 1836. For him the expedition was an immense success, particularly since he encountered in almost all the Kurds with whom he came into contact congenial and sympathetic qualities in such marked contrast to his Turkish associates in Baghdad. On leaving Sulaimaniyah the whole of his feelings were summed up in one strangely melancholy conclusion:

24 Kurdish soldiers recorded by Rich during his travels in the Sulaimaniyah area.

I quit Koordistan with unfeigned regret. I, most unexpectedly, found in it the best people that I have ever met in the East. I have formed friendships, and been uniformly treated with a degree of sincerity, kindness and unbounded hospitality, which I fear I must not again look for in the course of my weary pilgrimage; and the remembrance of which will last as long as life itself endures.[53]

Rich's journals are of course packed with information – the results of his diligent and conscientious inquiries on all subjects. Bearings were taken at all times, the temperature and weather recorded and even small excavations made when interesting ancient sites were discovered. But today the country he visited is mapped and familiar, the roads he travelled are surfaced for motor traffic and the young *aghas* are western-educated. So it is in no way surprising that his writings and notes have become a subject only of curiosity and admiration. For a human picture of the cavalcade which set out from Baghdad in the spring of 1820 in pouring rain on a journey to Kurdistan, and of its arrival and reception at Sulaimaniyah, one must turn to an appendix, included no doubt with considerable diffidence by Mary, and consisting of a fragment of her own journal. Here is a sample:

April 16. Mr Rich was already gone on to the garden of Hajee Abdullah Bey, about three miles from Bagdad, where he had been invited to pass the last night; and from thence our journey fairly begins. The night was very stormy and rainy. All of us were much astonished about ten at night to see Hajee Abdullah Bey's wife walk in. She had mounted her horse, and, in the midst of all the bad weather, had come three miles in the dark purposely to pass the last evening with me.

April 17. After getting a couple of hours' sleep, I rose by daylight, and, with unfeigned sorrow on both parts, took leave of my kind friends . . . we proceeded on to the Bey's garden, surrounded by my attendants on horseback. We were not, however, allowed to pass the house of our friends without dismounting and taking some refreshment. As Mr Rich was just mounting when we arrived, and as eastern etiquette makes it indecorous for a man to appear to care anything more about his wife than the *rest of his baggage*, or to allow her to form part of his more stately procession, I the more readily accepted the invitation, and had the advantage of eating a very good breakfast ere I commenced my journey, and in the mean time Mr Rich and his party got well on their road. . . .

Mary then gives some details of her actual method of travel, and that of her companions, Taqui, the Armenian lady's maid, and the obscure character called 'Minas's Mother', whose terror at every new development of the journey was a continual source of amusement.

I travel in a *takhterawan*, or litter, to give an idea of which I merely add, that it very much resembles a palanquin swung between two shafts before and two behind, to which are harnessed two mules. Over it is a covering of scarlet cloth, and it is ornamented at the four corners with gilt balls. My female attendants were in mohaffas, or a kind of cage, two of which are swung on one mule, and balance each other; but as Minas's mother is very stout and poor Taqui very slender, it was a difficult and nice operation to make the balance equal by throwing in a quantity of stones on Taqui's side. It is by no means a comfortable conveyance owing to the constrained posture the person is obliged to sit in. . . .

The early part of the journey northwards over the flat country beside the Diyala was made more than normally dreary by the weather. Eight days of almost continuous rain so late in the spring was most unusual and completely immobilized the little caravan.

The whole country was in such a state, and our tents and baggage so heavy and unmanageable from the wet, that we were obliged to remain stationary. . . . To add to our luxuries, the ground on which we were encamped was full of scorpions; and let it be remembered, the ground is our only seat. Everybody seemed out of humour at this succession of stormy weather, it being so very unusual in this climate. . . . I sat up most of the night in considerable alarm and at length lay down without undressing.

And on the following day:

Our situation is really very melancholy. The whole country, as far as the eye can reach, is one sheet of water, and there is no village to which we can retreat within three hours of our camp; besides which, there is a scarcity of provisions; our people are exposed to all the fury of the storm; and we ourselves are not much better off. We can neither go backwards nor forwards, and here we must remain. . . .

Under these conditions, which lasted almost as far as Kirkuk, it is not surprising that Mary has to record:

I was too unwell to admit either of our continuing our journey to-day, or of my accompanying the gentlemen in another *ruin-hunting* expedition. . . .

and a little later:

Claude very poorly from a violent bilious attack, and obliged to keep quiet . . . Mr Rich had a pretty tranquil night. . . .

Furthermore she was bitterly disappointed that they were compelled to leave the main road before encountering the *tatars*, whom they knew to be approaching with their mail from home. She complains:

Thus am I obliged, I own with a very ill grace, to wait many days ere I shall see the beloved Mardocks post-mark; and in what a place shall I receive the letters written by the most amiable, accomplished and beloved inhabitants of that pleasant retirement in the most refined and happiest country in the world! Oh that I could convey to you an idea of the barbarous, burning land we are in! Love your dear England!

But now they were out of the plain and travelling through low hills, with growing corn, pebbly brooks in the valleys and snow-mountains in the distance. Their spirits rose accordingly. At a point a little beyond Kirkuk, Mary writes:

A tent for us was pitched on a little elevation above my favourite river, which winding and meandering over its pebbly bed, through little *bosquets* of fig trees, mulberry trees and rose-bushes, together with the gentle green swelling bank on the opposite side, the extremely fresh appearance of everything around us, altogether made me very *pathetic*, as Claude called it, while he tried, though very unsuccessfully, to conceal how very, very much he sympathised with me. But from our very long privation of such a prospect it appeared like enchantment, and affected us more than the many celebrated spots we had visited in either England, Switzerland, or Italy. We rambled about the valley and through the beautiful grove, gathering roses and wild-flowers, till suddenly we came to a *wild rose bush*, for which everything else was abandoned and we almost worshipped the solitary exile, as it seemed, from England. . . .

The party's last camping-place was in a very beautiful garden outside and above the town of Sulaimaniyah. The place was full of the smell of roses and the song of nightingales, and Mary was extremely loath to leave it for less congenial quarters in the town itself. However the time was soon fixed for their official reception by the Pasha of Sulaimaniyah. Mary, of course, travelled with the scarlet curtains of her *takhterawan* lowered, and was only made aware at all of having entered the town by 'the low, continued sound of voices'.

Rich's travels in Kurdistan were not restricted to the Sulaimaniyah area. He penetrated far into what are now the Kurdish provinces of Iran, crossing the Zagros range and even reaching Sinna, where he was the guest of the Vali. Accompanying him now were Bellino and a Mr Bell, who had succeeded Hine as surgeon to the Residency. When he returned to Sulaimaniyah, Bellino left the party to pay an antiquarian visit to Kermanshah and Hamadan. It was during this trip that he was taken with a serious fever, and though he recovered sufficiently to rejoin Rich in Mosul,[54] it was there that his sad death occurred the following November at the early age of 29. Claudius remained some months in Mosul before returning to Baghdad. This time he took the opportunity of carefully surveying the ruins of Nineveh, and so paved the way for the sensational discoveries which were made there twenty years later. In search of early manuscripts, he visited all the Christian monasteries in the hills north of Mosul. Amongst these was Rabban Hormuzd, of whose chapel Gertrude Bell wrote: 'For English eyes it has an interest out of all proportion to its age, for upon the doorway are carved the names of James and Mary Rich, with the date 1820. . . .'[55] Like other famous travellers from Herodotus to Byron, the Riches seemed fond of carving their names in remote places. They did so over the little sacred spring in the east wall at Nineveh which they had christened 'Thisbe's Well', and Claudius remarked:

Some traveller in after times . . . may wonder, on reading the name of Mary Rich, who the adventurous female was who had visited the ruins of Nineveh. . . . He will not be aware that, had her name been inscribed at every spot she had visited in the course of her weary pilgrimage, it would be found in places compared with which Mosul is the centre of civilisation.[56]

In February 1821 Rich returned by *kelek* to Baghdad to find

25 Rabban Hormuzd, a Nestorian monastery north of Mosul, visited by Rich in search of early Christian manuscripts.

Da'ud Pasha, who had succeeded Sa'id, completely out of hand. He had been imposing increasing disabilities on British merchants trading through the port of Basra, and repudiated all European rights in Baghdad. To Rich, on his return, he was rude and disrespectful, and, when driven to ask for his passports, he refused him permission to leave the city. On returning to the Residency, Rich learnt through private sources that Da'ud was preparing to send troops and take him prisoner, so there was no alternative to putting the house in a state of siege. The sepoy guards were well armed and there were at the time several Indian Army officers staying as guests, so its defence presented no particular difficulty. Rich also had confidence in the fact that the townspeople were his friends almost to a man, and were only waiting for a shot to be fired in order to raise a general insurrection. The Pasha began his demonstration by picketing all the city gates and placing a gun to cover the Residency from the opposite bank of the Tigris. His regular infantry then advanced directly upon the house, but as soon as they saw Rich's defence preparations, they 'fell back and took up their station at a coffee house nearby'.[57] Their commandant was under an obligation to Rich, who had saved his life on a previous occasion, and now came forward to suggest negotiations, with the result that a little later two of the Pasha's ministers arrived at the Residency for a parley. Rich, of course, refused to take part in any kind of discussion until the troops were removed, and when Da'ud's envoys hesitated to comply, he completely lost his temper, and, seizing a stick, drove them ignominiously from the house.

This was the end of the siege, and Da'ud, who was growing progressively more uneasy about the whole incident and most anxious to be rid of Rich, was soon afterwards prevailed upon to provide passports. The yacht, which had been moored alongside the Residency terrace, was manned and loaded, and after a tumultuous and affectionate farewell from the population of Baghdad, having provided for the future of their dependants, the Rich family set sail for Basra. There they found an English vessel leaving for Bushire, and on 13 June 1821, with few regrets, they quitted the Pashalik of Baghdad for the last time.

Arrived at Bushire, where the Company maintained a factory, Rich received compliments and praise both from Bombay and Istanbul on his firm action in Baghdad. The time had now plainly come for a change of post, and he had in fact already been offered an important appointment in Bombay by the new Governor, Mountstuart Elphinstone. It was now merely a matter of awaiting direct instructions to proceed. There was no point in Mary's remaining in the appalling sticky heat of Bushire, so he decided reluctantly that she should precede him to Bombay, travelling on the *Volunteer* which had brought them from Basra. As the shabby buildings of Bushire began to dissolve in the heat-haze, Mary had her last glimpse of Claudius waving goodbye from the little jetty.

If Rich's conscience had permitted him to accompany his wife directly to Bombay, the tragedy which followed would have been avoided. As it was, his restless temperament soon tired of waiting at Bushire and he determined on a tour to Shiraz, for the purpose of visiting Persepolis, the Tomb of Cyrus and various other ancient sites. What followed is described in an anonymous notice which serves as a preface to the narrative:

While at Shirauz, the cholera morbus appeared in the city, and with such violence that it diffused universal dismay, six thousand inhabitants out of a population of forty thousand being carried off in a few days. The prince with all his family, all the chief nobles, and the higher classes, and such of the lower as were able, deserted the town. Mr Rich refused to quit the place, and continued nobly to exert himself to quiet the alarm of the inhabitants, and to assist the sick and dying. His time for many days was chiefly employed in visiting them, and administering the necessary medicines. The tribute of gratitude and respect which he received from the multitudes whom he assisted was gratifying to his heart. But the disease was already working in his own veins. On leaving the bath on 4th of October, symptoms of cholera appeared, and, in spite of every assistance and care, he expired on the following morning, the 5th of October. He was interred in Jehan Numa, one of the royal gardens in which he lived at the time, where a monument has since been erected to his memory.[58]

The explorer, Baillie-Fraser, and an old friend of Rich's, Dr Dukes, as well as Dr Tod, with whom he had been travelling, were all present at the funeral. Six years later a relative called Macdonald Kinneir had the remains disinterred and re-buried in the Armenian Cathedral at Isfahan.

CHAPTER SIX

The birth of Assyriology

When Rich's collection of antiquities reached the British Museum in 1825, attention was for the time being naturally focussed on the coins and Syriac manuscripts, since from the cuneiform inscriptions no scrap of information could at that time be obtained. In point of fact, the whole collection on arrival was split up into groups according to the various categories within which the objects fell, and no complete list has survived of what it comprised.[59] According to Wallis Budge's account, however, the cuneiform material accounted for one of the seven thousand pounds which Mary Rich received from the trustees and was by no means negligible in quantity. He mentions 'four historical baked clay cylinders, inscribed in cuneiform, thirty-two clay tablets and fragments inscribed in cuneiform, thirteen bricks stamped with inscriptions in the Babylonian character, a black stone memorial tablet inscribed in cuneiform, a large inscribed boundary stone, and several small miscellaneous objects'.[60] Apart from a few inscribed bricks sent back to Europe by Pietro della Valle and Beauchamp and others, collected for the East India Company, these for the time being represented all the portable examples of Babylonian inscriptions in the world. Yet by 1825 the first faltering steps had already been taken towards the decipherment of the wedge-writing, not on the basis of anything found in Iraq, but of the great, almost ineffaceable records of the Persian kings carved on rock among the Persian mountains.

Rich, on his last, fatal journey to Shiraz, like many previous European travellers, had seen and endeavoured to copy some of these inscriptions, particularly those in the vicinity of Persepolis–Takht-i-Jamshid, Murghab (the Tomb of Cyrus) and Naqsh-i-Rajab. But the even more important inscription on the great rock at Behistun, twenty miles from Kermanshah, he had only heard of from Bellino who had visited it shortly before his death. Almost all the other inscriptions had been copied with greater or lesser accuracy by Karsten Niebuhr late in the previous century. Like the Behistun inscription, they were trilingual; that is, the same cuneiform text was repeated in three different languages, which we now know to be Old Persian, Elamite and Babylonian. In Egypt, some years before, Napoleon's soldiers had discovered the famous

26 G. F. Grotefend, whose vital contribution in 1802 to the decipherment of cuneiform writing was ignored by German scholars, but vindicated ninety years later.

Rosetta Stone, with its parallel inscriptions in Greek and Egyptian hieroglyphs which served as a clue for the decipherment of the Pharaonic pictographs. Now these trilingual inscriptions in Persia were to fulfil something of the same function in deciphering cuneiform.

As early as 1802, working mainly on Niebuhr's copyings, a young German college-lecturer, called Grotefend, succeeded first of all in establishing that, on the basis of the smaller number of signs used, one of the three languages was probably alphabetical rather than syllabic. He therefore selected this version for further study. Grotefend recollected that in the later Pehlevi inscriptions the Persian kings were usually given the title 'Great King, King of Kings', so taking two short alphabetical cuneiform texts copied by Niebuhr from above the heads of royal figures carved in relief, he proceeded to do a lot of logical thinking. In each case the groups of signs at the beginning and end of the text were different, so he took each text to refer to a different king. But in the middle of each text the same group occurred twice and then a third time with certain additions. He at once realized that these additions could be taken to signify the genitive case, and that if the repeating group spelt the word 'king', here was the familiar formula of the Pehlevi. Next he noticed that the final group of each text also ended with genitive signs. So why should each not read: 'So-and-So, the Great King, King of Kings, son of So-and-So.' This, as it proved, fitted perfectly, and by a little judicious guessing he was even able to identify the two kings as 'Darius, son of Hystaspes' and 'Xerxes, son of Darius'.

Progressing ingeniously from the known to the unknown, Grotefend eventually succeeded in reconstructing a complete alphabet and in attributing the correct phonetic value to twelve of its letters. Yet, on account of the academic snobbery of contemporary German scientists, his discovery was refused publication by the Göttingen Academy and was not actually vindicated until ninety years later. Meanwhile others, working independently, had arrived at much the same results. Foremost among these was Henry Creswicke Rawlinson, whom we last saw leaving India for Persia as part of a military mission to the court of the Shah (Chapter One).

Lieutenant Rawlinson's little detachment arrived at Bushire by ship in the autumn of 1833, but were unable to cross the mountain passes to Teheran until the following spring. He was then able to make a preliminary examination of the Persepolis inscriptions on the way and was immensely intrigued by their possibilities. In March 1835 he found himself posted to Kermanshah in the capacity of military adviser to the Shah's brother, the governor of Kurdistan, and therefore within easy reach of the Rock of Behistun.

Actually the rock lies twenty-two miles to the east of Kermanshah, but it is only necessary to recollect Rawlinson's equestrian exploits as a subaltern in India[61] in order to realize how inconsiderable such a distance would seem. Budge, in fact, mentions that 'on one occasion, when it was necessary to warn the British Ambassador at Teheran of the arrival of the Russian agent at Herat, Rawlinson rode 750 miles in 150 consecutive hours'.[62] In any case, he at once began a series of regular visits to the rock, and between 1835 and

27 A drawing by the French artist Flandin and the archaeologist Coste of the trilingual cuneiform inscriptions at Behistun, as seen from the Hamadan-Kermanshah road. Their semi-inaccessible position is well illustrated.

1837 set himself the task of making exact copies of the inscriptions. The process required every bit of skill which he possessed as an expert climber and involved the continual and repeated risk of his life.

Let us now examine a much more recent visitor's account of the rock itself. Mr H. Filmer, in a travel book published in 1937,[63] says:

To obtain a sight of the great inscription and the sculpture surmounting it I had to descend from my automobile opposite a Persian tea house at the point of the rock by the road and then clamber over the strewn boulders at the foot of the mountain as far as it was possible conveniently to climb. From a corner of the rock thus gained, a view, although still somewhat indistinct, may be had of the smooth-faced ledges [*sic*] bearing in three languages a record of Darius' rule.

The sculptured panel, which is actually about 400 feet (122 metres) from the ground, represents Darius himself, standing in judgment upon nine rebel chiefs, including, at the end of the row, a strange-looking individual called 'Skunka' wearing a sort of dunce's cap. Also, the king is treading underfoot a figure representing the usurper, Smerdis, while the group is completed by two attendants, standing behind, and the god Ahuramazda in his winged disk.

The early visitors to the rock could by no means be expected to know all this, and, owing partly to the preference of western travellers for biblical associations, their conclusions were often sufficiently remarkable. Ker Porter, for instance, who examined the sculptures through a telescope, identified the minor figures as 'representatives of the Ten Tribes' standing before a 'King of Assyria and of the Medes', and surmised that Skunka's dunce-cap was probably 'the mitre worn by the sacerdotal tribe of Levi'.

During the process of copying, Rawlinson naturally made a minute examination of the rock-face. He consequently made certain discoveries which are not generally known. In the first place the whole prepared area – about 1,200 square feet of it (366 square metres) – had been carefully smoothed and the unsound portions of the stone replaced with better material embedded in lead. After this the whole face had received a high polish, 'which could only have been accomplished by mechanical means'. After the sculpture and inscriptions had been carved, it had been given a thick coat of hard, siliceous varnish to protect it. The varnish was plainly harder than the actual stone, for in certain places where moisture had broken out from the face of the rock it had pushed away great flakes of the varnish, which Rawlinson found fallen on the ledge beneath, sometimes still bearing the clear impression of the lettering which they had covered.[64]

During his early visits to the rock in 1835, Rawlinson began his copying of the Persian and Elamite inscriptions without the help of ladders or ropes, simply climbing down to the ledge beneath the panel. But the intentionally inaccessible location chosen by Darius for the sculptures made the area to be reached in this way very small, and during his return visits, in later years, ropes and ladders had to be used to read the remoter panels. Even so, the Babylonian inscription remain inaccessible until 1847, when a chance circumstance enabled Rawlinson to obtain 'squeezes'. He wrote:

At length, however, a wild Kurdish boy, who had come from a distance, volunteered to make the attempt, and I promised him a considerable award if he succeeded. The mass of rock in question is scarped, . . . so that it cannot be approached by any of the ordinary means of climbing. The boy's first move was to squeeze himself up a cleft in the rock a short distance to the left of the projecting mass. When he had ascended some distance above it, he drove a wooden peg firmly into the cleft, fastened a rope to this, and then endeavoured to swing himself across to another cleft at some distance on the other side; but in this he failed owing to the projection of the rock. It then only remained for him to cross over the cleft by hanging on by his toes and fingers to the slight inequalities on the bare face of the precipice, and in this he succeeded, passing over a distance of twenty feet of almost smooth perpendicular rock in a manner which to a looker-on appeared quite miraculous. When he reached the second cleft, the real difficulties were over. He had brought a rope with him attached to the first peg, and now, driving in a second, he was able to swing himself right over the projecting mass of rock. Here with a short ladder he formed a swinging seat, like a painter's cradle, and, fixed upon this seat, he took under my direction the paper cast of the Babylonian translation of the records of Darius.[65]

Fifty years later, after much exhibition, these same 'squeezes' were partly eaten by mice in the British Museum,[66] but they had by then fulfilled their function and the record had been fully deciphered.

Rawlinson's first clue to the decipherment of the Persian version, though he was probably unaware of it, was almost the same phrases as had so much helped Grotefend over thirty years earlier – 'Darius, the King, son of Hystaspes', and 'Xerxes, the King, son of Darius'. The identification of these phrases gave him enough phonetic values to identify many of the other proper names mentioned in the inscription, and by comparing them with possible Greek equivalents to compose an alphabet. By the end of 1837 he had succeeded in making a translation of the entire first two paragraphs of the inscription, which he sent in the form of a paper to the Royal Asiatic Society. It was on this paper and on a subsequent one written in 1839 that Rawlinson's claim to be the 'Father of Cuneiform' rests.

Yet much still remained to be done. There were still the syllabic Elamite and Babylonian languages to tackle, and these offered immensely more formidable problems. Rawlinson, as an active Army officer, lacked more than anything the leisure in which to apply himself to the task. He returned to India in 1839, just in time to take part in the Afghan War. In 1840, with the rank of major, he became Political Agent in Western Afghanistan, and later led a body of Persian cavalry with conspicuous success at the battle of Kandahar. With his return to India in 1842 his military career ended. During his early years in Persia he had once visited Baghdad for a month and it was thither he was now bent on returning to continue his cuneiform studies. Fortunately at about this time Colonel Taylor, Rich's successor as British Political Agent in Turkish Arabia, was due to retire, and Rawlinson had the great satisfaction of being offered the Baghdad Residency by Lord Ellenborough. On 6 December 1843 he landed in Baghdad from a British steamer under a salute of thirteen guns.

THE GREAT PLAGUE

Since this brings the thread of Assyriological research back to Mesopotamia, a short retrospect is necessary over the period of more than twenty years since Rich's death at Shiraz. We last saw Da'ud Pasha of Baghdad in disgrace with the Sublime Porte for his outrageous treatment of Rich. He indeed welcomed Rich's successor, Colonel Taylor, with well-simulated contrition. But the anachronism of his Mamluk rule and contempt for the Sultan's authority could not last for ever, and the crisis came in 1830, when, at the close of the war with Russia, the Sultan realized that the Pashalik of Baghdad had supplied no help whatever either in revenue or in kind. An envoy was dispatched to Baghdad with instructions to announce the deposition of Da'ud and the approaching appointment of a non-Mamluk governor in his place. He was met half-way between Kirkuk and Baghdad by an elaborately ceremonial deputation accompanied by a horse-drawn carriage, an almost unheard-of amenity in Baghdad at that time, and perhaps the ancestor of the ubiquitous *arabana* of later days. On arrival in Baghdad the envoy withdrew with ominous dignity to the apartments prepared for him, and there, a few days later, by the Pasha's orders, he was quietly strangled.

When the Porte was informed of the death of its envoy (which, as a matter of form, was attributed to cholera), it was clear that a reconquest of the Iraq province would be necessary. Accordingly, an individual called 'Ali Ridha was appointed in Da'ud's place, and, for his convenience, to the Pashalik of Baghdad was added that of Aleppo, so that he might reside in and administer the one, while making adequate preparations for the subjugation of the other. Da'ud, now officially branded as a rebel and an outlaw, must have realized that he had gone too far, for he sufficiently demeaned himself to ask the advice of Colonel Taylor as to his next move. The Resident, however, was saved the embarrassment of a reply by an entirely extraneous circumstance. Late in March 1831 the plague descended upon Baghdad.

The story of the appalling and complicated disaster which now befell the city is reasonably well known. In its way it is comparable with the fall of Nineveh or the destruction of Pompeii, and is made the more remarkable by the fact that, unlike either, Baghdad did subsequently survive as an inhabited city. Indeed, the significance of the whole episode lies in the fact that, having occurred only a century and a half ago, it is a circumstance without some knowledge of which one cannot fairly assess the modern character of Baghdad.

Baillie-Fraser,[67] another well-known traveller who visited Colonel Taylor at the Residency only three years afterwards, was astonished to find how little remained of the Baghdad depicted by Buckingham's now famous account of the city before the plague, which he quotes in full. In order to explain the contrast presented by the almost incredible poverty and squalor of the city as he found it, he adds a long and detailed account of the two tragic months in 1831 during which 100,000 people are said to have perished in the streets of Rusafah alone. The most moving passages in this are derived from the surviving journal of an English missionary called Groves who remained in Baghdad throughout, and by some providence contrived to survive.

Arriving with his wife and child in Baghdad in 1830, Groves had set up a modest establishment where, in the face of every kind of obstruction from Moslem bigotry, he had succeeded in starting a school for a score or so of Armenian children. A first fragment of his journal, describing his journey out through Russia and Persia and his first difficult months in Baghdad, was published in London in 1831, obviously before the story of his subsequent adventures had become known.[68] In turning its pages one is struck by his voluntary self-dedication to a task whose impracticability is as evident as its usefulness is doubtful. At the same time one cannot fail to notice that his conventional piety is tempered with common sense. This is perhaps best illustrated by a single entry on an occasion when he had just been informed that a *tatar* bringing mail from Istanbul had been attacked near Sinjar and robbed of all his letters. Groves says: 'This created a momentary disappointment, but quickly we remembered it was of the Lord and therefore for our good.' He then adds: 'and perhaps the tartar may have had no letters for us'.[69]

The sequence of events which Groves had to record in his diary during the spring months of 1831 may be briefly outlined as follows:

31 March. Colonel Taylor shut up the Residency and from then onwards nothing was received through the postern unless first passed through water.

10 April. Deaths in the city were now estimated at seven thousand. Of several large bands of people who had attempted to leave and go elsewhere, some were murdered and robbed by Bedouin, others were held up by floods, while the remainder carried the plague with them and died on the road. In spite of precautions in the Residency, a sepoy died and several other servants were infected.

12 April. Owing to prolonged rain the Tigris began to rise rapidly. It had already broken through its bunds to the northwards and flooded the low country around the city. It now began to reach danger-point in Baghdad itself with no one to attend to the embankments. Colonel Taylor decided to leave for Basra. Invited to accompany him, Mr Groves insisted upon remaining to give what help he could to his pupils and their families. The Residency party left in their own boats, now conveniently moored to the balcony of the house.

13 April. Groves' neighbours all died. He reports 50 bodies in the street within a space of 600 yards. The number of deaths per day rose from 1,500 to 1,800.

20 April. Part of the city wall fell and the flood burst into the city, inundating the whole of the eastern and northern districts. Houses began to fall, as their foundations were undermined, and 1,500 people were either drowned or crushed beneath the ruins within a few hours.

24 April. Groves visited the Residency, a part of which had fallen into the river. Out of the eighteen staff which Taylor had left to guard the house only one individual survived, mourning a family of fourteen.

25 April. The daily death-rate reached its maximum of 5,000 persons. (The population of Baghdad before the plague was less than 150,000.)[70]

4 May. The weather began to grow hot and the plague to decrease. The water in the town subsided, leaving a vast ruin-field covered in a deep layer of brown Mesopotamian mud, from which starving dogs began to exhume corpses.

7 May. Just as conditions in the town were improving, the plague entered Groves' house, and within a few days Mrs Groves and their child both succumbed. He himself afterwards removed to India, where he continued his missionary work for many years. The remainder of his journals were published posthumously.

In Baghdad a few thousand inhabitants remained crowded into the small section of the town where the houses stood high enough to have been clear of the flood. Other fugitives soon began to trickle back within the city from the surrounding country, but the ruined crops and flooded vegetable gardens now deprived them of their normal source of food, and famine added to the general distress. Da'ud Pasha himself, having failed in an early attempt to leave the city, had been stricken with the plague but miraculously recovered, and now emerged from the ruins of the Sarai where he had been attended by a single surviving retainer. On the arrival of 'Ali Ridha with a punitive force from the north, he gave himself up, and, partly no doubt in consideration of all he had gone through, was sent to Istanbul with a strong and, as it proved, effective recommendation to mercy. 'Ali Ridha then assumed legitimate control of the Pashalik, which he retained until 1842.

During these twenty years between Rich's death and Rawlinson's arrival in Baghdad, the course of archaeological exploration in Mesopotamia was rapidly approaching an important turning point. Up till now it had depended almost exclusively on the personal initiative of private individuals and such private funds as happened to be at their disposal. The time had now arrived for public institutions to take a hand and for public funds to make actual excavations possible. Meanwhile final contributions to the cause of surface exploration had been made by two individuals, one of whom has not yet been mentioned. This was a certain Captain Robert Mignan who, during Colonel Taylor's time, commanded the Residency escort. Almost every traveller till now had restricted his investigations of Babylonia to the sites directly accessible from the Euphrates route between Baghdad and Basra. Between 1826 and 1828 Robert Mignan set out to cover some of the large areas of country in southern Iraq which his predecessors had left unexplored. Where their activities had been hampered by retinues of formal attendants and military escorts, Mignan travelled light, 'accompanied only by six Arabs, completely armed and equipped after the fashion of the country, and by a small boat, tracked by eight sturdy natives in order to facilitate his researches on either bank of the stream'.[71]

Mignan's invaluable work was carried a stage further seven years later by Baillie-Fraser who adopted the same light method of travelling. In a journey of only one month, at the end of 1834, he was the first to venture across the *terra incognita* between the two rivers, and in the process discovered and recorded the names of mounds which we now know to be the remains of some of the most famous Sumerian cities, such as Tel Jokha, the ruins of Umma and Senkara, which is ancient Larsa.[72] He was also probably the first visitor to the ruins of Ur.

THE EUPHRATES EXPEDITION

The next enterprise in order of time, and one which already heralded the beginning of state-subsidized exploration, was of an entirely different character. This was the famous Euphrates Expedition, which is commemorated on a tablet rediscovered in Basra after the Second World War, and evidently part of some sort of monument.[73] The inscription reads:

This Fountain commemorates the awful event, which visited the Euphrates Expedition 21st May 1836, near Is Jaria, about 85 miles above Ana.

The Expedition was descending the river with full prosperity, when it was visited suddenly by a hurricane, with tremendous violence. Both vessels were placed in imminent danger, from which the *Euphrates* escaped. But the *Tigris* foundered, and with her were lost the chief part of the souls on board.

It then gives the names of twenty members of the expedition who lost their lives, and adds:

Sir Robert Grant and members of the Council at Bombay, in admiration of the labours and exertions with which the Expedition had surmounted its many and great difficulties up to the above moment and sympathising in the unhappy fate of the brave men who died, have raised this monument to their memory. And the British Residents in India with a generous and charitable liberality at the same time collected largely to afford pecuniary relief for the surviving relatives.

The tragedy in this way commemorated was really only a single incident in a prodigious and extraordinary undertaking. Over a century later it may still be said of the Euphrates Expedition that 'it stands really without parallel in the history of similar undertakings, alike for the novelty and magnitude of the enterprise, for the scale upon which it was got up, for the difficulties which it had to encounter and for the importance of the results obtained'.[74] Organized by the British Government under the especial patronage of King William IV, its official purpose was 'to survey the northern part of Syria, to explore the basins of the rivers Euphrates and Tigris, to test the navigability of the former, and to examine in the countries adjacent to these great rivers the markets with which the expedition might be thrown in contact'. Its ultimate intention was to establish regular railway or steamer communications with the Far East by way of the Euphrates valley. Yet the vision of its promoters ranged far beyond a mere route to India. In Mesopotamia they aimed 'to restore life and prosperity to a region renowned for its fertility in ancient times and generally regarded as the seat of the earliest civilization'.

Even when stated in its simplest terms the plan of campaign, as conceived in London, sounds fairly formidable. The component parts of two fairly large iron paddle-steamers were to be transported by ship to the mouth of the Orontes west of Antioch. From there they were to be carried overland by camel to Birejik on the Euphrates, re-assembled and manned for a slow voyage down that river to the Arabian Gulf. During this voyage a complete survey was to be made of the Euphrates valley. In fact it embraced an immensely larger task, whose scope can be judged from the bibliography afterwards associated with it.[75] Ainsworth alone, who was attached to the expedition as surgeon and geologist, but particularly interested in archaeology as well, covered an immense amount of ground in his incidental explorations. His own 'Narrative' account refers to surveys of the Syrian coast, the Gulf of Issus and Cilicia, the Orontes valley and Hollow Syria, the Upper Euphrates and ancient Comagene, the greater part of Babylonia, the Lower Tigris and Karûn valleys, the 'Persian Apennines and Persopolis, and finally a visit to Kurdistan in search of coal (there is an abundance of surface coal in the great valley between Amadiyah and Zakho).

In his publication of the results of all these varied investigations Chesney, with his passion for thoroughness, even went so far as to embody a definitive and comprehensive account of all the work previously accomplished in the same field, with the result, as Ainsworth points out, that the new facts tended to be buried in the vast mass of collected matter.

The equipment of the expedition, including the unwieldy components of the two steamers, were unloaded at the mouth of the Orontes in the spring of 1835, but owing to difficulties of transport, abnormal floods and continual sickness among the European per-

28 In 1836 the steamships 'Tigris' (shown here) and 'Euphrates' were reassembled at Birejik for launching on their exploratory voyage downstream.

29 The disastrous storm in which the steamship 'Tigris' was capsized and sunk with all her crew. The 'Euphrates' safely reached Basra.

sonnel, it did not reach the Euphrates until many months later. At Birejik, light earthworks were thrown up forming an enclosure, which was christened 'Fort William' and afterwards served as a base of operations. After enormous difficulties in assembling them, the steamers, now known as the *Tigris* and *Euphrates*, were eventually launched and started their journey down the river in March 1836. A surviving steel-engraving shows them with enormous side-paddles, very tall funnels heavily stayed, and foremasts intended for the auxiliary use of sails. Each day a navigating officer went ahead some twenty or thirty miles in a small boat to take soundings and plot a deep channel for use on the following day.

The disaster to the *Tigris*[76] occurred, not as is often supposed at Anah, but some eighty-five miles further up the river at a point a little below the confluence of the Euphrates and the Khabur. Here the Euphrates is hardly wider than, say, the river Thames at Richmond, and the manner in which the *Tigris* came to be capsized must appear quite incomprehensible to anyone unfamiliar with the astonishing freaks of weather which one comes to expect in Iraq. On a clear day in early spring mountains of black clouds will blow up in a few seconds, against the apparent direction of wind, and deluge the country in hail-stones heavy enough to knock a child unconscious. Pouring rain will turn suddenly into an opaque dust-storm, and later reappear through the same dust, spattering the earth with liquid mud. The sudden storms of wind do actually reach hurricane strength, and one has seen the entire contents of a camp kitchen blown nearly a mile across country.

Ainsworth's description, therefore, of the storm which hit the Euphrates Expedition on a Saturday in March 1836 is not only very vivid but entirely convincing. The two boats had spent the morning filling up with firewood and at midday moved off in bright sunshine with just enough breeze to ripple the water. The *Tigris*, as Chesney's flagship, was ahead, and the *Euphrates* had just come into line 150 yards behind, when a black cloud appeared low over the desert to the south-west. Ainsworth writes:

As the cloud neared us, the sky assumed an appearance such as we had never before witnessed, and which was awful and terrific in the extreme. A dense black arch enveloped the whole of the horizon, and the space beneath the arch was filled up with a body of dust, of a brownish orange colour, whirling round, and at the same time advancing towards us with fearful rapidity. . . . At this moment the hurricane came on us – a warm dry wind laden with the fragrance of the aromatic plants of the wilderness, followed in a few moments by a tremendous blast of wind with some rain in large drops. The crash broke upon us like heaven's own artillery, and the hurricane seemed as if bent upon hurling both steamers at once to the bottom of the foaming river.[77]

Chesney at once signalled to Cleveland, who was commanding the *Euphrates*, to follow as closely as possible, and turned his ship in towards the left bank. This she presently reached, but striking with some force, the recoil prevented the two sailors, who leapt out on to the bank with anchors, from making her fast, and the wind catching her bows she was swept clean round and back into midstream, narrowly missing the *Euphrates*, owing to the prompt action of Cleveland who violently reversed his paddles. By this time the whole scene was being enacted in almost pitch darkness owing to the thickness of the dust and the density of the clouds. The *Tigris* was being driven broadside on, heeled over so that her paddles would not function, with the wind tearing the boards off her paddle-boxes like dead leaves, and waves four or five feet high beating in through the broken saloon windows. She was already down by the bows and sinking when a gleam of light showed the left bank of the river only twenty yards away. Before reaching it she sank, and the entire crew of thirty-four, who had clustered in the stern, were flung into the turbulent water. The fact that twenty of them were drowned was afterwards partly attributed to the suction of the sinking vessel and partly to the fact that most of them were probably unaware in which direction they should swim. Chesney himself, who took a last-minute dive, was washed by the waves over the river bank into a cornfield, where he was presently joined by the sodden remains of his own Bible. When the storm moved on, leaving the same tranquil sunshine which had preceded it to mock its effects, he found himself lying amongst 'several cases of Birmingham and Sheffield goods, including guns and pistols, intended for presents, as also two casks of salt meat, nearly two hundredweight each, which had apparently been blown ashore by the force of the wind'.

The *Euphrates* meanwhile, after nearly being rammed by the *Tigris*, had reached the bank safely and succeeded in mooring herself securely, thus avoiding any danger of capsizing. Her officers, including Ainsworth, now hastened to the scene of the disaster. But little could be done. Some of the bodies of their drowned companions were found the following day disfigured beyond recognition by vultures. Others occasionally appeared during the following days, drifting alongside the *Euphrates* after she had progressed fifty or sixty miles further down the river. At Anah, Chesney left one of his officers to await the early autumn, when the river would reach maximum low-water, and to salvage all that he could from the wreck. He then proceeded in the one remaining ship to complete the main task for which the expedition had been financed. He successfully reached the Shatt al 'Arab and afterwards also navigated the Tigris upstream as far as Baghdad, but during an attempt to do the same by the Euphrates, there was a serious breakdown in the engines, and, the funds of the expedition being almost exhausted, the attempt was abandoned.

In his report to the British Government, Chesney's major findings were partly negative. The Euphrates would *not* be suitable for regular steam navigation owing to dangerous rapids and a rapidly shifting course. Also the construction of a railway parallel to it would present formidable engineering problems owing to the rocky character of much of the country on either side. Navigation of the Tigris, however, below Baghdad was shown to be not only practicable but easy, and Chesney's pioneer work resulted a little later in the establishment of the famous Lynch service of river steamers from Basra to Baghdad.

With Chesney's final assemblage and correlation of the results of all the exploration and research of previous travellers in Mesopotamia, surface exploration was brought to a temporary pause, and the stage was set for the melodrama of the first excavations. It was an ideally propitious circumstance that the discoveries in which they resulted were to have their counterpart in Rawlinson's study in Baghdad, where his brilliant work on the cuneiform texts made their interpretation increasingly practicable. Summer 1844 already found him comfortably established in the Baghdad Residency, which is now described as 'a house built on a grand scale with large and numerous apartments, necessitating an enormous staff of servants, cooks, grooms, stable-boys, attendants of all kinds, coffee-grinders, pipe-fillers, etc., etc.'[78] Of his work he wrote:

The interest in the inscriptions with which my original researches had inspired me had never flagged; it was sharpened perhaps by the accidents which had so long operated to delay its gratification; and I thus hastened, with eager satisfaction, to profit by the first interval of relaxation that I had enjoyed for many years, to resume the thread of the enquiry.

30 Henry Creswicke Rawlinson, a successor of Rich at the Residency in Baghdad, where his authority was undisputed. While holding the post he accomplished the final steps in the decipherment of cuneiform, which he had first studied during a military assignment in Persia.

Even the summer heat of Baghdad was not sufficient to deter him. Finding the house too hot to work during the day, he built a *chardag*, or summer house, overhanging the river at the end of the terrace. This was mostly constructed, like the *aghouls* used today, of aromatic camel-thorn, and imitating the cultivators of the upper Euphrates, he rigged up a tall water-wheel, turned slowly by the current of the river, which poured a continual stream of water over the little building.

The Residency in his day became filled with strange pets. A tame mongoose roamed loose about the house and grounds, while a leopard or lion-cub was often to be seen asleep beneath his chair as he worked. Under these conditions the greater part of his famous memoirs and dispatches were written.

CHAPTER SEVEN

Layard and Botta

AUSTEN HENRY LAYARD

Of all the great Englishmen whose names have appeared and re-appeared in this story, there is not one to whose writings one returns with greater relish than to those of Austen Henry Layard. It is not so much the content of his narrative, though that in itself is sufficiently fascinating; nor is it his style, which has little preten-sion to improve upon the familiar idiom of early nineteenth-century English. His special gift is enthusiasm. For, with the pos-sible exception of Buckingham, no writer whose youthful orienta-tion brought him eventually to the Middle East shows a zest so great and so apparent for the justification of his original predilec-tion. Rich's 'weary pilgrimage' was a concept which to Layard must have been incomprehensible. His energy never flagged and his high spirits were seldom abated, save when compelled by cir-cumstances to remain inactive or thwarted in an attempt to reach some remote goal.

In his early journeys he travelled light and unattended, and like many another, who in later days has attained an official position in which he found his freedom of movement and behaviour restricted by oriental convention, he afterwards recollected these days with increasing nostalgia. Writing in 1849, he says:

I look back with feelings of grateful delight to those happy days when, free and unheeded, we left at dawn the humble cottage or cheerful tent, and lingering as we listed, unconscious of distance and of the hour, found ourselves, as the sun went down, under some hoary ruin tenanted by the wandering Arab, or in some crumbling village still bearing a well-known name.* No experienced dragoman measured our distances or appointed our stations. We were honoured with no conversations by Pashas, nor did we seek any civilities from governors. We neither drew tears nor curses from the villagers by seizing their horses or searching their houses for provisions; their welcome was sincere; their scanty fare was placed before us; we ate, and came and went in peace.[79]

It is not altogether surprising that the almost crazily ambitious journey eastwards which Layard and Mitford planned together in London in 1839 (see p. 10) did not turn out exactly as they had expected. At Phillipopolis (Plovdiv) in Bulgaria, Layard fell ill with

---

* One is reminded of Flecker's line, 'Beyond the village which men still call Tyre'.

*31 Austen Henry Layard
by G. F. Watts.*

gastritis, and had to submit himself to the attention of 'an Armenian gentleman who had studied medicine at Edinburgh'. He says: 'He bled me twice copiously, and, moreover, made a large circle with a pen and ink on my stomach, which he ordered to be filled with leeches.' The consequent loss of blood so enfeebled him that it was some weeks before he was able to rejoin Mitford in Asia Minor. Reaching Jerusalem in January 1840 they again parted company, while Layard went off by himself on what Mitford rather disparagingly described as 'an excursion in the Hauran', but what was in fact an almost foolhardy escapade for which, having strongly discouraged him, the British Consul in Jerusalem washed his hands of all responsibility. Riding with a single Arab as a guide he passed through the bandit-infested Wadi Musa and reached Petra, his primary objective, without serious mishap. In the famous valley, though plagued and incommoded in every imaginable way by a resident band of Bedouin cut-throats, he made a fairly leisurely study of the ruins, and it is interesting to note that, unlike many visitors in more recent times, his criticism of the architecture was unimpaired by enthusiasm for the glamour of its setting. He did not in fact hesitate to call it 'debased and wanting both in elegance and grandeur . . . a bad period and a corrupt style'.[80]

Layard now set out to return northwards, with the idea of passing by Damascus and rejoining Mitford in Aleppo for the journey to Baghdad. Undismayed by a succession of extremely unpleasant adventures on the road, he succeeded in visiting Kerak, Jerash, Amman and other ancient cities on the way. Near Kerak he was set upon and robbed of all his clothes and equipment excepting his double-barrelled gun, in which he took a great pride and with which he now succeeded in defending his own life. By sheer pertinacity he persuaded a powerful local sheikh to insist upon the restoration of his property, and continued on his way with only minor losses. But before reaching Damascus he was robbed again and arrived eventually in pouring rain at the house of Mr Wherry, the British Consul, penniless, half-naked and on foot. He was able to recollect this occasion with some amusement thirty-eight years later, when he entered Damascus as the Queen's Ambassador to the Sultan, and was given a ceremonial reception by Midhat Pasha, who was then Governor.

Layard next took the road across the Lebanon to Beirut, visiting Baalbek on the way, and so travelled northwards to Aleppo, where he found Mitford impatient and about to continue the journey without him. 'He consented,' says Layard, 'to remain there a few days more, to give me and my mare a little rest, of which we were very much in need.' On 18 March they left together for Mosul, following almost exactly the same route, by Urfa and Nusaybin, which we have seen Buckingham take twenty-four years before. On 2 May they arrived in Mosul.

For Layard it was an eventful first visit, since it laid the seeds of his interest in the Assyrian mounds. Both Ainsworth and the British Consul, Christian Rassam, happened to be in Mosul at the time and they accompanied Layard and Mitford[81] on a vist to Qal'at Sharqat and the mounds of Ashur, which the Germans excavated seventy years later.

They encamped on the way near the sulphur springs of Hammam Alil, where today there is a rather squalid and ill-tended watering-place. Outside the village an ancient tell, or mound, rises to a considerable height, and from its summit, looking far down the Tigris valley, Layard had his first view of Nimrud, the great mound whose buried treasures were later to make his name a household word. At Hammam Alil it is also interesting to remember that he was within a few miles of Tell Hassuna, the earliest village settlement yet found in Iraq, whose excavation in 1944 has carried back the story of Mesopotamian civilization to a remote antiquity at that time unimaginable (see Chapter Fourteen). Having reached Sharqat, the party made a prolonged examination of the ruins of Ashur, now known to be the birthplace of the Assyrian nation, which Ainsworth shrewdly identified as probably 'associated with the Assyrian cities of Nineveh and of Nimrûd or Resen'. They then returned to Mosul, where Layard made his first investigation of the mounds of Nineveh.

Layard's first impressions of Iraq are most excellently described in a striking passage where he contrasts the 'Mediterranean' character of Syria with the very different aspect of the country he is now visiting for the first time. As he writes:

The graceful column rising above the thick foliage of the myrtle, ilex, and oleander; the gradines of the amphitheatre covering a gentle slope, and overlooking the dark-blue waters of a lake-like bay; the richly carved cornice or capital half hidden by the luxuriant herbage; are replaced by the stern, shapeless mound rising like a hill from the scorched plain, the fragments of pottery and the stupendous mass of brickwork occasionally laid bare by the winter rain. . . .

For the visitor to Iraq:

The scene around is worthy of the ruin he is contemplating; desolation meets desolation; a feeling of awe succeeds to wonder; for there is nothing to relieve the mind, to lead to hope or to tell what has gone by.

He adds:

These huge mounds of Assyria made a deeper impression on me, gave rise to more serious thoughts and more earnest reflection, than the temples of Balbec, and the theatres of Ionia.[82]

By his prompt appreciation of the obscure qualities which are the country's central distinction, Layard places himself in a class apart among European travellers.

For the moment, however, neither he nor Mitford had yet modified their initial intention of reaching India, and Baghdad was the next stage in the journey. They made their way down the Tigris by *kelek*, and as the creaking raft undulated over the rapids beside Nimrud, Layard obtained a new and even more tantalizing view of the principal mound with its conical peak representing the ruined ziggurat. He says:

The spring rains had clothed the mound with the richest verdure, and the fertile meadows, which stretched around it, were covered with flowers of every hue. Amidst the luxuriant vegetation were partly concealed a few fragments of bricks, pottery and alabaster, upon which might be traced the well defined wedges of the cuneiform character.

It must have been soon after this that he wrote to a wealthy merchant friend in England proposing that he put up some money for excavations, and maintaining that the antiquities to be discovered 'would amply repay the expense'. There is no record of his having received any reply.

Layard's first impression of Baghdad is perhaps sufficiently characteristic to be worth quoting:

We continued to float through these endless groves of palm trees, the air laden with delicious odour of the orange and citron trees, until, sweeping round a bend of the river, we came in sight of the city rising majestically on its banks – with its innumerable painted domes and minarets, its lofty walls and towers, its palaces and painted kiosks. It seemed to be all that I had pictured to myself of the City of the Caliphs and the sojourn of Haroun al Rashid.

He adds that after landing he was doomed to disappointment:

I found that, instead of the magnificent capital whose distant view had enchanted me, I was in the midst of an assemblage of mean, mud-built dwellings under a heap of ruins. . . .[83]

Arrived at the Residency, there is a prolonged reference to the character of the establishment and to Taylor, himself an erudite orientalist with whom this narrative by chance has so far been little concerned.★ The visitor observes:

Colonel Taylor's wife was an Armenian lady, whose family came originally, I believe, from Isfahan. He had two daughters, one of whom was married to Captain, afterwards Admiral, Lynch, who was then in command [*sic*] of the so-called Euphrates expedition. . . .

He also speaks with approval of Taylor's young officers, Lieutenants Jones, Campbell, and Selby:

Young men of enterprise and intelligence, taking a lively interest in all that concerned the country in which they were employed and its inhabitants, employing themselves while engaged in their professional duties in geographical and archaeological researches.[84]

Plainly Layard and Mitford enjoyed their short stay in Baghdad and the 'agreeable and intelligent society of the small English colony'. But the time soon came to continue their journey.

The two of them now joined a caravan making for Kermanshah and Hamadan. They followed the same route by which we have seen Ker Porter, Baillie-Fraser and others arriving in Iraq from Persia, and which in more recent times became a minor artery of American war-supplies for Russia. Visiting the rock-sculpture at Tak-i-Bustan, he encountered the French artist, Flandin, who afterwards collaborated with Botta in producing his brilliantly skilful records of the Assyrian reliefs found by the latter at Khorsabad.[85] For the moment, with the assistance of Coste, an architect-archaeologist, he was busy making drawings of these Sassanian and other sculptures on behalf of the French Government. At Hamadan they found the Shah encamped with his entire court and a shabby and disreputable-looking army. He had been contemplating a campaign against Baghdad, but had changed his mind and was now returning to Teheran. The circumstances afforded Layard and Mitford an opportunity for making a direct application for the *firmans* necessary to the continuation of their journey, and after just over a month of delay and procrastination these were granted. During this time Layard had the opportunity of studying the cuneiform inscriptions at Behistun, which greatly revived his interest in a subject already sufficiently absorbing. Combined with this a growing conviction of the possibilities offered by the Assyrian mounds now increased his reluctance to continue his journey eastwards. When the time came to leave Hamadan he and Mitford had already decided that their paths lay in different directions.

While Mitford made his way east, aiming for Kandahar and the Indian frontier, Layard conceived a new plan. This was to travel

★ H. J. Ross (1902, p. 34) says: 'Col. Taylor . . . was so good an Arabic scholar that when the Cadi or Mufti met with a difficult passage in some old manuscript and were not sure of the correct reading, they sent or went to him. He never left his house and was always to be found in his study poring over his Arabic books. Unfortunately, his knowledge died with him, as he never wrote anything.'

south from Isfahan through the territory of the wild Bakhtiyari tribes to Shuster and visit the ruins of ancient Susa. Leaving Hamadan, he was now accompanied by a rather objectionable Persian commissar, deputed for the purpose by the terms of his new *firman*, but well mounted on a horse requisitioned by this gentleman on the same authority. He still wore the Persian costume in which he had left Baghdad, and with the crown of his head shaved, 'leaving a ringlet on either side', and his hair and beard 'dyed a deep shining black with henna and rang', he must have made a handsome picture.

In Isfahan Layard was delayed some weeks, partly by the business of obtaining effective recommendations to the Bakhtiyari chieftains whose areas he would pass through, and partly by a recurrent fever. Here there was no lack of European society. He lived at first in the house of a French missionary, a M. Boré, whom he amusingly describes as 'a religious enthusiast, very ardent and zealous in promoting the interest of his country – a kind of politico-religious propagandism, much encouraged in the East by all French governments'. Flandin and Coste had also arrived from Kermanshah and for a time he saw much of the three Frenchmen. Later, however, their preoccupation with politics and offensive suspicion of his own motives in travelling became so tiresome that he was compelled to avoid their company. Of the three, Coste was probably the most sympathetic character, and Layard tells a good story to illustrate his capacity for absorption in his work. Asked by Layard to draw a finely carved Sassanian capital which he had found in a remote part of the city, Coste rode off at once to do so. 'Dismounting, he seated himself on a stone, and passing his arm through his horse's reins commenced his sketch. After finishing it he found to his surprise that his horse had disappeared. A thief had slipped the bridle off the animal's head, and had led it away, leaving the reins on the artist's arm.'

Once started again on his travels, Layard's curiosity carried him further and further from the beaten track. He spent many months in Khuzistan and among the Bakhtiyari, studying their life and speculating as to the possibilities of European trade with their various markets. The results of all his investigations he embodied, on his return to Baghdad, in a memoir which was eventually published in 1846 in the *Journal* of the Royal Geographic Society and earned him the Society's gold medal.

There is no space here to follow Layard's innumerable adventures amongst these wildest of all Persian tribes. In the early days, before his bona fides and prestige were established, it became a commonplace to be stripped and robbed every few days of his travels. Yet he invariably escaped with his life, and as time went on succeeded more and more often in recovering his property. The summer of 1841 found him at Shuster, deciding that personal considerations made it necessary to return to Baghdad, by way of Basra, and, as was now usual with him, he arrived at both places in turn, penniless and half naked. A sailor on board an English merchant vessel lying at anchor in the Shatt al 'Arab above Basra was astonished to be hailed authoritatively in English by what appeared to be a threadbare and dishevelled Arab. At Baghdad Dr Ross of the Residency,★ returning with a party of European ladies and gentlemen from an early morning ride, found himself at the city gate addressed by a grimy figure in a tattered *'aba* with bleeding feet and bare shaved head, who nevertheless spoke unmistakably with the voice of Austen Henry Layard. This last adventure had in fact come too near disaster to be pleasant. North of Hillah he had been set upon by a party of Shammar Arabs, and since he was wearing a *tarboosh*, mistaken for a Turk. On the point of being dispatched with a spear, he was rescued by the leader of the party, a young sheikh who, hearing him speak English, took him to be Dr Ross and ordered his release. Layard had completed the journey barefoot and hatless in great pain and privation. Ross himself, when he heard the story, at once sent a messenger to the paramount sheikh of the Shammar (then as now called Sofuk), who returned with the whole of Layard's property, a profuse apology, and a promise that he could, if he wished, in future pass through Shammar territory 'with a tray of gold upon his head'.

Layard remained in Baghdad long enough to receive replies to the letters which he now wrote home. During this time he declined Taylor's offer of hospitality for reasons of economy. In spite of perpetual thefts he had not yet exceeded the £200 with which he had left England over two years before, and did not yet wish to do so. He therefore rented a tiny mud hut, outside the Residency compound, but near enough to be within easy reach of Taylor's library.[86] Here he sat by day upon his well-worn carpet and slept at night upon the roof.

He did not, however, remain long idle. There were now on the Tigris two small armed steamers of the Indian Navy, called respectively *Assyria* and *Nitocris*. Layard made friends with Lieutenant Selby, who commanded the *Assyria*, and as soon as his mail arrived safely from England, the two of them went off together to Basra to satisfy Layard's curiosity as to the navigability of the Karun river, a waterway which he thought could bring Shuster within reach of the Shatt al 'Arab. He later paid another lengthy visit to Khuzistan.

Early in 1842 there were indications that the Sultan of Turkey was about to declare war on Persia. The quarrel concerned an alleged infringement of Turkish territorial rights at Mohammerah, and since Layard had been an eye-witness of much that had happened, Taylor requested that he should travel to Constantinople and inform the British Ambassador, Sir Stratford Canning, of the possibilities of mediation. Layard agreed to this proposal and left

★ H.J. Ross (1902, p. 37) says: 'I was sorry to have missed my namesake, Dr Ross of Baghdad, who has as great a love of animals as myself. Among the pets allowed to roam at will about his house is a leopard, who puts his paws on the window-sill and gazes down into the street below. When a sheep or a donkey passes he springs down upon them and breaks their necks, leaving the doctor to pay the damage.'

32 Paul Emile Botta, discoverer in 1843 and first excavator of Khorsabad. After his replacement in 1851 by Victor Place, he was relegated to a minor diplomatic post and little more was heard of him.

33 (Opposite) The city of Mosul in Canon Wigram's time (c.1912), as seen from the left bank of the Tigris, looking upstream.

Baghdad in June accompanied by a *tatar*. He was thus provided with the opportunity of paying a second visit to Mosul, and of meeting Botta, whom the French had just appointed as consular agent.

PAUL EMILE BOTTA

It was primarily the publication in Europe of Rich's *Memoirs* and *Narrative* which had been responsible for Paul Emile Botta's appointment. In particular, Julius Mohl of the French Asiatic Society had been inspired by the obvious possibilities of the excavations in the Mosul district to insist most strongly upon the careful choice and special briefing of the new agent. His convictions were now to prove justified beyond even his own expectations. Botta also was to show himself well qualified for the role allotted to him. Trained as a naturalist and son of a well-known historian, he already had considerable experience of diplomatic work in the Middle East, and soon adapted himself to the labyrinthine paths of Moslawi intrigue. The necessity for so doing perhaps needs some emphasis.

The city of Mosul has an individual character which differs as widely from the market towns of southern Iraq as that of Nineveh must have differed from the state capitals of Babylon. First recognizable as Xenophon's 'Mespila', it became a walled city early in the Christian era, and capital of a province which always approximated to ancient Assyria. It was often largely separated from southern Mesopotamia, and from late 'Abbasid times onwards often attained complete independence. On the map connected with the Sykes-Picot plan of May 1916 for the Allied partition of Turkey Mosul was even located within the French 'sphere of influence', and its inclusion in the state of Iraq was in doubt until some years after the

First World War. But whatever the reason for its basic individuality it is impossible to ignore the strangely conflicting sentiments to which it has tended to give rise among western visitors. Two British writers, for instance, who came to know it in the final years of the Ottoman Empire, found little good to say. One was Canon Wigram,[87] whose chapter on what he calls the 'Burden of the Newer Nineveh' begins with the cautious understatement: 'There are more pleasant places in the world than the city of Mosul.' Yet he gives the most racy and amusing account of life in the town, with whose 'corruption and confusion'* he plainly much enjoyed his temporary association. For Sir Mark Sykes, on the other hand, no abuse is too violent. He made his second visit to Mosul at about the time when the new railway seemed about to reach Iraq, and seriously proposed that the city should be by-passed, since 'the standing nuisance of this sink of disease and horror will not be mitigated, but rather increased by wealth; and if Mosul, in its present condition, becomes the chief town of a flourishing northern Mesopotamia, it will certainly contaminate the surrounding local-ity with the same sinister influence as Antioch of old spread over North Syria.'[88]

Sykes clearly did not like either Mosul or the Moslawis. Here is another passage whose violence creates the impression of personal bitterness:

By night robbers stalk untouched from house to house, and the time of rest and darkness is made fearful by the cracking of pistols and confused cries of strife. By day, drunkenness and debauchery are openly indulged

---

* H. J. Ross (1902, pp. 21–2) gives a good example of the sort of thing which could happen in Mosul at that time. He says: 'A most extraordinary thing happened here one day, the guard at the north gate sounded the alarm; and like a whirlwind a large troup of wild boar rushed through the town, scattering everyone they met like chaff before them; they tore through the narrow bazaars, upsetting sweetmeat-sellers and fruit and water vendors and, as though possessed of the devil, precipitated themselves down the city wall about sixty feet high and were all killed or maimed. It was supposed they had met a lion and losing in their terror all fear of man, had dashed straight through the town.'

in. The population is rotted by the foul distemper, corrupted and rendered impotent by drink, stupified and besotted by vice. The degradation of the city folk is not only physical but mental. Tales are whispered of dark and hideous sorceries and incantations – the noisome stench, as it were, of the charnel house of that dead Paganism which the Cross and Mohammed have slain, but have as yet been unable to annihilate.

These are strong words, which, sixty-five years after they were written, need not be taken with any great seriousness by a prospective visitor to modern Mosul. He will find an increasingly clean and orderly town, boasting an airport, one of the best public gardens in the country, as well as a railway station, first-class hotel, metalled roads, and a steel bridge across the Tigris; as a result of which its comfortable residential parts have extended into the area of ancient Nineveh.

Yet the Mosul in which Botta found himself must have approximated more closely to that of Wigram and Sykes. In those Ottoman days the morality of the Pashalik took its colour largely from the character of the Pasha himself, and the contemporary governor, Mohammed Keritli Oglu, was an unpleasant individual. Layard laconically observes that 'nature had placed hypocrisy beyond his reach. He had one eye and one ear; he was short and fat, deeply marked by the small-pox, uncouth in gestures and harsh in voice'. Having referred to his revival of the tax called *dish parasi* on villages which he visited, as compensation for wear-and-tear on his teeth while eating their food, and his well-known gambit of pretending to be dead in order to punish and confiscate the property of those who openly rejoiced, Layard also mentions the effects of his rule:

The villages and the Arab tribes had not suffered less than the towns-people. The Pasha was accustomed to give instructions to those who were sent to collect money, in three words – 'Go, destroy, eat'; and his agents were not generally backward in entering into the spirit of them. The tribes, who had been attacked and plundered, were retaliating upon caravans and travellers, or laying waste the cultivated parts of the Pashalik. The villages were deserted, and the roads were little frequented and very insecure.

Such was the authority with whom Botta had to deal in his negotiations for excavating facilities, and a false start was consequently understandable. Rich's mention of antiquities discovered beneath the houses on the Nabi Yunus mound led him first to make investigations in that quarter; but a storm of opposition from the guardians of the Moslem shrine induced him to transfer his attention to Kuyunjik. In December 1842 the first modest trenches were cut in the summit of the palace-mound, and thus was inaugurated an epoch of Mesopotamian excavation which continues to this day.

A chance circumstance now resulted in a second and this time momentous change of plan. While Botta was burrowing somewhat ineffectively in the surface debris of Kuyunjik, finding only inscribed bricks and fragments of alabaster, a native of Khorsbad,

34 Flandin's drawing of the palace mound and city walls of Khorsabad (c.1851). The village at the summit was removed by the French to the site which it occupies today.

a village fourteen miles to the north, brought news of another mound named after the village. His stories of sculptured stones★ eventually induced Botta to visit it, and to cut a long story short, in March 1843 he decided to transfer to Khorsabad the work which he had begun at Kuyunjik. Almost at once his workmen laid bare the tops of limestone slabs, sculptured in relief with Assyrian figures. Within a few days it was clear that an astonishing and epoch-making discovery had been made, and Botta was able to dispatch to Mohl in Paris his famous message: 'I believe myself to be the first who has discovered sculptures which with some reason can be referred to the period when Nineveh was flourishing.'

Let us now glance at the city discovered by Botta as we know it today. Dur Sharrukin, as it was originally called, was intended by King Sargon II to be the new capital of Assyria. At the end of the eighth century BC it was he who chose the site, laid out the mile-wide fortified quadrangle with its seven gateways and raised the vast platform at the centre of the north-east wall, on which his palace was to be built with its foundations twenty metres above the ground. The palace itself included a ziggurat and three small temples in its area, while larger temples and other secular buildings clustered around the base of the platform, enclosed in a powerful inner fortification.

When Botta came to Khorsabad in 1843, it was the mound representing the ruins of the palace and its platform which first attracted his attention. On its flat top were the houses of some Shebek peasants, and it was near these that he cut his first trench. It encountered the first of a hundred or so chambers, halls and corridors, many of

---

★ Here is a significant confirmation of the ignorance among Europeans of Arabic literature, referred to on the first page of this book, for – 'Khorsabad, or Khishtabad, is mentioned by the early Arab geographers. It is described as a village occupying the site of an ancient Assyrian city called "Saraoun", "Saraghoun"; and Yakuti [sic] declares that soon after the Arab conquest considerable treasures were found among the ruins' (Layard, 1849a, vol. I, p. 149). The astonishing accuracy of local tradition had deviated very little in twenty centuries from the true Assyrian name – Dur Sharrukin or 'Sargon's Town'.

which he opened up during the succeeding months, finding the walls of almost all of them to be lined with exquisite sculptured bas-reliefs representing gods, kings, battles, sieges and religious ceremonies. Between the sculptured pictures were large areas covered with raised cuneiform inscriptions. All the principal doorways were flanked by human-headed winged bulls or lions carved from gigantic monolithic slabs. When Botta's first dispatches began to reach Paris, the astonished French found themselves presented with a seemingly endless succession of pictures, portraying in the greatest detail the daily life, appearance and history of the Assyrians – a people till then remote and half-mythical, whose name was familiar mainly in connection with their ill-treatment of the biblical Hebrews. For the moment, in fact, Botta did not even know the name of the king who appeared in all his finery at the head of a procession in one of the reliefs.

The promptitude and enlightenment of the French Government's reaction to the situation and the munificence of their response to Botta's appeal for funds were most laudable, and characteristic. It was at once decided to send Flandin to copy the reliefs, and that on the way the Ambassador at Istanbul should acquire for him a *firman* protecting Botta from interference in his work by the local government. Unfortunately, however, there were delays, and Flandin did not actually arrive until May of the following year. By that time Botta had suffered every imaginable obstruction, and during the winter had been compelled to close the excavations.

In considering the events which followed this first marvellous discovery at Khorsabad, one may be permitted to wonder whether it did not come a century too soon. The unskilled labour and consequent crudity of excavating method, the bigoted ignorance and vandalism of the peasants, the distracting opposition and deliberate obstruction of the local authorities, aggravated by the perversity of its motives, and finally the complete lack of proper facilities for packing and transporting the sculptures, all combined to try the patience and test the ingenuity of Botta and his successors almost beyond human endurance, while they spelt ruin and destruction for a great part of their finds. Many of the Khorsabad slabs, for instance, were cracked and insecure. When Mohammed Pasha maliciously boycotted Botta's work, temporary wooden struts were fixed to hold them in place; but the peasants stole the wood at night and the slabs were shattered. One of the finest bull-colossi had to be abandoned on the road to Mosul, owing to the collapse of the trolley conveying it, and was burnt into gypsum by the peasants. The disaster at Kurnah sent a great part of the Khorsabad collection to bottom of the Tigris (see Chapter Ten). It is hard to resist the reflection that much of this wastage would have been avoided had the Assyrian palaces remained safely embosomed in the earth until the infant science of archaeology had reached maturity, and the land of the Assyrians attained a more equitable rule.

35 Sir Stratford Canning, British Ambassador to the Sublime Porte, whose generosity enabled Layard to open excavations at Nimrud in 1845.

LAYARD MEETS BOTTA

Botta had made great friends with Layard when he passed through Mosul in 1842 on his way to Istanbul. The *tatar* with whom he was travelling had a three-day wait for dispatches, and this gave the two young men an opportunity to discuss at length the relative merits of mounds they had both seen. Layard afterwards confessed to finding the Frenchman good company, but commented unfavourably on his weakness for opium-smoking, a habit which he had picked up in China. Botta was at that time still preoccupied with Kuyunjik, and Layard did not hear of the Khorsabad discoveries until some months after reaching Istanbul.

The British Ambassador at the Sublime Porte, to whom Layard's introduction was addressed, was Sir Stratford Canning. He was a remote and dignified personage and Layard at first had some difficulty in obtaining access to his presence. In his anxiety to deliver his dispatch, he had only permitted himself time to 'add a few details of European dress' to his Bakhtiyari costume, so his appearance for one thing was probably against him. At all events, after being kept waiting a great while, as he says, 'a fashionably-dressed young gentleman appeared, asked me roughly for the dispatches of which I was the bearer, informed me that the Ambassador was too much occupied to see anyone, and turning on his heel left the room without deigning to listen to what I had to say'. Layard, who had been riding day and night across Asia Minor at Taylor's request and with the express purpose of seeing Canning, was excusably angry at this brusque treatment. He accordingly wrote a letter of protest to the Ambassador and prepared to continue his journey as far as Vienna. He was in fact about to embark in a ship bound for the mouth of the Danube when overtaken by a *kawass* bringing a letter of apology from Canning. It assured him that the 'gentleman of the Chancery' had been reprimanded, and ended with the words: 'Instead of going away, come and dine here to-morrow.'

This was the beginning of a most fruitful association. Canning with his experience and judgment at once appreciated the peculiar talents of the young explorer, and saw that the Anglo-Russian mediation between Turkey and Persia now foreshadowed could be based on his first-hand knowledge of the controversy. He therefore proposed that Layard should enter and remain in his service until such time as the preliminary negotiations might be complete, and that meanwhile he should temporarily occupy himself with certain unofficial political missions in the Balkans. 'Mediation' in the Mohammerah dispute did not, as Canning had expected, take place until many months later. The solution then accepted by the British Government in deference to Russia bore no relation whatever to the joint recommendations of himself and Layard and could hardly have been more grossly unjust to Turkey. Yet it fell to his lot to communicate to the Porte both the nature of the decision and the intention to enforce it. Through adversities such as these a strong friendship grew up between Layard and Canning. Layard remained in the service of the Embassy for over two years, during which time he undertook a succession of ever-more complicated missions and eventually became one of Canning's most intimate counsellors. But in spite of Canning's urgent representations to the Foreign Office that his services should be rewarded by an official appointment, by 1845 there still seemed little hope of this materializing. As his disappointment increased, he began to grow restless.

All through the time he remained in Istanbul, news had continued to reach Layard of Botta's discoveries at Khorsabad. His intense interest in the subject was shared by Canning, and it is plainly to Botta's credit that he magnanimously allowed the two Englishmen access to his periodical reports, which passed through Istanbul in transit to Paris. Layard had continually expressed a conviction that Khorsabad could be only one of many mounds covering the ruins of Assyrian palaces, and had repeatedly pointed to Nimrud as another promising example.* Early in 1845 Canning, who was himself about to return to England on leave, and no doubt felt some qualms of conscience about the future of his young protégé, began seriously to consider providing a sum of money to enable Layard to put his theories to the test. In the autumn of the same year he informed him that he was prepared temporarily to incur the expense of excavations at Nimrud in the hope that the results would justify a subsidy from more official quarters for their continuation.** It need hardly be said that Layard wasted little time in taking advantage of this offer. Once the *firman* authorizing him to excavate had been obtained from the Porte, he took only twelve days to reach Mosul.

* His interest in Nimrud had been revived by an English missionary called Badger, who visited it in 1844 and made an even more detailed examination. When he visited Istanbul on his way home to England, Layard had the benefit of his impressions, which were not actually published until some years later. (See Badger, 1852, vol. I, p. 86ff.)
** In later years the acquisition of the Halicarnassus Marbles by the British Museum was largely due to Canning's initiative.

CHAPTER EIGHT

Nimrud

From this point onwards the story of Layard's excavations is taken up by his own narrative in *Nineveh and its Remains*, a book which on publication in 1849 attained instant popularity. He mentions in a letter to Mitford that a year's sales had been 8,000 copies, 'which will place it side by side with *Mrs. Rundell's Cookery'*.[89]

Arrived in Mosul, he was introduced by Christian Rassam, the British Vice-Consul, to Mohammed Pasha, in whom he at once recognized a familiar type. He did not therefore satisfy the old Cyclops' obvious curiosity as to the purpose of his visit. Instead he enlisted the help of H.J. Ross, the well-known sportsman, who was at the time in commercial partnership with Rassam. Together they loaded a *kelek* with horses, greyhounds, guns and other paraphernalia as if for one of Ross's usual hunting expeditions.[90] Surreptitiously they included in the equipment a certain number of excavating tools and engaged a stonemason. On 8 November they set off down the Tigris for Nimrud. In contrast to Layard's impressions on his previous visit in the spring, they found the country everywhere parched by the summer heat and ruined by the predatory rule of the Pasha. At Nimrud, which they reached the same evening, the mound itself was stripped of all foliage and the surrounding villages in ruins, the Arab settlers having withdrawn to safety beyond the Zab river and resumed the Bedouin habit of living by raids. At Naifah they found a single Jehesh sheikh in hiding with his family and it was in his hovel that they spent their first night.

Layard could not sleep. Anticipation of what the next few days held in store had overtaxed his imagination and now brought a succession of half-waking dreams:

Visions of palaces underground, of gigantic monsters, of sculptured figures, and endless inscriptions, floated before me. After forming plan after plan for removing the earth, and extricating these treasures, I fancied myself wandering in a maze of chambers from which I could find no outlet. Then again, all was re-buried, and I was standing on the grass-covered mound.

The sheikh meanwhile had travelled by night to the nearest settlement and returned at dawn with six Arabs who were prepared to work. Layard put them to dig at two widely separated points in the main mound, and by the evening of the same day they had in each case partially cleared a chamber lined with slabs of alabaster and decorated not with reliefs, but with neat cuneiform inscriptions. In a single day's work, with six men, he had in fact discovered two of the principal palaces of the Assyrian kings.

The ancient city of Kalhu, Calah of Genesis, of which Nimrud is the site, was the second capital of Assyria, after Ashur and before Nineveh or Khorsabad. It occupies a very fertile tongue of land in the angle between the Tigris and its tributary, the Greater Zab. Today the river is separated from the ruins by about half a mile of low ground, but its ancient bed is easily distinguishable washing the foot of the city walls. The extent of the city itself is less clearly defined, but, as at Nineveh and Khorsabad, by far the most formidable feature is the platform upon which the palaces were built. This is a double square 300 metres wide with its long axis oriented northwards. At the north-west corner a high conical excrescence represents the ruins of a small ziggurat. The two buildings which Layard's first soundings had encountered were afterwards known as the North-west and South-west Palaces.[91]

During the next few days he increased his gang to eleven men and among other things cut a trench in the conical mound at the north-west corner of the platform, which surprisingly proved to be solid mud brick. The function of a ziggurat as the emplacement for a raised shrine was, of course, completely unknown at that time, and it did not occur to him to connect it with the similar structure at Khorsabad, which Botta had provisionally identified as an 'observatory'. Meanwhile there could be little doubt that the news of his activities must by now have reached Mosul, and at the end of the week he felt that the time had come to visit the Pasha and offer some explanation. His instinct was correct. After greetings and an exchange of compliments, Keritli Oglu congratulated him on his discovery of buried treasure and to prove that his information was well substantiated, produced a grubby morsel of paper containing a minute fragment of gold leaf. In the filling of one of the chambers which he had already cleared, Layard had come upon a delicately carved object which was in fact the forerunner of the now famous Nimrud ivories. It still retained traces of gilding, and what he now saw was a tiny flake of gold detached from the ivory, which he had not bothered to recover.

Layard's suggestion that on his return to Nimrud he should be accompanied by an agent of the Pasha's to take charge of any gold which he had already found or should find in the future provided a temporary solution of the problem, but he was no longer under any illusion as to the opposition which was in store for him. What he did find regrettable was that, when it came, a good deal of it proved to have its origin in the French Consulate. From Botta he had never received anything but open-minded friendship and co-operation. With Rouet, Botta's temporary replacement, things were different, for he at once introduced an atmosphere of petty jealousy and

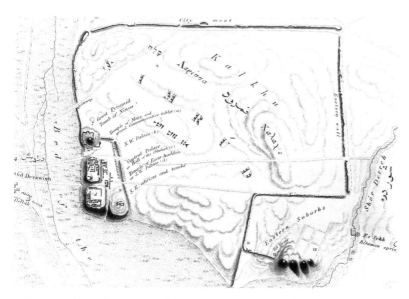

*36 Captain Felix Jones' map of the Nimrud ruins: part of a survey commission-
ed by the British Museum in 1852. The area marked 'Eastern Suburbs' later
proved to be 'Fort Shalmaneser' (see Chapter Fourteen).*

international rivalry. Before Layard returned to Nimrud he found
that Rouet's agents were travelling round the country 'opening up
mounds' at random, in a feverish race to stake their claims to new
discoveries. He himself felt obliged to join in an undignified
scramble in which neither side was rewarded with any success.

Meanwhile work continued at Nimrud with thirty men directed
by a foreman. Winter rains had now started and in his hovel at
Salamiyah, Layard lived in considerable discomfort. The roof
leaked continually and his nights were spent 'crouched up in a
corner or under a rude table surrounded by trenches to carry off the
accumulating waters'. In the South-west Palace he continued to
clear chambers lined with inscribed slabs, but these appeared from
certain indications to have originally belonged to an earlier building
and to have been re-used. Finally, on 28 November, the tops of
two slabs appeared, covered with bas-reliefs. At the moment of
their discovery there was a violent storm, but the workmen, now
greatly excited, continued to work in the streaming rain until the
sculptured pictures were completely cleared. The reliefs on each
slab were in two registers separated by a band of cuneiform inscription, and represented battle scenes, in one of which the siege
of a walled city was dramatically depicted. They also were evidently
in secondary use and had been somewhat damaged in the process
of re-setting.

A few hours after this discovery Layard received a call from
Da'ud Agha, captain of the Turkish irregular troops stationed
nearby, with whom he had already become close friends. Da'ud's
manner now made it plain that he had bad news, and Layard at once

assumed quite correctly that he had instructions from the Pasha to stop the excavations. In Mosul that evening Keritli Oglu informed him that his excavations were disturbing some Moslem graves on the summit of the Nimrûd mound and must therefore be discontinued. Returning disconsolately to Salamiyah he again encountered Da'ud Agha, who reluctantly admitted that, if there were no graves, he had instructions to *make* some, and that he and his men had spent an exhausting day removing head-stones from a neighbouring cemetery. 'Indeed,' he said, 'we have destroyed more real tombs of the True Believers, in making sham ones, than you could have defiled, between the Zab and Salamiyah.'

Actually Layard had little difficulty in persuading the Pasha's *cawass*, who now accompanied him, that it would be necessary to retain some of his workmen for purposes of cleaning and recording the slabs already exposed, and as the Turk rarely considered the three-mile ride from Salamiyah to the mound as part of his duties, he was able to continue with a good deal of surreptitious excavation. In this way he discovered a variety of new sculptures including 'a crouching lion', a pair of damaged winged bulls, and 'a human figure nine feet high'. Having thus established beyond all possible doubt that important antiquities were contained in the mound, he decided to inform Sir Stratford Canning of the necessity for a *firman* protecting him from interference of the sort he had already experienced. Soon after his letter had been dispatched to Istanbul, one of his principal stumbling-blocks was suddenly removed, by the deposition of Keritli Oglu and his replacement by a just and enlightened official of the new school. Accordingly, while awaiting new developments in the local administration, Layard determined temporarily to re-bury his sculptures and to spend Christmas with Rawlinson in Baghdad.

It will be remembered that Rawlinson had arrived in Baghdad to take up his appointment as Resident in 1843, and Layard had not since then visited the Residency. This, therefore, was the first meeting between the two men. Contrasting their characters in his *Memoir*, Canon Rawlinson's disparagement of Layard's academic attainment makes commendation of his practical ability seem patronizing. ('He was not a scholar, or a man of any great culture, or of any wide reading.')[92] Yet it is possible to maintain that qualities such as linguistic ability and unfailing ingenuity, combined with imaginative sensibility and good taste, are a possible substitute for other forms of 'culture'. In any case, Layard's brief stay at the Residency on this occasion saw the beginnings of an association most profitable to science and of a life-long friendship.

Returning to Mosul in early January, Layard found that many changes had taken place. The new governor, Isma'il Pasha, had already to a large extent conciliated the tribes. Many had returned to their villages and a lot of belated cultivation was in progress. Furthermore, the heavy rains which had fallen almost continually since he had been away had clothed the countryside in an early

37 Hormuzd Rassam, Layard's locally born assistant and successor, in the costume of a Moslawi grandee.

garment of green. Isma'il made no objection to his continuing his excavations, but opposition now came from a new source. This was the *qadi*, or principal judge of the town, an elderly bigot who had succeeded in stirring up some of the more fanatical religious elements with a cock-and-bull story about Layard's inscriptions being subversive of the principles of Islam. Layard therefore judged it best to postpone any obvious activity for the time being, and did not in fact restart work until mid-February. He had now enlisted the help of Hormuzd Rassam, an intelligent Chaldean Christian and brother of the British Vice-Consul who had greeted him on his arrival in Mosul. Rassam became from now onwards his overseer and general agent, and later, as it will be seen, developed some pretensions to be an archaeologist. Security in the Nimrud district was now so greatly improved that it was possible to move their headquarters from Salamiyah to the village close by the mound and known by the same name. A team of thirty Nestorians, or as they are now called, 'Assyrians', formed the nucleus of their workmen, and these encamped on the summit of the mound. Layard had no difficulty in establishing friendly relations with the sheikh of the Abu Salman★ who had now returned to his settlements, so there was no lack of unskilled labour.

★ It was he who about this time took Layard to see Negub (The Tunnel), an underground water channel dating from Assyrian times and entered from the bank of the Zab River. Here he discovered 'a slab covered with cuneiform characters, which had fallen from a platform and been wedged in a crevice in the rock'. In the half light he could see that it bore 'a genealogical list of kings', but returning some days later to remove it, he found that he had been anticipated by a party of Arabs who had maliciously or otherwise broken it in pieces. See Oates (1968, p. 46) on this subject.

Soon it was spring again, and once more Layard found himself enchanted by the ephemeral beauty with which the Mosul country-side adorns itself during this short season of the year. The pastures were deep in grass and flowers, and he describes how his saluki greyhounds, tired from hunting, 'issued from the long grass dyed red, yellow or blue, according to the flowers through which they had last forced their way'. Finding the village huts verminous, he had moved out to camp in the open, as in fact is the almost universal practice among the people of that district during the month of April. Colloquially it is called *waqt al barriyyah*, 'the country time', and has something in common with the Jewish Feast of the Tabernacles (cf. Leviticus xxiii: 34). Arab peasants bring dusty black tents to pitch on the greensward about their village; Kurds or Yezidis build *chardags*, which are shelters of leafy branches over or beside a stream of running water. The children pick flowers, which their elders wear behind their ears or tucked into their headdress. Even Christians of Mosul migrate to the temporary hospitality of monasteries outside the town.

Seated before the door of his tent in the evening, after a successful day's work among the relics of another age, Layard was extremely happy. Here is how he recollected the scene afterwards:

As the sun went down behind the low hills which separate the river from the desert – even their rocky sides had struggled to emulate the verdant clothing of the plain – its receding rays were gradually withdrawn, like a transparent veil of light, from the landscape. Over the pure, cloudless sky was the glow of the last light. The great mound threw its dark shadow far across the plain. . . . The Kurdish mountains whose snowy summits cherished the dying sunbeams, yet struggled with the twilight. The bleating of sheep and lowing of cattle, at first faint, became louder as the flocks returned from their pastures, and wandered amongst the tents. Girls hurried over the greensward to seek their fathers' cattle, or crouched down to milk those which had returned alone to their well-remembered folds. Some were coming from the river bearing the replenished pitcher on their heads or shoulders; others, no less graceful in their form, and erect in their carriage, were carrying the heavy load of long grass which they had cut in the meadows. Sometimes a party of horsemen would ride up to my tent and, driving the end of their lances into the ground, they would spring from their mares, and fasten their halters to the still quivering weapons. . . .

The plain now glittered with innumerable fires. As the night advanced, they vanished one by one until the landscape was wrapped in darkness and in silence, only disturbed by the barking of the Arab dog.[93]

For Layard's readers at home, this passage must more than anything have evoked the world of the Old Testament. For those who have followed where he led, it is a nostalgic reality.

Now, indeed, he had good reason to be satisfied with the progress of his work. Temporarily he had abandoned the exploration of the South-west Palace. The building proved to have been destroyed by fire, and the sculptures, which had suffered considerably as a result, had also at some time deteriorated owing to long exposure to the weather. But a new sounding on the side of a deep

gulley, which runs far into the mound on the west side, had produced most gratifying results. Here was an older palace from which,
as he presently realized, some slabs must have been taken for re-use
in the south-west building. But the sculptures which remained
were undisturbed and in a fine state of preservation. The morning
after this discovery, returning from a visit to the Abu Salman
sheikh, he encountered two horsemen coming from the direction
of the mound, who greeted him excitedly with the words: 'Hasten,
Bey, to the diggers, for they have found Nimrod himself.' 'Nimrod' he found to be the head of a perfectly preserved winged bull
colossus, which had just been exposed in one of the trenches.
Rightly suspecting it to be one of a pair, Layard measured the
distance according with a square-proportioned gateway, and by
evening a second similar head had appeared above the ground.

The reactions of Layard's workmen can be imagined. Most dis-
concerting was that of one man who, on the appearance of the first
head, at once flung down his basket and made off for Mosul, hardly
pausing for breath until he reached the bazaar, where his semi-
articulate tidings set the whole town in an uproar. This was a less
fortunate circumstance, since poor Isma'il Pasha again found himself prevailed upon to summon Layard to his presence and temporarily veto any further discoveries.

Things had now reached a point where, without proper support
from official quarters, Layard's individual efforts could not be
expected to go further. He wrote to Canning, contrasting the
magnitude of his new finds with the legal and pecuniary deadlock
which he was at present facing, and asking for advice. As a result,
one of his major difficulties was successfully solved. Canning, on
retiring from his post as Ambassador, was provided by the Sultan,
partly as a gesture of goodwill, with a *firman* for Layard of a most
generous character, and so strongly worded as to be capable of
protecting him in the future from any kind of official interference.
His second request, however, provided Canning with a more formidable problem. Suggestions which he had already made to the
Trustees of the British Museum that Layard's finds were now of a
nature to become the responsibility of a public institution, rather
than of an individual, had so far been coldly received. He could
now only repeat them in stronger terms, stressing that if the
Treasury would subsidize the continuation of the work, the whole
of the finds so far made should become the property of the Museum.
Failing this, he threatened to club together with Rawlinson and
make it a private enterprise, adding in fun, 'even at the expense of
my daughter's expectations!'

It was perhaps Layard's own reports and sketches which, on
reaching London, eventually convinced the Trustees of the generosity of Canning's offer. Yet the sum of £2,000, which they were
then induced to put at Layard's disposal, can hardly have seemed
other than parsimonious. We have already remarked how Botta,
at Khorsabad, in spite of the much more generous support afforded

by his government, was still not in a position either to conduct his search or to handle his finds with the care and attention which their importance merited. So also Layard was now driven, against his own conscience and inclination, to expedients which have in later times laid his sponsors open to criticism. His purpose from now onwards was 'to obtain the largest possible number of well-preserved objects of art at the least possible outlay of time and money'.

A generation later, when the first American Assyriologists entered the excavating field, their comments on this subject were openly censorious. We may quote, for example, Hilprecht, who towards the end of the century directed American excavations in Babylonia:

In the interests of science it remains a cause of deep regret that after his great discoveries, Layard did not at once find the same hearty support in England as his more fortunate French colleague so speedily had obtained in Paris. Not even an artist was dispatched to draw the sculptures and copy the inscriptions, though many of the monuments 'were in too dilapidated a condition to be removed', and though Layard 'had neither knowledge nor experience as a draughtsman – a disqualification which he could scarcely hope to overcome'. He was thus practically prevented by his own government from making a methodical exploration of Nimrûd. And this lack of method, system and thoroughness unfortunately remained a characteristic feature of most of the following English excavations in Assyrian and Babylonian ruins, – a lack felt by nobody more keenly than by Layard, Loftus and all the other great British explorers.[94]

Even C. J. Gadd, who later dedicated a beautiful publication[95] to the memory of Layard, *ad gloriam redintegrandam viri apud majores praeclari*, refers, albeit in measured terms, to the limitations, which could only have been imposed on his work, 'by a body of men so inexperienced in excavation as the Trustees of that time necessarily were'.

And finally there is Layard's own apologia for the makeshift character of his own excavating. He says:

The smallness of the sum placed at my disposal compelled me to follow the same plan in the excavations that I had hitherto adopted, *viz.* to dig trenches along the sides of the chambers, and to expose the whole of the slabs, without removing the earth from the centre. Thus, few of the chambers were fully explored, and many small objects of great interest may have been left undiscovered. As I was directed to bury the building with earth after I had explored it, to avoid unnecessary expense, I filled up the chambers with the rubbish taken from those subsequently uncovered, having first examined the walls, copied the inscriptions and drawn the sculptures.

AN EXPEDITION TO HATRA

During the late spring of 1846, while Layard was awaiting his *firman* and a decision about the future of his work, he passed the time by making a number of enjoyable expeditions into the sur-

38 *Deprived in the early days of a professional artist, Layard recorded many of the Assyrian reliefs himself, often working under difficult conditions in a poor light. Here S. C. Malan has depicted him sketching relief slabs at Kuyunjik.*

rounding country. One of these was to the strange, eerie ruins of the Parthian city of Hatra, far out in the desert called Al Jazirah, between the two rivers (see Chapter Fourteen). On this occasion he was accompanied by 'a cheerful party of Christian and Mohammedan ladies and gentlemen from Mosul', and the freedom with which this considerable cavalcade travelled across country was a tribute to the improved security which Isma'il's rule had brought about. Layard's picture of the party leaving Mosul by the Cannon Gate and cantering southwards over the flowery uplands is a pleasant one:

Our tents, obtained from the Pasha, and our provisions and necessary furniture, were carried by a string of twelve camels. Mounted above these loads, and on donkeys, was an army of camel-drivers, tent-pitchers, and volunteers ready for all services. There were, moreover, a few irregular horsemen, the cawasses, the attendants of the Mosul gentlemen, the Mosul gentlemen themselves, and our own servants all armed to the teeth. Ali Effendi [al 'Umari] was mounted on the Hebdan, a well-known white Arab, beautiful in form and pure in blood, but now of great age. Close at his horse's heels followed a confidential servant; who perched on a pack-saddle, seemed to roll from side to side on two small barrels, the use of which might have been an enigma had they not omitted a very strong smell of râki. The English lady [Mrs Rassam] was equipped in a riding habit and hat. The two Englishmen, Mr Ross and myself, wore a striking mixture of European and oriental raiments. Mosul ladies, in blue veils, their faces concealed by black horsehair sieves, had been dragged to the top of piles of carpets and cushions, under which groaned their unfortunate mules. Greyhounds on leashes were led by Arabs on foot. . . . The horsemen galloped round and round, now dashing into the centre of the crowd, throwing their horses on their haunches while at full speed, or discharging their guns and pistols in the air. A small flag with the British Colours was fastened to the top of a spear and confided to a Cawass.[96]

Hatra lies in the centre of the Shammar territory, and it was then usual to obtain guides for the final stage of the journey from the Shammar *shuyuk*. The main body of the tribe were to be found at spring pastures somewhere between Hatra and the Tigris, and, for so distinguished a party, a visit to Sofuk, the paramount sheikh, was essential. In this case it was not at once easy to obtain news of his exact whereabouts, and such scattered outposts of the tribe as they encountered were uncommunicative. He had naturally been on poor terms with Keritli Oglu and was for the moment taking no chances with the new Pasha. Finally, however, mounting a ridge above the Wadi Qassab, Layard was confronted with the magnificent sight of almost the entire tribe on the move – the whole plain for miles covered with camels, asses, flocks and herds and strings of beautiful horses. For him Arab bloodstock had a particular fascination, and during this short sojourn among the breeders of some of the finest in the world, he was continually lost in admiration. On the previous day the sight of a young filly had drawn from him superlatives of the sort which, unlike Buckingham, he never wasted upon his fellow-humans. 'Light and elegant as a gazelle', she was struggling to free herself from the spear to which she was tied. 'Her limbs', he says, 'were in perfect symmetry; her ears long, slender, and transparent; her nostrils, high, dilated and deep red; her neck gracefully arched, and her mane and tail of the texture of silk. We all involuntarily stopped to gaze at her.' Within the next few days, between the Wadis Qassab and Jernaf, he was to be shown animals by whose pedigrees Shammar history was dated.

The party's entertainment by Sofuk is described by Layard with a great deal of picturesque detail. But since in recent years goat-hair tents and whole-roasted sheep, together with multiple matrimony and tribal lore, have become so much the stock-in-trade of Middle East travel literature, the changeless routine of such an occasion may here perhaps be taken for granted. As for the ruins of Hatra, they have now been extensively excavated, as described in Chapter Fourteen.

Back in Mosul, Layard found time to make a few soundings in Kuyunjik. In spite of the expostulations of the French Consul, which to him seemed little justified, he dug enough trenches to satisfy himself once and for all that remains similar to those at Khorsabad and Nimrud existed somewhere in the mound. Next he made some excavations at a point in the northern line of mounds enclosing the city, which we now know to have been the 'Nergal Gate', and came upon the largest pair of winged figures yet seen. These were afterwards thought to have been destroyed, but in 1941 one complete bull and part of another were revealed by a heavy rainstorm, and today this section of the walls, together with the gate and bulls, has been fully restored. Layard then returned to Nimrud itself and, anticipating the favourable outcome of Canning's negotiations with the British Museum, continued work on the new building with a fairly large gang of men. Slab after slab was laid bare and the wealth of beautiful sculpture became almost bewildering. Layard was amused by the reaction of his workmen and their curious identification of Assyrian figures. 'If it was a bearded man, they concluded at once that it was an idol or a *jin* and cursed or spat upon it. If a eunuch, they declared that it was the likeness of a beautiful female, and kissed or patted the cheek.' Soon he felt that enough was accumulated to send a representative collection to England. The fact that the first consignment of cases from Khorsabad had reached Baghdad and was about to be transferred to Basra, where a French naval vessel, *Le Cormoran*, was awaiting them, introduced a quaint element of competition and was undoubtedly an extra incentive. Captain Felix Jones, who now enters the story for the first time, was then in charge of the little Tigris steamer *Nitocris*, and at Rawlinson's suggestion an attempt was now made by him to bring his vessel as far as Nimrud. Unfortunately he failed to get beyond the first rapids above Tekrit. In this way, much of the summer was wasted and Layard was compelled in the end to ship his slabs to Basra by *kelek* and country-boat, having first reduced their weight by sawing off their backs. Since they did not eventually reach England till nearly a year later, the unedifying little race was lost by a wide margin.

So preoccupied had Layard been, that he had hardly noticed the increasing heat of the summer sun. But soon it could no longer be ignored. He writes:

The change to summer had been as rapid as that which ushered in the spring. The verdure of the plain had perished almost in a day. Hot winds coming from the desert had burned up and carried away the scrub; flights of locusts, darkening the air, had destroyed the few patches of cultivation, and had completed the havoc commenced by the heat of the sun.

In Baghdad, Rawlinson would now be working in his damp little *chardag* overhanging the Tigris; so Layard, taking a leaf out of his book, ordered a recess to be cut in the bank of the river, where it rose perpendicularly from the water's edge. By screening the front with reeds and boughs of trees, and covering the whole with similar materials, a small room was formed. He admits, however, 'I was much troubled with scorpions and other reptiles which issued from the earth forming the walls of my apartment.' In the end, it is not surprising that he began to feel the strain on his health of all his exertions, and by August had decided temporarily to close the excavations, and spend the time, until autumn brought cooler days, travelling among the mountain tribes.

This time his first objective was the villages of the Nestorian Christians in the Tiyari mountains between Van and Urmia. His interest in this ill-starred minority had probably been aroused by the missionary Badger's account of his visit to their houses and again stimulated by the band of tough 'Assyrian' pick-men who formed the nucleus of his working gang at Nimrud. He gives a fairly accurate account of their rituals and beliefs as contrasted with those of the Chaldean or Uniate branch of the same Church, whose principal villages, Tell Kaif and Tell Usquf, he visited on his return to Iraq. On the first day of this journey he took the opportunity of inspecting the site of Botta's now abandoned excavations at Khorsabad. 'Since M. Botta's departure', he writes, 'the chambers had been partly filled up by the falling-in of the trenches; the sculptures were rapidly perishing; and, shortly, little will remain of this remarkable monument.'

THE YEZIDI TRIBES

Another delightful experience which had fallen to Layard's lot while travelling in the Shaikhan hills north of Mosul was that of attending the famous Spring Festival of the Yezidis in their sacred grove at Shaikh 'Adi. He learnt a great deal about this much-persecuted people and the obscure beliefs which centre around their propitiation of the evil principle. He observed the cleanliness and simple good taste of their villages, and in their shrines, to use the words of a modern writer, 'their capacity to be still and worship'. On his return to Mosul, therefore, finding by chance that Tahya Pasha was preparing an expedition to Jebel Sinjar, around which more Yezidi tribes are grouped, he offered to accompany him. Layard's impressions of the Yezidis make an intentional contrast with his description of the scene in the courtyard of the Sarai, where the Pasha's retinue were making ready to start.

The attendants of his Excellency were hurrying to and fro, laden with every variety of utensil and instrument; some carrying gigantic telescopes, huge bowls, in leather cases; others labouring under bundles of pipe-sticks, or bending under the weight of calico bags crammed with state documents.

Finally the preparations were complete,

and as his Excellency placed his foot in the stirrup, the trumpets sounded as a signal for the procession to move onwards. First came a regiment of infantry, followed by a company of artillery-men with their guns. The trumpeters, and the Pasha's own standard, a mass of green silk drapery, embroidered in gold, with verses from the Koran, succeeded; behind were six led Arab horses, richly caparisoned with coloured saddle-cloths, glittering with gold embroidery. The Pasha himself then appeared, surrounded by the chiefs of the town and the officers of his household. The procession was finished by the irregular cavalry, divided into companies, each headed by its respective commander. . . .[97]

Needless to say, the commissariat arrangements had been entirely neglected, and at the first halt both men and beasts went supperless to bed.

39 The sacred shrine at Shaikh 'Adi of the Yezidi sect (often wrongly described as 'devil-worshippers'), visited by Layard in 1846.

Tahya had been at pains to impress on Layard that this expedition was being made, 'not with any hostile intention, but for the purpose of examining the state of the country'. At Tell 'Afar, the picturesque Turkoman market-town on the easternmost spur of the *jebel*, Layard had an opportunity of judging exactly how welcome to the country people this sort of visit would be. 'The commissariat was replenished from the scanty stores of the inhabitants. The houses were broken into and a general pillage ensued.' While the ingredients of the evening meal were in this way being obtained, Layard climbed to the ruined castle above the town and from this point of vantage he looked southwards over the once-fertile farmlands of Assyria, now rendered barren by misrule and insecurity. 'As the sun went down', he says, 'I counted above one hundred mounds, throwing their dark and lengthening shadows across the plain.'[98]

Jebel Sinjar itself is a strange, isolated range of hills, high enough to be snow-capped in winter, but entirely surrounded by flat, arable country and pastureland. Its southern flank is chased with deep, rocky gorges, honeycombed with caves, and the principal Yezidi settlements are usually terraced into low foothills at the mouths of these gorges. In times of peace and security their cultivation spreads out into the plain, beyond the fruit gardens immediately surrounding the villages. Danger drives them back into the mountains to live precariously in caves. So now, in sight of the first of these settlements, the Pasha and his army were greeted by a deputation of Yezidi elders, not, however, including the headmen of Mirkhan, the village which they were approaching. Having failed to convince them of his peaceful intentions, the Pasha sent a troop of irregulars forward to enter the village; but these were met with a volley of rifle-fire from the rocks above and two of them fell dead at the feet of Layard, who was with them. With such provocation the sequel was inevitable; the now-deserted village was promptly plundered and burnt.

A few aged women and decrepit old men, too infirm to leave with the rest, and found hiding in the small dark rooms, were murdered, and their heads severed from their bodies. Blazing fires were made in the neat dwellings, and the whole village was delivered to the flames. Even the old Pasha, with his grey hair and tottering step, hurried to and fro among the smoking ruins and helped to add the torch where the fire was not doing its work.

Next morning military operations were undertaken in earnest against the Yezidis hiding in the gorge behind the village. But every time a detachment of troops entered the valley they were decimated by accurate rifle-fire from the caves above. Eventually, their losses becoming serious, they were compelled to desist. On the second morning the Pasha ordered a fresh attack and, to Layard's astonishment, in order to encourage his men, advanced himself into the gorge and had his carpet spread on a rock.

Here he sat, with the greatest apathy, smoking his pipe, and carrying on a frivolous conversation, although he was the object of the aim of the Yezidis.

Even this characteristically eccentric piece of bravado did not, however, improve the lot of his attacking troops, and another day passed without a single Yezidi casualty. On the third morning there was no opposition; the caves were found empty, their occupants having slipped out in the night and escaped to safety over the watershed. The engagement was ended.

While the Pasha's retinue lingered at Mirkhan attending to their dead and wounded, Layard took the opportunity of proceeding alone to visit the remaining Yezidi settlements, including Beled Sinjar, the chief town of the district. In the latter he did not for some reason recognize the Roman fortress of Singara, so often mentioned by Marcellinus and other Latin writers, for he says:

It would be difficult to point out, with any degree of certainty, ruins at Beled Sinjar more ancient than the Mohammedan conquest.

Returning, still alone, to Mosul, he had the rare privilege near Tell 'Afar of seeing a fairly large herd of wild asses drinking at a spring. He must afterwards have been reminded of this occasion when the famous hunting-reliefs came to light, in the palace of Ashur-banipal at Kuyunjik.

CHAPTER NINE

Subsidized exploration

On 1 November 1846 Layard reopened excavations at Nimrud on a large scale. He now had the responsibility of administering public funds, and was subject in his work to the limitations imposed by the very detailed instructions received from the Trustees. He proceeded to build a modest expedition house just outside the village at Nimrud and to establish his Nestorian workmen in a camp on the mound itself. From now onwards Hormuzd Rassam joined him permanently and proved an extremely efficient major-domo and general assistant. In the trenches he distributed his gangs at four widely separated points – in the old North-west Palace, in the South-west Building, whose sculptures had suffered so much from fire and exposure, in a 'Central Building' where little had so far been discovered except for the two winged colossi, and at a fourth point in the south-east corner of the mound.

The weeks which followed were more astonishingly rich in finds than perhaps any similar period in the history of Assyriology. 'Scarcely a day passed without some new and important discovery.' Layard had as yet had no opportunity of discussing his inscribed material with Rawlinson and was therefore still unable to identify the names of kings associated with the different palaces and the genealogical lists. Right up to the end of this first season's full-scale excavations, he still used expressions like, 'the Khorsabad king' or 'the son of the builder of the North-west Palace'. In the marvellous reliefs surrounding the reception rooms of the latter building he could not recognize the life and accomplishments of Ashur-nasirpal (883–859 BC), nor read the name of Esarhaddon (680–669 BC) on the slabs removed from here to the South-west Building and there set up with their faces to the wall ready for their backs to be re-sculptured. The Central Building also seemed to have been used as a quarry for the adornment of some later structure, for he discovered over a hundred sculptured slabs, 'packed in rows, one against the other, and placed in a regular series, according to the subjects upon them'. What could have been a more acceptable find for one in search of removable antiquities and hampered by limited funds? Yet there was better still to come. A few metres further on his workmen encountered the corner of a polished black stone, and

40 The famous Black Obelisk of Shalmaneser III, discovered by Layard at Nimrud in 1846. The panel (second from the top) depicting 'Jehu, son of Omri' (sic) bringing tribute to the Assyrian King, created a first historical link with the Old Testament.

soon uncovered the now famous Black Obelisk of Shalmaneser III (858–824 B C) – today one of the choicest antiquities in the British Museum. Sculptured on all four sides, it has twenty small reliefs depicting, for the most part, foreign princes bringing tribute to the Assyrian throne. Could Layard but have known it at the time, it also created the first and most dramatic link between the Assyrian sculptures and the Old Testament, for the long inscription beneath the reliefs recorded, amongst much other matter, the receipt of gold and silver from Jehu, son of Omri (*sic*), King of Judah (cf. Kings xix: 16, and 2 Kings ix and x).

In addition to these major finds, Layard's trenches produced many minor sculptures and small objects – carved sphinxes, lion-pedestals, the famous Nimrud ivories with their curiously Phoenician-looking designs, copper objects and vessels of glass or alabaster. But so poorly equipped was he by modern standards to extract and handle anything but the best-preserved and most portable antiquities, that a pathetically small proportion can have survived except in his memory, or been adequately recorded in his faltering sketches. As a more fortunate successor in the same field, one may perhaps be excused for reiterated regrets on this score. Criticism of Layard's methods is at once disarmed by his frankness on the subject. Yet the impression left by his own account is none the less disturbing. One phrase in particular occurs with monotonous and painful regularity. It is a phrase made familiar by the early discoverers of Egyptian mummies, but which nowadays would carry little conviction – '. . . entire when first exposed to view, it crumbled into dust as soon as touched. . . .'[99] Thus Layard says, for instance, of 'several [copper] helmets, some with arched crest', 'they fell to pieces as soon as exposed';[100] a sculptured pedestal consisting of twin lions, 'had been so much injured by fire, that I was unable to preserve it';[101] iron armour was 'in so decomposed a state that I had much difficulty in detaching it from the soil. Two or three baskets were filled with these relics';[102] 'copper vessels of peculiar shape . . . fell to pieces almost immediately on exposure to the air, and I was unable to preserve one of them entire'; where walls were covered with painted frescoes, 'the plaster fell from the walls in flakes, notwithstanding all my efforts to preserve it'; most of the famous ivories 'on their discovery fell to pieces almost upon mere exposure to the air . . .';[103] and so on. Today it is tempting to reflect how much could have been done with a little paraffin wax or plaster of Paris.

By the end of April 1847, in the North-west Palace alone, Layard had explored twenty-eight halls and chambers, some having plastered walls ornamented with brightly painted frescoes, but the greater part lined with sculptured slabs. He had also located thirteen pairs of gigantic winged bulls and lions. Since the British Museum had insisted that all discoveries which could not be removed must be reburied, the period during which this great array of sculptures and paintings remained exposed to view was an extremely short

41 *Layard supervises as a winged bull sculpture is removed from a doorway at Nimrud and lowered on to a wooden platform.*

one. There was, however, at least one Englishman who visited the excavation before the dispersal began – a certain Mr Longworth, who has left the most interesting record of his impressions in the form of a letter to the *Morning Post* of which he was a correspondent.[104] Like so many people seeing a Mesopotamian excavation for the first time, he was surprised to find Layard's palaces apparently so far beneath the ground and to have to descend into them by precipitous staircases. Yet his description must have effectively conveyed to the *Post*'s very large circle of readers the most vivid impression of the romantic character of the Assyrian finds.

Layard himself meanwhile returned to the problem of transport. On the last day of December 1846 he had watched a *kelek* laden with a second consignment of twenty cases float off down the Tigris, to be shipped from Basra to England by way of Bombay. By May 1847 yet another consignment of sculptures was ready to leave. Included among them was the Black Obelisk and all the remaining slabs which for the moment he felt justified in sending to England. Yet Layard still hesitated to fill in his trenches. In regard to the winged colossi, the British Museum had rightly decided that they should not be sawn up into sections for re-assembling after reaching Europe, as had been done by the French at Khorsabad, but should remain in place with earth piled over them 'until some favourable opportunity should present itself to remove them entire'. To Layard this was the greatest disappointment, as he was naturally most anxious that examples of them should be seen in England as soon as possible. Finally, he decided to use his own initiative in the matter. He selected one lion and one bull from amongst the best-preserved sculptures and prepared for the prodigious task of loading them on to a raft. A little tackle was obtainable in Mosul – hemp ropes, a couple of pulley-blocks and a pair of screw-jacks. In addition he ordered one enormous cable to be made of palm-fibre, and constructed a powerful wooden cart, mounted on a pair of iron axles, which Botta had used for the same purpose at Khorsabad. Botta had, in fact, met with very little success in his early attempts to bring his bulls over the fifteen miles of ploughland from Khorsabad to the river, and one had had to be abandoned half-way. His 'cart' had wheels nearly a metre thick and was pulled by a gang of 600 Yezidi and Shebek workmen (as may be seen in a fine engraving in Place's publication).[105] On this subject Layard, in a letter home, permitted himself to be critical, saying that Botta could not be induced to abandon brute force in favour of mechanics. Yet, when himself eventually faced with the same problem, the only mechanics which he could contrive was a team of oxen, and these, perhaps intimidated by the nature of the object in the cart, refused to pull.

But first there was the task of transferring the colossi from their upright position to the horizontal, and so to the cart which awaited them at the foot of the mound forty or so metres away. Since the writer was responsible in 1939 for a similar operation in connection with the transport to Baghdad of the last two bulls discovered at Khorsabad (found in the Citadel Gateway in 1934 by the Oriental Institute of the University of Chicago: now ornamenting the Assyrian Gate, Baghdad), it may be of interest here to compare sizes and weights. The colossi are invariably carved, partly in situ, from a single slab of stone 46–61 centimetres (18–24 inches) thick. Layard's bull and lion measured about 3 metres (10 feet) square and a good deal of stone was sawed from their backs before dispatch.

42 Preparations for the removal by the present author in 1939 of two winged bull sculptures, discovered by Gordon Loud at the entrance to the Citadel at Khorsabad. Each was cased in a steel framework.

43 A winged bull being moved on a cart to the river, under Layard's supervision. In the background is the Nimrud mound.

At Khorsabad these would have been comparatively small slabs. The pair moved from there in 1939 were 4·4 metres (14 feet 6 inches) square and weighed a little over 20 tons each. The single bull with its head facing sideways which the Oriental Institute transported in pieces to Chicago in 1929 (one of a pair flanking the entrance to the throne-room in King Sargon's palace) was 5 metres (16 feet 6 inches) square, and the largest fragment weighed 14 tons. Two even larger bulls facing forwards in the same entrance are also in fragments and have never been removed. They measure 5·5 metres (18 feet) square, and are as far as one knows the largest of which traces have yet been found. Nevertheless, if one calculates Layard's monoliths, when ready for lowering, at a minimum weight of 10 tons, the task was still a formidable one. They had first to be bound up in felts and matting in order to deaden the shock of any blow they might receive; their descent was then checked by ropes twisted around the projecting masonry behind them and hauled on by struggling gangs of workmen. Wooden props, used as a secondary check, were gradually and precariously removed as the great stone began to tilt over.[106]

It is hard to know whether Layard's own description or his dramatic coloured illustration[107] give one the more vivid impression of this tense moment. In the trench, scores of half-naked Arabs directed by Mr Rassam are hauling on the ropes or pouring water to cool them as they smoke and crackle, while the Nestorians easing the wooden props are in increasing danger of being crushed beneath the descending stone. On the surface of the mound above is a motley crowd of onlookers – Bedouins with their horses and camels and all the women from the village. In front of them stands Layard himself, his beard and long hair blowing in the wind, vainly attempting to make himself heard or to attract attention by throwing lumps of earth. As the angle of the stone increases, the shouts of the men and the excited screaming of the women rise to a crescendo. Finally,

44 An Assyrian relief from Kuyunjik showing transport of a bull sculpture by river from the quarry. The figure is carved 'in the rough', to be completed after placing in situ.

with a metre and a half to go and the props no longer useful, the ropes all break together and the sculpture settles with a crash on to the wooden platform prepared for it. As the dust clears away and the noise dies down, Layard leaps down, and finds to his enormous relief that no damage is done.

Meanwhile, a sort of railway-cutting had been dug from the palace to the edge of the mound and along this the bull was now moved on rollers (in exactly the same manner as it had been brought from the river by the Assyrians two-and-a-half millennia earlier), and finally coaxed on to its wooden cart. Again it may be interest-ing to compare the writer's experience of the same manœuvre with the Khorsabad bulls in 1939. Cased in situ in wood and steel, these slabs weighed considerably more than twice as much as Layard's; yet now at last 'mechanical' methods could be used. In each case the mud-brick wall behind the bull was cut down to a convenient shelf at half the height of the stone. The head of the slab was then tilted back on to the shelf, its base was raised by jacks and tackle on an overhead beam, and the transport, which consisted of 20-ton 'White' trucks supplied by the oil company, was backed into the cutting and slipped beneath the load.

Layard's bull again met with a major adventure on its short journey from the mound to the river bank. One wheel of the cart having stuck in the soft earth it became necessary to postpone further progress overnight. In the small hours the workmen who had remained on guard were attacked by a band of robbers, and the precious bundle received a direct hit from a musket-ball. The mark on the stone is visible to this day as the bull stands in the British

Museum. The whole process was repeated with the winged lion, which, however, received a bad crack in the process of loading and eventually fell in half. In the end both halves were successfully loaded on to *keleks* composed of 600 skins each, and on 22 May 1847 Layard watched this new consignment of sculptures float off to Basra, and returned to the mound to fill in his trenches.

A little money still remained from the British Museum grant, so before returning to Mosul Layard determined to make another attempt at Qal'at Sharqat. He unearthed a much-damaged life-size statue in black stone, covered with an inscription of Shal-maneser II, which was already known to exist there and which was eventually safely transported to London. But apart from this he was extremely puzzled to find that his workmen encountered almost nothing at all. This was not, in fact, explained until more than half a century later, when the ruins of Ashur were most systematically excavated by the Germans, and its temples and palaces found to be constructed without the use of stone. The trenches of Layard and other early excavators were then found cutting through the crude brick walls, which they had not had sufficient knowledge to detect or skill to trace. Ashur was the earliest capital of Assyria and by the most skilful research the Germans followed the material remains of its history back to Sumerian times. From theirs and other excavations we now know that in the Babylonian palaces of the second millennium BC painted frescoes adorned the lower parts of the walls.[108] The use of sculp-tured reliefs for the same purpose did not begin until after the Assyrian capital had moved to Nimrud in about 880 BC.

Disappointed at the failure of Sharqat to produce movable anti-quities, Layard returned to Mosul and expended what little money

45 *Another Kuyunjik relief depicting Assyrians moving a bull colossus by leverage and manpower.*

remained on yet another sounding in Kuyunjik. He now had the measure of this peculiar mound to some extent, having realized that continued occupation in later years had left the Assyrian remains buried beneath some twenty or so feet of accumulated debris. He therefore began trenching deeply in the south-west corner, and this time, after some days, he met with success. In fact, when the first calcined and crumbling slabs of the now famous Palace of Sennacherib were found, Layard himself was not present, having gone for a brisk morning walk on the Mosul side of the river. His stout foreman, Toma Shishman, therefore set off over the bridge at an exhausting jog-trot to bring the good news to his master and claim the traditional reward. He had the misfortune, however, to be outdistanced by two Kurdish girls, wives of the workmen, who swam directly across the Tigris on inflated sheep-skins, and almost without pausing to readjust their clothing, breathlessly announced the discovery to Layard.

Having finally established the existence of at least one Assyrian palace in the main mound at Nineveh, Layard at once realized that this was a fitting juncture to terminate his work. On 24 June 1847 he left Mosul for Istanbul and London, taking Rassam with him.

There could be no doubt that his two years' work among the Assyrian ruins had produced results of which he could be proud. He had identified the sites of the biblical Calah (Nimrud) and of Nineveh itself, and discovered the remains of no less than eight Assyrian palaces connected, as was subsequently proved, with such illustrious names as Ashur-nasirpal, Sargon, Shalmaneser, Tiglath-pileser, Adad-nirari, Esarhaddon and Sennacherib. He had completed his own part in the transporting to England of some hundreds of tons of Assyrian sculpture. The official appreciation which awaited him at home may be recorded in his own words: 'As a reward for my various services and for my discoveries, I was appointed an unpaid attaché of Her Majesty's Embassy at Constantinople.' (This is the final sentence of his *Early Adventures*.)

LAYARD IN ENGLAND

On his journey to England Layard took the opportunity of travelling through Italy and so renewed acquaintance with many family friends and haunts of his childhood. In Paris he again encountered Botta, who treated both him and the story of his discoveries with the generous enthusiasm so characteristic of him. Layard even found himself prevailed upon to face an assembly of the French *Académie des Inscriptions*, and the excited discussion aroused by his account of the Nimrud sculptures prolonged itself into an extraordinary session on the following day. With the willing and generous co-operation of the French Government, who supplied a naval vessel for the purpose, Botta's own finds had already reached Paris in December of the previous year, and he himself was now at work on his magnificent publication, *Monument de Ninive*,[109] five sumptuous volumes, four of which consisted of steel-plate reproductions of Flandin's beautiful drawings. So appreciative were the French of the real value of his finds that in fact the sum granted for this production equalled, if not exceeded, that which originally made the excavations possible.

A few months later, on the establishment of the Second Republic, the Consulate at Mosul was suppressed, and Botta was banished to an insignificant post in the Levant. He died in 1870.

In London, meanwhile, Layard as usual found that official enthusiasm over his discoveries manifested itself in a much less tangible form. An initial proposal by the Trustees that £4,000 should be spent on a publication similar to Botta's was refused by a Treasury too preoccupied by events in Paris to give much thought to archaeology, and the privilege of producing a folio of engravings from Layard's drawings eventually fell to the lot of John Murray's enterprising publishing house. Layard himself meanwhile devoted the next eighteen months to more popular accounts of his excavations from which we have already repeatedly had occasion to quote. Nor did the transport of his actual finds from Basra to England arrange itself with the ready facility which Botta had experienced. Even the journey to India involved transhipment at Bushire, and at Bombay there was a further delay of many months during which no suitable vessel seemed available. Finally, fifty cases were loaded on to a newly built naval sailing ship which sailed for England on 12 April 1848. 'On the 23rd she was caught in a great storm, dismasted, and in considerable danger of foundering, but succeeded at last in weathering the tempest, and making Trincomalee in Ceylon, where she was ordered to refit.'[110] She reached Chatham in October.

When Layard attended at the museum to see the cases opened in the presence of the Keeper, an exasperating discovery awaited him. The larger sculptures had arrived in fairly good condition, but not so the cases containing small objects.

He found that there was within a mere jumble of fragments, so carelessly packed that they had suffered great damage. What was as bad was that the order in which he had himself placed the antiquities was disturbed, so that much information as to the origin of the pieces was lost, and even the fragments of broken objects which had been placed together were utterly dispersed. Worst of all, certain things of a portable size were no longer to be found, and appeared to have been abstracted.[111]

A protest lodged with the Bombay Government through the East India Company eventually elicited the explanation that while the cases were lying on the quay at Bombay the local British community had been overcome by curiosity to the extent of opening and examining their contents. There was even a record of a certain clergyman having given a lecture on the subject illustrated with 'squeezes' from the Black Obelisk! One favourable result of the considerable scandal which this discovery caused was that from now on the Bombay port authorities showed the most unwonted alacrity in transhipping and forwarding any further freight addressed to the British Museum.

Layard till now had little reason to be grateful for the encouragement which he had received from official quarters. With the public, however, things were different. As soon as the sculptures began to be exhibited, and *Nineveh and its Remains* to be read in English homes, there was no limit to the interest and enthusiasm which they aroused. For the mid-Victorian Englishman, vindication of his belief in the Bible and, at last, authentic details of the appearance and character of places and people mentioned in the Old Testament were a primary consideration. But, as Campbell Thompson suggests,[112] it may also be that there was something in the aggressive self-assurance of the Assyrian character and the nature of its contribution to human progress, which found a particular response in the imagination of contemporary Englishmen; that in fact 'these enormous Assyrian bulls had something in common with the ponderous conservative philosophy of the mid-Victorian period, with its unshakeable faith in the best of all possible worlds, with its definite social castes duly prescribed by the Catechism, all doubtless to be maintained *in saecula saeculorum*'. Soon their poets, from the Laureate downward, began deftly to introduce into their writings erudite references to the Assyrian finds rhymed in a jingle as irritating as Byron's reference to Claudius Rich. In schools Nimrud and Khorsabad became subjects for prize essays, and a generation later we find them filtered through into such popular productions as *Helen's Babies* (1877) and the *Pirates of Penzance* (1880).

Even in these early days the measure of popular enthusiasm over Layard and his finds did not escape the Trustees of the Museum. By 1849 they showed signs of proposing a new campaign of excavations, and even applied to the Treasury for a grant of £4,000. For Layard himself the strain of satisfying popular curiosity had been considerable, and knowing his own particular predilection, it is not difficult to understand that life in England had begun to pall. He had no fondness for soft living and did not submit with any great enjoyment to the process of social lionization. His attitude could indeed be summed up in the words of General Gordon: 'I would rather live like a Dervish with the Mehdi than dine out each evening in London.' This being so, he had already dealt most effectively with the situation by getting himself appointed to the new Turko-Persian Frontier Commission, and was already on his way back to Mesopotamia. In Istanbul he received a direct request from the Prime Minister Lord Palmerston to resume charge of the Assyrian excavations, and had no alternative to acceding to his wishes, though he had already learnt that the sum of £4,000 requested by the Trustees had been reduced to £3,000 and was to be spread over a period of two years. By October 1849, he and Rassam were back in Mosul and a new campaign of excavating had begun.

LAYARD'S SECOND EXPEDITION

Layard's second expedition to some extent differed in character from the first. The Trustees sent out a succession of young artists to assist in copying the reliefs, but all of them for one reason or another turned out to have been unsatisfactorily chosen; Cooper was poorly when he arrived, and before long broke down completely in health; Bell was drowned while bathing, contrary to everyone's advice, in the Gomel river at Bavian; Hodder was so hopelessly young and inexperienced that he could take no responsibility. The funds did not suffice for the employment of any other European assistant. So it was not that the expedition was particularly better staffed or equipped than the previous one. It was rather a change in the relative importance of finds – a shifting of emphasis from sculpture to inscriptions.

Thanks to scholars such as Rawlinson, the science of Assyriology had so greatly progressed during Layard's absence in England that simple cuneiform inscriptions could now be read with increasing facility. The two great Assyrian libraries which he and Rassam were about to discover thus assumed an importance and fascination surpassing that of the now familiar sculptured reliefs.*

Yet the new sculptures which began to appear were in themselves by no means to be despised, especially since their subjects had suddenly become easily identifiable. For the past two years Ross and Christian Rassam between them had contrived to substantiate and maintain the British Museum's claim to the south-west corner of Kuyunjik by keeping a few men continually at work there, so it was in Sennacherib's palace that Layard now renewed his excavations. A few months later he was able to record:

In this magnificent edifice I had opened no less than seventy-one halls, chambers, and passages, whose walls, almost without exception, had been panelled with slabs of sculptured alabaster recording the wars, the triumphs, and the great deeds of the Assyrian king. By a rough calculation, about 9,880 feet, or nearly two miles, of bas-reliefs, with twenty-seven portals, formed by colossal winged bulls and lion-sphinxes, were uncovered in that part alone of the building explored during my researches.[113]

Pictures in one chamber recorded the adornment of Nineveh and the building of the palace. The Kuyunjik platform is recognizable in the process of construction by a gang of war-prisoners, and it appears protected on all sides by the waters of the Tigris and the Khosr. The royal guard, with their crested helmets, shields and spears, look on while another gang drag into position the partly-carved bulk of a winged bull colossus. Beyond are the wooded slopes of the mountains of Kurdistan and, over all, an inscription:

---

* During the early days of his work at Nimrud, Layard still did not know what a tablet was, and considered those he found as 'bits of pottery decorated in an unusual manner' (cf. Budge 1925, p. 83). It is extremely probable that much valuable inscribed material was lost in this way.

Sennacherib, King of the Universe, King of Assyria; white limestone, which at the command of the God was discovered in the land of Baladai, for the work on my palace, the people of hostile towns and the men of hidden mountains, conquered by my hands, quarried with picks and mattocks of iron, and I made it into colossal bulls for my palace-gates.[114]

Then there is the famous 'siege of Lachish' where one sees the whole violent panorama of an attack on a walled city. Protected by covering-fire, the Assyrian sappers bring a penthouse against the wall and the assault is made up a prepared slope, while showers of stones, arrows and flaming torches fall from above. Over the figure of the king an inscription reads: 'Sennacherib, King of the Universe, King of Assyria, sat upon a throne; the spoil of Lachish passed before him.'[115] In recording this inscription, Layard adds with pardonable pride: 'Little doubt, I trust, can now exist in the minds of my readers as to the identification of the builder of the palace of Kuyunjik, with the Sennacherib of scripture.'

All through these excavations odd fragments of cuneiform tablets had been coming to light, but these had not sufficed to prepare Layard for the astonishing haul which awaited him in the King's Library. It consisted of two large chambers, of which the whole area was piled a foot or more deep in tablets. The contemporary method of excavating, which consisted of tunnelling along the base of the walls, would not suggest that their removal was accomplished with any high degree of scientific care. However, when they reached the British Museum a number of them were still intact and others could be pieced together from scattered fragments (one tablet, for instance, numbered K. 2570, is composed of eleven fragments derived from the finds of six different expeditions). Furthermore, the sequence of tablets, formidable in itself, was completed three years later by Hormuzd Rassam's discovery in the palace of Sennacherib's grandson, Ashur-banipal, of what appears to have been the remaining part of the state archives.

The total of documents represented by the two successive discoveries was by that time literally immense.

The total number of pieces which have been given a separate registration is round about 26,000, and of them something less than 2,000 are 'joins'. This leaves us with approximately 24,000 whole and fragmentary tablets, of which doubtless there are still many joins to be made.[116]

The tablets are divided according to their content into five groups: (1) historical literature; (2) the King's private library; (3) the library of the Temple; (4) correspondence; and (5) certain contracts. Historical texts were often inscribed on large baked-clay prisms or cylinders, and these again seem to have presented some difficulty in removal, since the phrase 'unfortunately crumbling to pieces when exposed to the air' reappears in Rassam's account. Their content was doubly important since they sometimes contained copyings verbatim by Assyrian scribes of ancient documents connected with Sumerian history.

46 *Excavation at Kuyunjik by tunnelling, with light shafts from above. Sketched on the spot by S. C. Malan.*

But by far the greater bulk of tablets belong to the Royal Library, in which a great variety of subjects are represented.

Myths are represented by the Seven Tablets of the creation, wherein is described the beginning of all things and the creation of Man: the twelve tablets of Gilgamesh, who seeks that problem which has exercised the mind of man from time immemorial, what will happen after death, and how to obtain eternal life: the legend of Etana, who was carried up like Ganymede, on an eagle's back: Adapa, who having broken the wings of the south wind, was hauled before Anu in heaven to answer for his crime: Zu, the bird who carried off the Tablets of Fate; and many others. . . . Science held high place: medicine proper (distinct from magic) is accorded due position on some five hundred tablets, which give good, honest, practical prescriptions for every ill under the sun, from ear-ache and ophthalmia to childbirth and the restoration of the apparently drowned, showing a knowledge of some five hundred drugs: botany had recorded some hundreds of names of plants, with a vast display of knowledge of their properties: the chemist had already discovered the practical use of a large number of minerals from red lead to magnetic iron ore, and he has left an invaluable treatise on the components of glass and the glazes for pottery. The charlatan of the observation of the future by omens is equally represented: but as it gives us an insight into the tremendous knowledge of the heavens, the sun, moon and stars, it deserves in part to be promoted to the category of science. Philology too has its abundance of dictionaries.

In fact:

We are still only halfway over the threshold in our knowledge of what this library once contained.[117]

During these years (1849–51) of his second expedition, Layard's activities were by no means limited to Nineveh itself. Simultaneously with Kuyunjik, his excavations at Nimrud were renewed on a fairly large scale and with considerable success. He also found time to make soundings in many of the larger mounds of the Mosul district. Amongst those which to him seemed more or less disappointing were 'Bahshiqah', the mound now known as Tell Billah, where American archaeologists have since excavated a mid-second millennium city of great interest;[118] Tell Abu Maria, where there now appears to have been a hunting-lodge of the Assyrian King Ashur-reshishi; Sherif Khan, the ancient Tarbisu, a few miles north of Kuyunjik, where he even discovered two Assyrian temples and inscribed limestone slabs from a palace which Esarhaddon had built for his son, Ashur-banipal; and other mounds, such as Karamles, Lak and Shemamyk, concerning which nothing further is known. In a renewed attempt on Qal'at Sharqat he found terracotta prisms of Tiglath-pileser I, while having carried his explorations as far afield as the banks of the Khabur river, today beyond the frontier of Iraq, a tunnel driven into the mound called Arban encountered the most interesting archaic sculptures, including winged bulls carved and inscribed in the Assyrian manner and what appears in his sketch to be a really magnificent lion.[119] These were, presumably, simply left exposed and have, as far as one knows, never been further investigated.[120]

For Layard, perhaps understandably, the criterion of interest in a mound corresponded to its content of portable antiquities. So it is not surprising that an attempt which he made in the autumn of 1850 to investigate some of the principal mounds of Babylonia proved one of the major disappointments of his career. From the beginning the prospect was a dismal one. Deprived of the support of Rassam, who was seriously ill, and suffering himself from malaria, he found little encouragement in Baghdad, whence he had intended to start his operations. Rawlinson he had seen off to England some months before, after a characteristic episode when, descending into one of his own trenches at Nimrud, he found the great man lying wrapped in his travelling cloak and fast asleep, having covered the first stage of his journey to London on his own horse at a speed reminiscent of his earlier feats when a subaltern in India. Furthermore, a characteristic tribal disturbance made travelling south of Baghdad for the time being impossible. He had temporarily to content himself with making ineffectual holes in one of a group of small mounds, some four miles beyond the city walls, which have in more recent times yielded buildings and tablets of first-rate importance (Tell Abu Harmal, called by Layard Tell Mohammed, excavated by the Iraq Government in 1945 (see Baqir 1946)). Later he contrived to reach Babylon, where he excavated for four weeks without any satisfactory results, and Nippur,[121] where he was no more successful. For, in truth, the patience and skill necessary to trace the remains of mud-brick

47 The mound of Arban, on the Khabur river, investigated by Layard c.1850.

buildings were beyond the capacity of his temperament and the limitations of his funds, as one may judge from a remark which he subsequently made to Fresnel:

There will be nothing to be hoped for from the site of Babylon except with a parliamentary vote for £25,000, and if ever this sum should be voted, I would solicit the favour of not being charged with its application.[122]

In April 1851 Layard once more turned his face homewards, rich in new honours, but, as he himself said, 'with a heavy heart'. By that time more than 120 cases of his Assyrian finds had been sent to Baghdad for examination by Rawlinson before being shipped to England. Two years later he was able at last to submit the total results of his researches to the public in the form of definitive publications, and was belatedly accorded the official recognition which his work had so well merited.[123]

CHAPTER TEN

The scramble for antiquities

The beginning of the second half of the last century marks an interesting stage in the progress of Mesopotamian exploration. Rawlinson returned in 1851 to a second period of residency in Baghdad as Political Agent, more than ever preoccupied with archaeology, having by that time published his famous memoir, *On the Babylonian Translation of the Great Persian Inscription at Behistun*, which unequivocally established the fact that the Assyrian-Babylonian language written in the cuneiform script was now capable of translation. Politically he now occupied a unique position in Baghdad. British prestige and the respect in which the Resident was held had scarcely decreased since the time of Rich, and Rawlinson's formidable personality had soon earned him a reputation throughout the Pashalik, which after his departure became legendary. When Wallis Budge visited Baghdad in 1888, out of curiosity he made some enquiries on the subject from an elderly official. After confirming the story of Rawlinson having knocked together the heads of two recalcitrant members of the *majlis* (council), he concluded:

The Balios Beg [a term of unknown derivation used when referring to consuls] lived here for twelve years, and each year his power in the country became stronger. And towards the end of his time here had he taken one dog and put his English hat on his head and sent him to the Sarai, all the people in the bazaar would have made way for him, and bowed to him, and the soldiers would have stood still and presented arms to him as he passed, and the officials in the Sarai would have embraced him; and if he had sent another dog with another of his hats across the river to Kâzimên, the Shi'ites and the Sunnites would have stopped fighting each other and would have asked him to drink coffee with them.[124]

Layard, meanwhile, had disappeared permanently from the field and his excavations for the present were closed. The French had in 1851 appointed as successor to Botta, the skilful architect and antiquarian Victor Place, and had furnished him with funds for the resumption of excavations at Khorsabad. Other funds had been provided for 'a scientific and artistic expedition to Mesopotamia

48 William Kennett Loftus, the first excavator of Warka (Uruk) and Larsa.

and Media'. This enterprising but ill-fated attempt to wrest from the mounds of Babylonia treasures such as had already been found in Assyria owed its conception partly to the new interest aroused in Babylonia by Loftus' attempt on the vast ruin-field at Warka.

WILLIAM KENNETT LOFTUS

William Kennett Loftus[125] was geological member of the same Turko-Persian frontier commission to which Layard also had been originally appointed. Finding much time on his hands, and actuated by a 'strong desire to explore a region which from our childhood we have been led to regard as the cradle of the human race', he had already visited the better-known Babylonian ruins, when in the last days of 1849 the Commission was at last ordered to proceed to Mohammerah, the scene of the original international dispute. While the rest of the party sailed from Baghdad in the armed river-boat *Nitocris*, commanded by Captain Felix Jones (the same who in 1846 had made an unsuccessful attempt to fetch Layard's sculptures from Nimrud), Loftus and his friend, H. A. Churchill, took the bold step of travelling on horseback diagonally across the desert and marshes of Chaldea from the Euphrates to the lower Tigris. Everywhere they were astonished to find traces of advanced ancient civilization and extensive cultivation existing incongruously amidst the barren heritage of the unruly southern tribes, and were able to take note of now-famous ruins such as Al Muqayyar (Ur), Niffar (Nippur), Warka (Uruk or Erech) and others which have still not been further investigated, such as Hammam and Tell Jid. On re-joining his colleagues, the whole of his discoveries made such an

49 The earliest known picture of the ziggurat at Ur, as seen by William Kennett Loftus in 1849, while exploring the mounds of southern Mesopotamia.

impressive story that the head of the Mission, Colonel Williams, eventually agreed to his returning to make small-scale excavations at Warka, presumably with funds from the budget of the Commission. Layard once in a fit of irritation had drawn an unfavourable comparison between the latter and the funds provided by the Treasury for his own expedition, considering the potential results of the two undertakings. The new situation must have intrigued him.

Under great difficulties and with inadequate assistance, Loftus accordingly undertook three weeks' excavations at Warka, and two years later, when in the employment of the newly-created Assyrian Excavation Fund, continued the same work for another three months, accompanied by his friends Boutcher, the artist, and Kerr Lynch. At the end of that time he had come to realize something of the colossal task which would face anyone attempting systematic excavations there. Warka, the site of biblical Erech, home of the mythical Sumerian hero Gilgamesh, was a city occupied continuously for nearly four thousand years, and its ruins, which are nearly six miles in circumference, compare in importance with those of Babylon. There are, for example, at least three ziggurats and a gigantic Parthian temple. Hilprecht, at the beginning of this century, estimated that its adequate excavation would require fifty years' digging and a fund of 500,000 dollars.[126] The continuing work of the German expedition which started in 1924 has shown this to be true.

What, then, was the result of these first rather superficial diggings, actuated, as Loftus admitted himself, by 'a nervous desire to find important large museum pieces at the least possible outlay of time and money'? He at least discovered the Parthian cemetery, which until quite recently has proved an almost inexhaustible source of glazed 'slipper' coffins. 'After many fruitless trials and the demolition of perhaps a hundred specimens', he found a way of strengthening them with paper and paste, so that a few examples could be removed intact to the river for dispatch to Europe. He partly excavated (though he could neither understand nor date it to within a thousand years) the great Parthian temple. Even more incomprehensible and of an antiquity quite unimaginable at that time was a section of walling, ornamented with the coloured mosaic-work of terracotta cones, now a familiar architectural feature associated with the Proto-Sumerian builders of the fourth millennium, for whose technical designation the name of this site (Uruk) is still used. There was little else; a few cuneiform tablets, some of them in 'envelopes', a figurine or two and some decayed copper objects. In the end the party was not sorry to turn its attention to other neighbouring sites – Sinkara, Medina and Tell Sifr.

Loftus moved his camp to Sinkara, which lies on the banks of the ancient canal, Shatt al Kar, within sight of Warka, and spent a few days in cutting some trenches in the highest part of the mound. His work was at first a good deal interfered with by the nightly attention of a family of lions, who had previously been the only occupants of the ruins. The lioness seemed particularly to resent the barking of the dogs which gave warning of her approach to the camp at night, and accordingly proceeded to remove them. Loftus says:

Gradually their number decreased, until our greatest favourite, Toga, alone remained. One pitch-dark night Toga was more energetic than usual in warning us of our enemies' position; at last, apparently tired of his exertions, he returned sullenly into camp, and lay down close to my tent-ropes, growling audibly. Soon afterwards a sudden rush, followed by two or three hounds, making the very ground tremble like the galloping of horsemen, informed the whole encampment that the dog-devourer was among us. Poor Toga was heard to give one stifled yelp, and all was over with our last guardian; he was carried off and demolished at a meal. . . .

The camp never recovered its composure again that night, and the following day's work was but a sorry one.[127]

Yet, in spite of these and other interruptions of Loftus' work, the results of his investigations enabled Rawlinson, to whom he sent any inscribed material which he discovered, to identify Sinkara as the site of the ancient city of Larsa, the 'Ellasar' of the Bible (Genesis xiv: i). He was even able to infer that the terraces of kiln-baked brick which his trenches encountered formed part of a temple and ziggurat dedicated to the sun-god, Shamash. Rapid and haphazard as his excavations had been, the inscriptions which he found were of considerable importance. There were duplicate foundation cylinders of Nebuchadnezzar II, many inscribed bricks bearing the name of a king of Ur, and one giving for the first time the name of a Kassite king ruling over Babylonia in the mid-second millennium B C. In addition there were many tablets, terracotta plaques and other objects from a group of interesting vaulted tombs. These finds represented a considerable advance on any previous attempt to excavate a Babylonian site.

Of the other two mounds which Loftus 'tried', Medina proved unproductive, but at Tell Sifr he experienced one of those remarkable pieces of luck which occasionally cheer the heart of the least sanguine excavator. Riding over from Sinkara with a handful of workmen, he dug straight into the remains of what appeared to be a coppersmith's store, and, after a few days' work, had accumulated 'a large collection of cauldrons, vases, dishes, hammers, hatchets, knives, daggers, fetters, mirrors and other instruments and utensils', in addition to nearly one hundred tablets which dated these objects to Babylonian times. Tell Sifr has since that time received no attention from legitimate excavators, though, like Sinkara itself, it has suffered at times from illicit digging.[128] Loftus himself was compelled to terminate his excavations by the overflowing of the Kar and the consequent rapid rise in the level of the marshes, which threatened to cut off his retreat. He consequently loaded himself and his finds on to two 'country-boats' and sailed down the Euphrates to Basra.

Meanwhile the three Frenchmen, Fresnel, Oppert and the artist, Felix Thomas, who had been sent out by their government in 1851 to excavate in Babylonia, had met with even less success than Loftus. Baffled by the seemingly featureless mountains of broken bricks and other debris which they found at Kish and Babylon, they were forced, after two years' work, to return almost empty-handed to Paris, leaving a few cases of the now familiar inscribed bricks and terracotta figurines, to follow by raft and ship. Even these, as will be seen later, never reached France, for in 1855 they were involved in an accident which sent them to the bottom of the Tigris in company with the greater part of the new consignment of sculpture which Place had been laboriously extracting from his extended excavations at Khorsabad.

In Sargon's palace, two years had sufficed for Place to accomplish the task which he had set himself. The complete plan of the surviving buildings at the summit of the mound had been recovered or conjecturally restored, and may be seen today, enhanced by fine draughtsmanship, in his publication.[129] His method of excavating, like that of his predecessors, consisted of tunnelling along the face of the walls and obtaining light by occasional vertical shafts from the surface. Accurate surveying in the underground warren thus created must have been virtually impossible; so one must forgive him if, as more recent work on the palace has shown,[130] the actual remains of the building do not correspond in every detail to his plan. It is equally understandable that to save himself time he should have occasionally assumed in the Assyrian architect a most un-oriental passion for symmetry. The only major fault which is observable in his records is that buildings investigated in other parts of the city have plainly been located on his site-plan quite arbitrarily, and from memory, after returning to Paris.

It will be remembered that, almost simultaneously with Place's arrival at Khorsabad in 1851, Rawlinson had returned to his post as Resident in Baghdad. Layard had by that time decided definitely against taking any further part in Mesopotamian excavations,

partly owing to the recurrent fever to which he had become subject, and partly on account of his new orientation towards politics.[131]
Rawlinson had accordingly agreed to take charge of British
archaeological interests in Baghdad and Mosul, and had at the same
time been provided by the Trustees of the British Museum with a
considerable sum of money for the resumption of excavations. It
was clear that his official duties would prevent him from taking
personal charge of any work of this kind and his first intention was
to detach Loftus from his work in the south and send him to Mosul.
This, however, proved unnecessary, since in 1852 the British
Museum sent out their usual rather sickly young artist (the third in
succession), shortly followed by Hormuzd Rassam. So again the
narrative of discovery 'is resumed in the English language, but this
time by a native of Mosul'.[132]

HORMUZD RASSAM

Rassam has hitherto appeared in this story as Layard's indefatigable
helper and reliable adjutant. With the great pioneer's own work
and writing setting so high a precedent, that of his pupil and
successor perhaps inevitably suffers by comparison. It is in any case
certain that once he began operating independently, save for the
remote control of Rawlinson in Baghdad, there was something in
Rassam's conduct as an explorer which induces a peculiar distaste,
and the written account of his adventures falls correspondingly flat.
Without laying oneself open to a charge of prejudice, one may
perhaps be allowed to suggest that the picture of an Englishman
such as Layard frustrating by patience and good humour the importunities of oriental malice and bigotry appeals to one more than
that of Victor Place who, by all accounts, was an equally conscientious and otherwise sympathetic character, being outwitted
by a born Moslawi in what can only be described as an undignified
scramble for archaeological loot. In fact Rassam's accomplishments
were considerable. He did, as we shall see, acquire for the British
Museum an Assyrian Royal Library and perhaps the finest of all
Assyrian relief sequences – the Lion-hunt from the palace of
Ashur-banipal which would otherwise have fallen to the French.
With Mosul as a base, he did, either personally or by proxy,
'examine' mounds 'within an area of nearly two hundred miles';
he did acquire for London the famous bronze gates of Balawat;
and he did discover what seemed to be inexhaustible mines of
Babylonian tablets at southern sites such as Sippar. Yet at times his
gangs of workmen were scattered over the countryside in such a
way that any kind of adequate supervision was out of the question;
the clay documents of the library were grubbed up in fragments
from his dark and awkward tunnels at Kuyunjik; no proper plans
were made or records kept of the circumstances of his discoveries
and, in the case of the bronze gates, a doubt at one time arose as to
whether they really came from Balawat at all.[133]

Returning to Mosul in 1852 as representative of the British Museum, Rassam found the Turkish Government itself taking a hand in the now popular process of 'mining' in the ruins of Nineveh. The head of a winged bull had come to light in the *sirdab* of a house in the village of Nebi Yunus, some property had been bought which made space available for small-scale excavations, and gangs of convicts from the local gaol had been detailed for the actual work. Digging was continued for some months, but produced little beyond the original bull-colossus, which could not be removed, and an inscribed marble tablet, later known as the 'Nebi Yunus inscription' of Sennacherib. It can be well imagined that holes dug beneath the floors of already rickety houses by workmen 'inexperienced and hampered by heavy chains' were unlikely to fulfil the Turks' very considerable expectations, and the accumulating expense of compensating the residents eventually made it impossible to continue.

Rassam and Hodder meanwhile, having been refused access even to the village of Nebi Yunus while the work was in progress, had turned their attention once more to Kuyunjik; and here from the beginning an embarrassing situation arose in connection with the rival claims of the French to an important section of the mound. The British Museum's *firman* entitled its agents to excavate without hindrance in all lands which were Crown property, but it chanced that the summit of Kuyunjik was privately owned, and from the first some question had arisen as to the necessity of compensating the landlord. By a curious coincidence, when Layard was in Istanbul in 1849, he had chanced to encounter this gentleman in person at a moment when he was in very serious financial straits, and had seized the opportunity of helping him out of his difficulties, in return for a loose concession in connection with his property at Nineveh. Bearing in mind the vague prerogative thus acquired by the British Museum, Place, on arrival in Mosul in 1851, had sought Rawlinson's permission to make further soundings in Kuyunjik, and as a result had been generously assigned a large area at the northern end of the mound, which had thus become rigidly divided into national concessions. When, therefore, Rassam reopened excavations in the southern or British area, he found gangs of men employed by the French Consulate already at work to the north. For a time, at Kuyunjik, the line of demarcation carefully worked out by Rawlinson prevented any open dispute. But when efforts were made by both sides simultaneously to restart work on other mounds, where national prerogatives were even more debatable, there was bound to be trouble. Place's agents, working their way surreptitiously towards Nimrud, found Rassam's men already installed; but at Qal'at Sharqat two representative parties converged simultaneously on the mound and an embarrassing scuffle ensued.

So the last months of 1852 and the whole of 1853 passed with Rassam working sporadically at Kuyunjik, Nimrud and Sharqat, and pecking restlessly at new and less reliable mounds. Six statues of the god Nebo, fragmentary stelas of Shamsi-adad IV and Ashurnasirpal II from a new temple at Nimrud, and a beautiful white obelisk covered with reliefs and inscriptions from the southern part of Kuyunjik, combined with important inscribed material from Sharqat, would have satisfied most excavators today, but compared with the immense accumulation of Layard's finds they did not seem to Rassam anything like an adequate return for the financial outlay. Meanwhile, in the French concession at Nineveh, he had the discomfort of watching Place's workmen rapidly approaching what he considered the most promising spot of the whole mound. In the end, at the risk of 'getting into hot water with Mr Place', he decided on an experimental examination of it himself at night with the help of a few trustworthy workmen. The result must be told in his own words:

It was on the night of the 20th of December, 1853, that I commenced to examine the ground in which I was fortunate enough to discover, after three nights' trial, the grand palace of Assur-bani-pal, commonly known by the name of Sardanapalus. When everything was ready I went and marked three places, some distance from each other, in which our operations were to be commenced. Only a few trenches had been opened there in the time of Sir Henry Layard; but on this occasion I ordered the men to dig transversely and cut deeper down. I told them they were to stop work at dawn, and return to the same diggings again the next night. The very first night we worked there, one of the gangs came upon indications of an ancient building; but though we found among the rubbish painted bricks and pieces of marble on which there were signs of inscriptions and bas-reliefs, I did not feel sanguine as to the result.[134]

On the second night, having concentrated the whole of his workmen on this one spot, to his great delight the bottom of a slab was found in position, on which were recognizable the feet of Assyrian soldiers and captives. Rassam at once sent off a dispatch to the British Museum claiming to have found a new palace, and was consequently much perturbed to discover later that his slab was not part of a continuous wall but isolated in a mass of debris. As he says:

This put a damper on my spirits as I had on that day reported both to the British Museum authorities and to Sir Henry Rawlinson the discovery of what I considered to be a new palace, as I was then fully convinced of its being so. I knew, also, that if I failed to realize my expectations, I should only be found fault with and laughed at for my unrewarded zeal. However, I felt that as I had commenced, so I must go on, even if only to be disappointed. The next night I superintended the work in person, and increased the number of men, placing them in separate gangs around the area, which seemed the most likely place for good results. The remnant of the sculptured wall discovered was on a low level, running upwards, and this fact alone was enough to convince an experienced eye that the part of the building I had hit upon was an ascending passage leading to the main building: . . . my instinct did not deceive me; for one division of the workmen, after three or four hours' hard labour, were rewarded by the first grand discovery of a beautiful bas-relief in a perfect state of preservation, representing the king, who was afterwards identified as Assur-bani-pal, standing in a chariot, about to start on a hunting expedition, and his attendants handing him the necessary weapons for the chase. More than half of the upper part of the sculpture came into sight in an instant, as it happened that while the men were busily engaged in digging a deep trench inside what was afterwards found to be a long, narrow saloon, a large part of the bank which was attached to the sculpture fell, and exposed to view that enchanting spectacle.

The discovery could now, of course, no longer be concealed, and soon, as may be imagined, brought Place riding over in great haste from Khorsabad. His reaction to the obvious infringement of a 'gentleman's agreement' was on this occasion really beyond praise, and even Rassam has to record with some surprise that Place seemed inclined to acquiesce in the *fait accompli*, 'and before we parted he congratulated me on my good fortune'. But he adds in a footnote:

The loss of this prize had such a bad effect on M. Place's mind that in the work he published in 1866–9 of his researches, entitled *Ninive et L'Assyrie*, he quite ignored the fact of my discoveries, but made it appear that Mr Loftus, and even his artist, Mr Boutcher, were the successful explorers.

It was now necessary to clear the great 'lion-hunt' gallery and follow the wall-faces through its doorways into the adjoining room of the palace, so examining its plan and contents. If ever there was an archaeological occasion which called for leisurely and methodical work, this was it. The chambers proved to have had the function of a library as well as a picture gallery, so that a wide area of floor in the centre was stacked high with a great mass of priceless tablets, among which, as it proved, was the Assyrian account of the Deluge and 'Noah's Ark'. Built into a section of wall which Rassam unintentionally demolished was a tall terracotta prism covered with inscriptions. This, of course, 'crumbled to pieces when exposed to the air', but, as though Ashur-banipal had foreseen the necessity for making his own immortalization as nearly as possible foolproof, a second duplicate prism was installed nearby and this was miraculously rescued intact. It contained the annals of the King's reign. From all points of view the building proved a precious storehouse of historical documents and works of art, and would have justified any expenditure of time and money. Yet Rassam was short of both. Owing to Place's admirable restraint, the palace could be explored without the embarrassment of conflicting claims to its contents. But, as C. J. Gadd admits in a most impartial discussion of the episode,[135] in all other respects the discovery was positively 'inopportune'. He says:

In general, its [the palace's] excavation was conducted in a hurried and unobservant manner, without any such record as Layard had kept; little but sculptures and tablets was preserved, and there was no adequate planning. These were the faults of inexperience, universal at the time; and it must be added that the absence of any European supervisor from the work was a very serious handicap. But they were not the only disadvantages. This immense discovery was made but a month or two before the

50 The tablet recording the Assyrian account of the Deluge which was recovered by Rassam from Ashurbanipal's palace at Kuyunjik.

expedition, for want of funds, must come to an end. Rawlinson was detained by pressing official business in Baghdad, and could pay only a flying visit to Mosul to view the new wonders. Deeply impressed by what he saw, he could only select a number of slabs to be packed for the British Museum, lament that the treasure had not appeared a year earlier, and try to formulate plans for getting Loftus and Boutcher to abandon the south, and carry on at Kuyunjik when the time came, in March, for Rassam to leave. Yet another misfortune was that Hodder, whose services would never have been so precious, was now completely incapacitated by an intestinal malady, and could do no more drawing. . . .

In April 1853 Rassam packed up and returned to London. Some months later he accepted a political appointment in Aden and temporarily abandoned antiquity-hunting.

Rawlinson now succeeded in his plan to detach Loftus from his not over-productive work in Babylonia. The Assyrian Excavation Fund, by which his excavations were financed, was an organization recently instituted by a group of private individuals, interested as connoisseurs or in other capacities in the acquisition of Mesopotamian antiquities, and its representatives from the first seemed doomed to find themselves in an undesirably competitive relationship with those of the British Museum. Furthermore, its commercial appearance could not but be misunderstood when it was known, for instance, that Boutcher was directly employed by a firm of Bond Street art dealers. It is hardly surprising, therefore, that when Loftus first arrived at Kuyunjik after Rassam's departure, friction was inevitable between rival gangs of workmen employed by two separate institutions. Soon, however, the position was regularized by the transfer of the Fund's remaining resources and the direction of its representatives to Rawlinson, so that Loftus and Boutcher were able to continue Rassam's work at least for a few short months until recalled by the British Museum.

From the whole of the above account it will be possible to gather that the beautiful and famous palace of Ashur-banipal at Nineveh never was and, in spite of some subsequent work on its site, never has been properly and completely excavated. In addition to this, many of its sculptures were lost completely, leaving neither trace nor record in the transport mishap of 1855. The loss occasioned by this disaster,[136] which took place near the head of the Shatt al 'Arab at Qurnah, was literally immense. The country-boats and rafts, which were waylaid by Arab brigands and maliciously capsized owing to the disappointing character of their freight,[137] were carrying not only the entire results of the French Babylonian expedition and 120 cases of Khorsabad material, but 80 cases destined for the Prussian Government, and 68 further cases of sculpture from Ashur-banipal's palace, which Rawlinson had allowed Place to select for the Louvre. In the case of the Khorsabad material, the reliefs had fortunately already been meticulously drawn and recorded by Felix Thomas (who had providentially offered his services to Place when the work at Babylon proved unproductive) and could subsequently be published in a new folio as lavish as that already produced by Botta.[138] Boutcher's drawings of the lost Kuyunjik slabs, however, were themselves lost in England before being adequately published,[139] a fitting end to the whole unedifying scramble.

The loss of 300-odd cases of antiquities at Qurnah was only one of several mishaps to the Assyrian sculptures on their journey down the Tigris. On another occasion two of Rassam's rafts reached a point on the lower Tigris where the spring floods had broken through the enclosing dyke and the water was pouring through into a great desert lake; one of the rafts was swept through the gap and eventually ran aground nearly a mile from the river-bank. The situation was only saved by the courage and ingenuity of Captain Felix Jones who, arriving at the scene in the *Nitocris*, took his craft boldly through the gap in pursuit and succeeded with much difficulty in rescuing the sculptures.

CAPTAIN FELIX JONES

Captain Jones himself at this point merits a considerable digression, particularly in view of the great topographical contributions which he made to Mesopotamian archaeology during the years which we have just been chronicling. In 1846 he had set out to chart the course of the Tigris from Baghdad northwards, and though on reaching Tekrit the power of his engines proved unequal to any further navigation, he had by then already acquired the most valuable information.

His next enterprise, undertaken two years later, carried him farther afield into a region hardly less remote today than it was in those days. His own careful account of it, which was subsequently buried, like all his other reports, in the Records of the Bombay Government,[140] was entitled 'Narrative of a Journey undertaken in April 1848, by Commander J. F. Jones, Indian Navy, for the purpose of determining the tract of the Ancient Nahr Awân Canal; accompanied by Preliminary Remarks on the Canal, with a glance at the past History of the Territory of the Nahr Awân.'

One of the most famous of Iraq's ancient waterways, Nahr Awan (see Chapter Fourteen) has always had a special appeal to the imagination as a 'lost river'. Bringing under cultivation, as it did up to the fourteenth century A D, a vast area of land to the east of the Tigris, it left the parent Tigris a little below Tekrit and, flowing far out into the eastern alluvium, rejoined it nearly 200 miles further south near Kut al 'Imara. Today it is a dry bed, partly filled with drifting sand and its farms and ploughlands are *chol*-desert visited only in the spring by the Bedouins with their flocks. Its upper reach from Daur to Baqubah is known as the Qatl al Kisru or 'Chosroes Cut', being attributed like so many other remnants of ancient engineering feats to the great Persian conqueror. When in the ninth century the 'Abbasid caliphs built Samarra, and the land between Chosroes Cut and the Tigris came to be covered with palaces and gardens, Al Mutawakkil attempted to reopen its channel; but after spending several hundred thousand *dirhams* his engineers had to abandon the attempt. Up to Baqubah the Nahr Awan was in the true sense a canal, constructed scientifically with its controlling weirs and affluents, but at this point it received the waters of the Diyala river and the whole flowed out eastwards into the plain to find its own course to Kut. As a result the southernmost part has no spoilbanks, and has the appearance merely of a huge dry river-bed. But it can easily be traced and takes much the same line as the railway constructed in 1942 by British engineers as a link in the eastern transport route for American aid to Russia. Where in the old days one would have sailed down the Nahr Awan in a ship, as did the medieval Arab geographers,[141] observing the prosperous cities and gardens on its banks, today one may drive along its bed in a car and endeavour to follow Felix Jones' identification of some of the forlorn ruinfields which mark its course.

Next after Baqubah comes the bridge-town, Jisr Nahr Awan, where the Baghdad–Khorasan road spanned its waters. Somewhere about here a smaller canal branched off along the present line of the lower Diyala, to water the orchards and vegetable gardens east of Baghdad and rejoin the Tigris below the city. The next bridge was called Burar, after the wife of the Caliph Al Ma'mun. Below this was the city of Abarta with its famous Persian markets, and here the ruins of a great brick tower still form an eerie landmark in the otherwise empty desert. Sixty miles onward, as far as Madharayah, near Kut, where the Nahr Awan finally rejoined the Tigris, one can identify city after city, and observe scanty remains of a once-prosperous agricultural province. If we are to believe Ya'qut, a traveller in Iraq at the time, it was the Seljuk Sultans of the twelfth and thirteenth centuries whose neglect of the canal wasted the district. He records their omission to dredge and repair the dykes, and adds: 'Further their armies had made a roadway of this same canal whereby both district and canal have now gone to ruin.' Felix Jones plotted the whole course of the Nahr Awan most carefully, and has left a curious hand-coloured map[142] which is still frequently consulted by irrigation engineers.

In 1852, the Captain reappears actually in the employ of the British Museum. We are told that, 'yielding to a general desire of seeing a complete picture of Assyria in her present desolation', the British Museum officially commissioned him to undertake a survey of the country between the Tigris and the Greater Zab, already partially mapped by Rich earlier in the century. He was assisted on this occasion by a Dr Hyslop, who had become doctor to the Baghdad Residency on the death of Dr Ross, and who was perhaps more interested in flora than antiquities. The result was a most admirable map (published as a supplement to the work of the Chesney Expedition)[143] which remains today the principal authority for the geography of Assyria. In presenting it, Jones paid the following remarkable tribute to Rich:

His survey of [Nineveh and Nimrud] will be found as correct as the most diligent enthusiast can desire; indeed, were it not for the renewed enquiry into Assyrian subjects, the present survey we have the honour of submitting to the public might have been dispensed with, for its value chiefly consists in corroborating the fidelity of his positions, and otherwise, though quite unnecessary, stamping his narrative with the broad seal of truth.

Other enterprises which are meticulously recorded in the captain's *Memoir* included 'Researches in the Vicinity of the Medean Wall of Xenophon, and along the Old Course of the River Tigris; and Discovery of the site of the Ancient Opis', also illustrated by a map and a number of almost incomprehensible engravings crudely ornamented in water-colours; 'A Journey to the Frontier of Turkey and Persia through a part of Kurdistan; undertaken in company with Major (now Lieutenant-Colonel) Henry Creswicke Rawlinson, K.C.B., late Political Agent in Turkish Arabia', and a 'Plan of the enceinte of Baghdad' with a commentary on the province. The latter is ornamented with more crude engravings, including views of the contemporary British Residency, which appears to have been located on the left bank at a point a little south of the present Ahrar Bridge.

After presenting the Honourable East India Company with the last of these notes for their records, Felix Jones was offered and accepted the post of British Agent in Bushire, where certain of his relatives have survived to this day.

In 1855 the Crimean War temporarily put a stop to all Middle Eastern exploration. By this time the British Museum was confessing to inadequate exhibition-space and an 'Assyrian Room' was arranged in the newly-named Crystal Palace on Sydenham Hill. At Nineveh and Nimrud, distributions of sculptures had been made by Rawlinson, before finally leaving the country, to other museums in Europe and also for the first time to America. When Bouvet, who had succeeded Place as French consul at Mosul, asked for money to continue excavations, 'Non, répondit le Ministre, les fouilles sont finies, on a trop dépensé'.

For almost a score of years no authorized excavations took place; yet at Nimrud the sound of pick and shovel were still not infrequently heard. All pretence of historical research had now been abandoned, and the place of the archaeologists had been taken by commercial speculators. In this way during the 1860s at least two consignments of sculpture were dispatched to Europe by Baghdad merchants.

CHAPTER ELEVEN

Smith and Rassam

In 1872 Western interest in Mesopotamia seemed suddenly to revive, and subsidized excavations began once more to be considered. George Smith, the British Museum copyist, was first in the field, on the trail of a missing fragment of the now famous 'Deluge Tablet'. Then came an ageing but still indefatigable Hormuzd Rassam. The French consul, de Sarzec, working for the Louvre in 1877, made the first of his astonishing discoveries at Telloh, and soon afterwards the first American expedition started work at Nippur.

Yet during this last quarter of the nineteenth century there were signs of at least two new developments in the character of archaeological research. In the first place both French and Americans elected to apply themselves to the prolonged excavation of a single site. The funds with which they were provided were in both cases adequate and their work, after a disastrous false start in the case of Nippur, was comparatively leisured and deliberate; so at least it seemed probable that the hectic scramble of the earlier days would not be repeated. Admittedly Rassam, as 'Supervisor of Excavations' for the British Museum, continued to flit about the country depositing gangs of workmen to dig tunnels in widely separated mounds, and either removing them when they failed at once to find large and obvious antiquities, or leaving them unsupervised for periods of up to a year. But this policy was at last beginning to be frowned upon, even by the Turks. The second new development was a reorientation of interest towards Babylonia, now considered to have been the cradle of the culture which had blossomed with such magnificence and ostentation in Assyria.

While the first systematic excavations of Babylonian cities were in progress and the last of the Assyrian inscriptions were being deciphered and published by the museums of Europe, historians gradually became aware of a more remote and shadowy race, who had taken possession of the biblical land of Shinar in an earlier age, and from whom, it now seemed, the Assyrian and Babylonian civilizations had themselves originally been derived. These were the Sumerians, a people whose very existence was not suspected until the re-copyings of some of their literature by Assyrian scribes began rather disconcertingly to appear amongst the tablets from Kuyunjik – re-copyings which themselves had been made 1,500 years after the disappearance of Sumer as a political entity. Fortunately among these documents there were also bilingual texts and syllabaries which sufficed to identify the language as non-Semitic and pre-Babylonian. The very small collection of bricks, tablets and seals obtained at various times by the British Museum, whose archaic inscriptions appeared to correspond to this earliest known form of speech, were consequently at once invested with a new interest. By now the earliest royal title of Babylonia, 'King of Sumer and Akkad' was already familiar, and, since the Akkadians had been recognized as the first Semitic arrivals in Mesopotamia, the new non-Semitic language came rightly to be called Sumerian.

The Sumerians, as we now know, were already established in southern Mesopotamia at the beginning of the third millennium B C. At that time they occupied a number of walled cities, mostly situated on the various branches of the lower Euphrates. Each city had its villages and farms grouped around it to form a city-state, and each of these states was ruled by an *ishakku* or governing prince. There was perpetual rivalry between them and quarrels, usually about irrigation water, often resulted in small-scale wars. One state would as a rule emerge victorious from all its battles and for the time being exercise a sort of loose hegemony over the remainder, and as senior state its *ishakku* would assume the traditional title, 'King of Sumer and Akkad', and the curious designation 'Shepherd of the Black-headed People'. In this way the cities of Uruk, Ur, Kish, Lagash and many others successively provided dynasties of kings to rule with varying success over the whole of Mesopotamia.

Amongst the authentic Sumerian relics, which in 1869 enabled Oppert definitely to postulate the existence of a non-Semitic pre-Babylonian people, were inscriptions which derived from actual excavations which had already taken place on the sites of at least two of the above-named cities. As early as 1854 we have already seen Loftus at Warka, the site of Sumerian Uruk, puzzling over the traces which he found of a then unimaginably ancient civilization. While he was so employed, Rawlinson also arranged with J. E. Taylor, the British Vice-Consul at Basra, to make some soundings in Tell Muqayyar near Nasiriyah. Muqayyar even in those days possessed the most completely exposed and best-preserved ziggurat staged-tower of any Babylonian site, into which Taylor proceeded in the manner of the time to cut a tunnel. Having satisfied himself that it was entirely constructed of solid brickwork, he almost by chance discovered an inscribed cylinder built into the masonry at one corner, and rightly concluded that duplicate cylinders would be found in corresponding positions at the remaining corners. This enabled Rawlinson to identify the site as Ur-of-the-Chaldees, the biblical home of the Patriarch, Abraham, and seat of one of the earliest Sumerian dynasties. Two further Sumerian cities were identified in this way, both as it has since proved, religious centres with little, if any political history. First a group of mounds far out in the desert to the south of Ur were investigated by Taylor and proved to be the biblical Eridu (see also Chapter Fourteen).[144] Secondly, in Birs Nimrod, the ruin west of Babylon most often considered by early travellers to be the Tower of Babel, Rawlinson himself had discovered foundation cylinders showing it to be the ancient Borsippa.

But now, twenty years later, the Sumerian site at Telloh (thought until recently to have been ancient Lagash: see note on p. 158) was to be the first southern mound selected for prolonged and methodical excavation. It is no exaggeration to say that one of de Sarzec's major accomplishments during the first months after its discovery was in protecting it from the attentions of Rassam and his gangs of treasure-seekers. To understand this it is necessary first to examine the general trend of archaeological activity sanctioned and subsidized by the British Museum after its sudden renewal of interest in Mesopotamia in 1872. For this purpose further mention must be made of George Smith.

GEORGE SMITH

It has not been possible in this story to make individual reference to the many names of scholars who contributed to the development of Assyriology. Yet that of George Smith cannot be omitted, if only because he was the first to meet his death in the field. Originally apprenticed to a firm of banknote-engravers, he devoted every minute of his spare time to reading about the Assyrian excavations, and his dinner-hours to studying the sculptures and inscriptions exhibited in the British Museum. His absorption in the subject eventually drew the attention of an official of the museum, who succeeded in obtaining for him a minor post in the Assyrian department. There he soon developed a peculiar genius for decipherment and was allotted the task of sorting and 'joining' the broken tablets from the Ninevite libraries. It was while engaged on this work that he made his sensational discovery. His first care had been to classify the fragments roughly according to what appeared to be their subjects, and in this way he had put aside a fairly large pile labelled 'Legends and Mythology'. He says:

Commencing a steady search among these fragments, I soon found half of a curious tablet which had evidently contained originally six columns. . . . On looking down the third column, my eye caught the statement that the ship rested on the mountains of Nizir, followed by the account of the sending forth of the dove, and its finding no resting-place and returning. I saw at once that I had here discovered a portion at least of the Chaldean account of the Deluge.[145]

On 3 December 1872 Smith read a paper on his discovery before the Society of Biblical Archaeology and, as can be imagined, it created a very considerable sensation. He had by then discovered further fragments of the original document, and, by combining with them the equally fragmentary remains of a duplicate text, had succeeded in completing a large section of the story. But there was still a most tantalizing gap. As soon as his discovery was authenticated, the London *Daily Telegraph*, gauging the extent of public interest, offered a sum of £1,000 to equip an expedition to Nineveh for the purpose of finding the missing fragment, providing only that George Smith himself would take charge of the investigation and send occasional accounts of his work. Smith, of course, showed no reluctance to do so, and left England for Mosul in January 1873. Owing to difficulties in obtaining a *firman* from the Porte, it was not until early May that he was able to begin work at Kuyunjik. But by an astonishing piece of luck, he accomplished almost at once the primary purpose for which he had been sent out. He trenched through the debris thrown out by the previous excavators (there was no lack of scattered tablets) and he himself again relates how on the evening of the fifth day

I sat down to examine the store of fragments of cuneiform inscriptions from the day's digging, taking out and brushing off the earth from the fragments to read their contents. On cleaning one of them I found to my surprise and gratification that it contained the greater portion of the seventeen lines of inscription belonging to the first column of the Chaldean account of the Deluge, and fitting into the only place where there was a serious blank in the story.[146]

In spite of this prompt reward for its initial generosity, the *Telegraph* showed no inclination to pay for the continuation of the excavations, and Smith consequently returned almost immediately to London. During the next few years the museum sent him twice more to dig at Nineveh, but the days of large-scale discoveries at Kuyunjik were over, and Turkish interference in the activities of foreign excavators were on the increase. Writing of Smith, Budge insists that the repeated delays and obstruction which invariably resulted from his contacts with the local government were the result of his naïve directness and inexperience in the most elementary forms of oriental 'graft'. Be this as it may, they did eventually prove disastrous. Having waited in Istanbul from October 1875 until March 1876 for a third permit to excavate, he eventually reached Mosul too late to begin work, and having decided to return to London, set out, contrary to everyone's advice, to make the cross-desert journey to the Mediterranean in the early summerheat. He was taken ill with dysentry on the way and died in Aleppo.

RASSAM RETURNS

It was now necessary for the British Museum to find somebody to take Smith's place in the field, and the first person who suggested himself was Rassam. Rassam had now resigned his political appointment in Aden, after a number of adventures which included the peculiar experience of being temporarily held prisoner by King Theodore of Abyssinia, and had returned to London. Partly as a result of having been absent from England almost continuously since his discovery of the Palace of Ashur-banipal, he had up to now received remarkably little credit for his part in the Assyrian excavations. As he remarks rather plaintively himself:

The consequence was, that not many years afterwards some of my acquisitions were attributed to others, and, actually the Assyrian legends of the Creation and Deluge tablets, which I found in Nineveh, in Assur-bani-pal's palace in 1853, were credited to Mr George Smith's exploration, which he undertook for the proprietors of the *Daily Telegraph* twenty years afterwards, because, forsooth, he was the first Assyrian scholar who had deciphered them.[147]

Even the discovery of the Lion-hunt was usually attributed to Rawlinson. Nevertheless in 1876 when the Trustees again approached him to undertake the supervision of their continued excavations at Nineveh, he welcomed the opportunity of returning once more to Mosul, and it must be said in his favour that, in return for a free hand in the conduct of the work, he renounced any kind of salary.

Like Smith, Rassam was held up a long while in Istanbul attempting to obtain a *firman*, but here in the end a great piece of good fortune awaited him. Early in 1877 Sir Henry Layard was made British Ambassador to the Porte.

Layard's political career on which we last saw him embarking in 1852 had in some ways been almost as remarkable as his Assyrian discoveries. Early in that same year we read that

DON LAYARDOS IN MADRID.

51 Caricature in Punch, 6 November 1869, of Layard arriving in Madrid as British ambassador.

52 *Layard in old age.*

After holding this post for a few months, however, the Government fell, and Layard, turning his attention to the Commons, was returned as Liberal member for Aylesbury. Afterwards for a time he became Chief Commissioner of Works, and eventually in 1869, returning to the Foreign Office, he was appointed Her Majesty's Minister Plenipotentiary at the Court of Madrid. (In a contemporary number of *Punch* there is a humorous picture of him in diplomatic uniform riding into the Spanish arena on a stout and smiling Assyrian winged bull.)[149] In 1877, as we have said, he was knighted and sent in a similar capacity to the seat of the Ottoman Government.

With Layard to intercede for him Rassam obtained a concession which must have exceeded his most sanguine hopes. It authorized him to excavate almost unconditionally on all Crown lands in the Pashaliks of Baghdad, Aleppo (which included Mosul) and Van in eastern Anatolia, and permitted him to retain all his finds with the exception of duplicates. He reached Mosul early in 1878 and began the first of a series of excavating campaigns, which lasted until 1882.

Rassam's instructions from the Trustees were perfectly well defined. He was to concentrate on the mounds of Nineveh with the purpose of augmenting the Museum's collection of tablets from the library of Ashur-banipal. But being, in his own words, disinclined to restrict himself to 'this tame undertaking', he determined to use his own judgement. 'Although', he says, 'that was the first object of my mission, I was, nevertheless, more eager to discover some new ancient sites . . . and to bring to light some important Assyrian monument.'[150] The way he went about it was characteristic. Hilprecht says:

Owing to the large geographical area included in his permit, it was impossible for him to superintend all the excavations in person. As a rule he directed them only from the distance, sometimes not visiting the same ruin for weeks and months, and in a few cases even for a whole year. During his absence from Iraq the British Resident at Baghdad undertook a general control of his excavations in Babylonia, while at Mosul his nephew, Nimrud Rassam acted most of the time as his agent in connexion with the operations conducted on several Assyrian sites. A number of intelligent native overseers . . . carried on the work as well as they could and as far as possible in accordance with their master's instructions. One can easily imagine how unsatisfactory such an arrangement must prove in the end, as diametrically opposed to all sound principles of strict scientific investigation, and in part as contrary to the very explicit instructions received from the British Museum. It was the old system of pillage in a new and enlarged edition.[151]

This criticism is understandable from one who had himself concentrated for many years on the patient and methodical excavation of a single Babylonian site. And although, more recently, any American reflection on the methods employed by Layard and other British pioneers always met with a storm of dignified protest from their successors at the British Museum,[152] in the case of Rassam, it will presently be seen to have been completely justified.

Nevertheless, from the Museum's point of view there is no doubt that Rassam did most effectively 'deliver the goods'. Within a few weeks of his arrival at Mosul in 1878 he made another sensational discovery. About a year before returning to the East he had received in London (through the good offices of an interpreter in the French consulate at Mosul) fragments of two bronze plates ornamented in relief with Assyrian figures and decoration. Once he had reopened excavations at Kuyunjik and Nimrud, his first concern was to discover where these plates came from, and this presented no difficulty. Their place of origin was a small mound called Tell Balawat, about twelve miles north-east of Nimrud, and they had been found by a peasant from the nearby village of Balawat while engaged in digging a grave on the mound. When Rassam visited the site, this was easily explained, as almost the whole top surface of the mound was covered by a graveyard. Even his *firman* prohibited him from disturbing graves, yet in this case he felt the prospect of an important find to be 'well worth the risk of getting into hot water with the authorities, and even with the village'. The term 'hot water' was an underestimation of the difficulties which he encountered when he began to dig.

The inhabitants of the village were 'Shebeks', members of one of the several non-Moslem minorities within the Mosul area, but this fact did not in any way diminish their religious susceptibility.

53 Miniature reliefs in repoussé bronze from the Balawat Gates (now in the British Museum), showing Shalmaneser III's campaign of 858 BC on the Levant coast. The city of Tyre on its rocky island (top left), sends tribute by boat to placate the king. Below, he departs in his chariot, leaving his camp empty.

Exercising the greatest tact and caution Rassam selected the most respected religious notables of the village to supervise the proceedings, and went to work in a part of the mound which was free of graves. Within a few hours he encountered more copper plates like the ones he had received in London, and ascertained to his great delight that the enormous object of which they formed a part was located outside the limits of the cemetery. Three days' work sufficed for Rassam to clear a large part of it and obtain some idea of the extraordinary character of his find. As he later wrote:

The monument was very much corroded and injured from the length of time it had been lying in damp soil. As soon as the relic was exposed to the air it began to crack, and I had very great difficulty to remove it entire. It was lying on its face and spread like a gigantic hat-rack with the top part rising to within four feet of the ground, and the lower part gradually descending to about fifteen feet deep. The plates seemed to have belonged to the covering, of a monument, which proved to be a huge gate with double leaves. . . . Each leaf had seven panels eight feet long; and, according to the way they were lying, it appeared as if they were used to cover the wooden frame in the shape of belts . . . each leaf had a thick bronze pivot, which is shown by the bend at the end of the panels in the shape of a scroll. These revolved in hard stone sockets, that were found still standing in their former position. . . . The plates, which are embossed with a variety of subjects, such as battle scenes, triumphal processions, and religious performances, are divided into two panels surrounded by a border of rosettes.[153]

These were the Bronze Gates of Shalmaneser III, which are now one of the choicest exhibits in the British Museum.[154]

All went well in Rassam's relations with the villagers as long as he himself was present. But on the fourth day, which was Sunday, he found it necessary to return to Mosul, leaving his foreman in charge. As he explains himself rather naïvely:

I had about five hundred men working in the old trenches at Kuyunjik and Nimrud, and I was obliged, therefore, to give fresh directions to the overseers at short intervals to prevent waste of time and labour.

In his absence, fighting broke out between his Arab workmen and the Shebeks, and on the Monday he was compelled, although suffering acutely from sciatica, to ride back to Balawat in a heavy snowstorm. He found the Shebeks all on strike; but the Arabs, who were still at work, had discovered 'a scientifically built Assyrian well', which greatly interested them.[155] He was also relieved to find that the gates themselves, which he had covered with a sprinkling of earth before leaving, had suffered no damage on the previous day.

With an ingenious combination of tact and persuasive humour, which would have been impossible for anyone not locally born, and a liberal distribution of small presents, Rassam coaxed the Shebeks into an improved frame of mind, assuring them that any extension of his excavations would be made by tunnelling deep beneath the graves, and that if necessary arches of masonry would be built to prevent their falling in. Eventually they returned to work, and, with occasional quarrels and other interruptions, the digging was continued. Sixty feet to the north-west of the first gates, Rassam encountered

another copper monument half the size of the first; but instead of the plates being ornamented like those of the former with double rows of figures, they had only one set on each, and the representations were larger.

In the case of this second pair of gates he was relieved of the responsibility of their removal, for

they were found very much injured and as soon as they were exposed to the air, they crumbled to pieces. . . .

Rassam next gives an explanation of the respective setting of the gates, which, as will be seen later, is doubly important, not only because he made no adequate plan and published no other information on the subject, but because of the doubt which was subsequently thrown on the whole circumstance of the find. He says:

In front of each of these monuments there was a T-shaped marble platform, with a brick border constructed so coarsely that it looked more like the work of the Sassanians than that of the Assyrians. . . . The monument stood in front of the narrowest part, and on a level with it; the sockets being fixed at each corner so that when the two leaves were opened they rested against the sides of the narrow ledge, as far as the widest part.

This is an impossibly confusing description, but sufficient to show that the doors had stood in some sort of architectural setting. He then continues:

Some Assyrian scholars have supposed that these relics were the gates of a temple, but I am of a contrary opinion, and consider them to have been mere monuments set up on the mound of Balawat in commemoration of certain events. In the place where they were discovered no trace of any wall or building was found [this was not surprising, since Rassam was rarely capable of recognizing sun-dried brickwork]; and, considering that the trophy itself must have stood at least twenty-four feet high, the huge building could not have vanished without leaving a trace even of its foundations. Moreover, when we consider that the other monument which was fixed parallel with it, about sixty feet apart, was not half its size, it would have looked unsightly whether in the same building or separately. Within the same distance, and forming almost a square with these two platforms, I found two others which must have had other monuments in front of them, but no trace of them was seen.

In another part of the mound Rassam's men came upon a marble coffer containing two beautifully inscribed tablets hewn of the same material. (These tablets gave the ancient name of Balawat as Imgur-Bel.) After further digging they found that this coffer

was placed at the entrance of a room which had been burnt down and proved afterwards to have been a temple. At the northwest of this chamber there was an altar ascended by five steps, on which we found an inscribed marble tablet of the same size and shape as the other two which were found in the coffer.

All these antiquities, including even the marble coffer, Rassam succeeded, with the help of a large cart, in transporting safely to Mosul, and so eventually to England. But unfortunately fighting had broken out anew among the workmen, and, being disinclined to be the cause of further bloodshed, after clearing out the temple, he closed the excavations and himself returned to Mosul.

As has already been said, Rassam made no adequate plan or drawings of the layout of the site or the relative positions of his discoveries. Yet his rather full description of the work and its difficulties, of which the foregoing account is an abbreviation, creates for one a clear enough picture of the mound and village of Balawat. The next reference to it in archaeological literature is therefore all the more surprising. This is by Budge, who visited the site with Nimrud Rassam in 1890, long after the gates had been exhibited, published and generally become famous. He bluntly asserts that 'none of the natives had ever heard of the discovery of the bronze plates', and adds that: 'Mr Rassam questioned them closely, and was convinced that someone had made a mistake.'[156] In his book, *By Nile and Tigris*, he amplifies this by saying:

If the two sets of gates were found at Tell Balawat there must have been a palace at this place, but this is impossible for there is no room in the mound for a temple still less for a temple and a palace however small. An explanation of the difficulty is hard to find, but it seems very probable that the natives deceived Mr H. Rassam and did not tell him where they found the plates which were sent to Paris. Mr H. Rassam may have obtained from Tell Balawat the plates and the coffer, etc., which he sent home, but if he did the natives must have taken them there.

However extraordinary this contention may seem, it is a fact that the British Museum authorities still considered the provenance of the gates to be in doubt until the site was revisited by the present writer in 1942 during the course of departmental duties.[157]

The mound is about 275 metres in diameter and two-thirds of the summit is occupied by graves. In the unoccupied space and among the outlying graves are the remains of Rassam's trenches and collapsed tunnels, perfectly matching the dimensions and dispositions which are mentioned in his account. At another point near the edge of the mound, his 'Assyrian well' is still exposed, and near if a 'brick aqueduct' which he also mentions. Amongst the older villagers the story is still told of the visit of the *Balios* and the antiquities which he found.

As Rassam had anticipated, in spite of the enormous gangs of men employed, finds at Nimrud and Kuyunjik were now few and far between. So in 1879 he decided on another attempt at Nebi Yunus, where the villagers and religious guardians had so far frustrated all attempts to excavate.

He prepared the way by spending much of his time in the village in order to gain the confidence of the little community which lived there. Next, as he had expected, he found more than one householder whose home was in a dilapidated condition, prepared to sell for a reasonably good price. In this way he gradually acquired quite a large amount of property on the mound, and, without actually demolishing the buildings, began to excavate in their *sirdabs* and connect his shafts by tunnels. There is no knowing what effect this method of procedure would eventually have had on the palace of Esarhaddon, whose existence Layard had established beneath the village, or for that matter on the buildings above ground. As it proved, Rassam had hardly begun his underground operations when a counter-intrigue among the religious notables of Mosul became evident, and an appeal by them to the Minister of Public Instruction in Istanbul resulted in an official ban on his work.

He now had excavations in hand both at Babylon and Birs Nimrod, but these did not prevent him extending his explorations to the borders of Syria and the remote shores of Lake Van. His excavations at Van do not fall within the province of this story, but the following is an example of his discoveries on the Khabur:

There is a mound at the junction of the Jarajir [Jaghjagh?] River with the Khaboor, wherein I made some tentative excavations, and after a few days' labour some important sculptures were discovered; but as soon as the local authorities at Ras-al-ain heard of the find they sent and turned away my workmen, and took possession of the relics, which I was told consisted of crouching lions and a bas-relief on which were represented horses and other animals. The only object my overseer was able to come away with was a fragment of black basalt, whereon there were engraved a few hieroglyphic figures, which I brought to the British Museum. Unfortunately I could not go there myself. . . .[158]

Babylon and Borsippa were naturally unproductive according to

54 *The famous stela of Nabu-*
apla-idinna (870 BC), found by
Rassam at Sippar (Abu Habbah).
The image is that of Shamash
the sun-god in his shrine called
Ebabarra.

Rassam's standard, as indeed were most of the other southern mounds which he 'opened'. Tell Ibrahim, for instance, where the ruins of the Babylonian city of Kuthah are buried beneath six metres of later occupational debris, completely defeated him: 'Although it had no less than twenty tunnels and trenches opened in it, there was no indication whatever in them to give me any hope of finding Babylonian remains.' When he found bricks stamped with the name of Nebuchadnezzar, he surmised that 'they might have been taken there from another place'.

It was not until the end of 1880 that Rassam made his first major find in Babylonia. This was the site of the biblical Sepharvaim (2 Kings xvii: 24, 31), which today is called Abu Habbah. Abu Habbah is located about twenty miles south-west of Baghdad near the Yusufiyah canal, and is easily recognizable as the ruins of a walled city with a small ziggurat in the centre, surrounded by a group of public buildings. Here Rassam was fortunate from the first. Starting work near the ziggurat mound he found a chamber with a bitumen-covered pavement, which some strange impulse induced him to break through. Beneath it he found an inscribed terracotta box, closed with a lid, and inside it the now-famous marble tablet of King Nabu-apla-idinna with its beautiful relief of the sun-god in his shrine. An inscription in front of the shrine at once provided both the identification of the city and the name of

55 *Rassam in old age, proudly displaying photographs of the Balawat gate reliefs, whose provenance was at one time doubted by officials in the British Museum.*

the temple of which this chamber formed a part. It read: 'Image of Shamash the Great Lord, dwelling in Ebabarra in the city of Sippar.'

Rassam estimated that the buildings surrounding the ziggurat comprised about 300 chambers grouped around several courts, and the mud-brick walls must in this case have been unmistakable, for he has even left a primitive plan showing the disposition of a number of them. During the eighteen months which followed he excavated about 170 rooms and obtained an immense volume of inscribed cylinders and tablets from them (his own estimate was 40,000–50,000). The content of one cylinder alone is sufficient to show their great interest. It was an inscription of Nabonidus, the last King of Babylon, whose life, up to the time when his son Belshazzar saw the 'writing on the wall', was dedicated almost wholly to antiquarian research. It describes how, interesting himself in the original foundation of this very temple, he had determined to check his theories by excavating. Eighteen cubits beneath the contemporary pavement his workmen had come upon a foundation-stone originally laid by Naram-Sin, son of Sargon of Akkad, 'which for 3,200 years no previous king had seen'. As dating evidence alone this cylinder was a priceless discovery.

Unlike the Kuyunjik library the Sippar tablets were of unbaked clay, and accordingly very fragile. They lay in heaps, clinging together in the clayey soil and could not be removed without many breakages. Of their general content Hilprecht gives an extremely good summary:

For the greater part these documents are of a business character, referring to the administration of the temple and its property, to the daily sacrifices

of Shamash and other gods, to the weaving of their garments, the manu-
facture of their jewelry and vessels, the building and repairing of their
houses, and to the execution of various orders given in connexion with
the worshipping of their images and the maintenance of their priesthood.
At the same time they make us acquainted with the duties and occupations of the many classes of temple officers and their large body of
servants, with the ordinary tithes paid by the faithful and with many
other revenues accruing to the sanctuary from all kinds of gifts, from the
lease of real estate, slaves, and animals, and from the sale of products
from fields and stables. As tithes were frequently paid in kind, it became
necessary to establish regular depots along the principal canals, where
scribes stored and registered everything that came in. Among the goods
thus received we notice vegetables, meat and other perishable objects
which the temple alone could not consume, and which, therefore, had
to be sold or exchanged before they decayed or decreased in value. No
wonder that apart from its distinct religious sphere the great temple of
Shamash at Sippara in many respects resembled one of the great business
firms of Babel or Nippur.[160]

In 1882 Rassam left Mesopotamia for the last time. A late portrait, which serves as a frontispiece to *Asshur and the Land of Nimrod*,
shows, against a map of Assyria, an old gentleman with white hair
and beard, holding up to the camera a large photograph of the
Balawat Gates, as though determined that with these at least his
name should be associated by posterity.

CHAPTER TWELVE

The birth of a conscience

Reference has already been made at the beginning of the last chapter to the Sumerian site at Telloh, whose impressive ruins, once thought to be ancient Lagash but now linked with the name of ancient Girsu,* are situated at the tail of the Gharraf canal, and to the chance by which its excavation eventually fell to the lot of the French. The story of how this came about is coloured by an atmosphere of almost childish international rivalry perfectly in accord with the old Mesopotamian tradition.

Ernest de Sarzec, being in 1877 French Vice-Consul at Basra, found himself 'longing for a more serious occupation to fill out the ample time left him by the slight duties of his consular position'. At Basra we are told that

An occasional ride into the desert, with its bracing air, and the hunting of the wild boar, francolin and bustard are the general means by which the members of the European colony try to keep up their energy and vitality in the hothouse atmosphere of this tropical region. But such an aimless life was very little to the liking of de Sarzec.[161]

He accordingly emulated his earlier compatriots in Mosul by interesting himself in archaeology, and though, as will presently be seen, his initial impetus was largely commercial, its eventual outcome was greatly to the advantage of the French nation. De Sarzec first heard of Telloh from Mr J. Asfar, of the steamship company then known as Strick-Asfar, who had himself been a dealer in antiquities in a small way. He was dissuaded from applying to Istanbul for a permit to excavate, partly by fear of attracting Rassam's attention to the mound, and partly owing to the very independent status of south Babylonia at that time under the Muntafiq chief, Nasir Pasha (founder of Nasiriyah and afterwards first Vali of Basra). He, therefore, without more ado, set about a general examination of the site by a series of trial trenches. Asfar had already told him of

* This incorrect identification of Telloh with Lagash is explained in the author's recent book, *The Archaeology of Mesopotamia* (1978, p. 106), as follows: 'It was not until 1953 that a study by Th. Jacobsen drew attention to a neighbouring site called Tell Al-Hiba, fifteen miles to the southeast, where excavators from the Metropolitan Museum and New York University have now located the true Lagash, capital of a state, one of whose religious centres was ancient Girsu, now Telloh.'

fine diorite statues which purported to have been seen among the ruins, and several of these he found exposed to view on his arrival. The excavations, which he carried on from March until June 1877 and reopened from February to June in 1878, produced further statues and a great quantity of inscribed material, all of which he successfully transported to Paris, and disposed of to the Louvre for a sum of 130,000 francs.[162]

While de Sarzec was absent in France, Rassam also found time to take a look at Telloh. He was at first disconcerted to find that, not being technically included in the Pashalik of Baghdad, the site did not fall within the area assigned to him by his *firman*. But directly he heard that de Sarzec had already made soundings there without any permit, he determined to follow suit. Hastily collecting a gang of local Arabs, he set them to work on the highest mound, and within a few hours they had unearthed a pair of inscribed pivot stones, memorial cones, tablets and a number of red stone mace-heads which he supposed to be 'weights'. The largest of the diorite statues de Sarzec had postponed removing until his return, and had consequently reburied, but Rassam says: 'As I wished to take a squeeze of the inscription on it for the British Museum, I had it wholly dug out.' As can be imagined, it was broken up by local Arabs after his departure. Nor was the provenance of the pivot-stones, one of which reached England, ever exactly located.

After three days' digging, fighting broke out among Rassam's workmen and he was compelled to abandon the excavation. He hoped, however, by application to Layard, to obtain a special concession for excavations at Telloh before de Sarzec returned. In this design he was thwarted, as he found on inquiring that de Sarzec himself had already obtained one. He says:

I did not know at first that M. Sarzac was negotiating for a concession to excavate at Telloh, but supposed only that he had asked the French Government to give him a grant for exploration in Southern Babylonia, which they had refused to do; and this put me off the scent.

He ends almost peevishly:

From what I have seen of the place of M. Sarzac's discoveries I am certain that if I had continued my researches there one day longer, I should have come upon the nest of black statues which were discovered in the highest mound. . . .

Happily for de Sarzec, who, armed with a *firman* and subsidized by the French Government, could now at least be free from interference or molestation by Rassam's gangs, it was not a matter of 'continuing his researches one or two days more' in order to find a 'nest of statues'. His annual seasons of excavation were to be continued almost uninterrupted until the end of the century, and the whole vast site systematically examined. Actually it would be absurd to pretend that there was yet much 'system' in the process of excavation. It was still only possible to follow the best-preserved and most obvious mud-brick walls, and the plans which de Sarzec

56 Diorite statue found near Telloh (part of the ancient state of Lagash), probably depicting the governor, Gudea, himself, to judge by the characteristic headdress. Statues such as this, discovered in the 1870s, were the first evidence of pre-Assyrian art in Mesopotamia.

left are scanty and incomplete. (More than thirty years after his death one of his successors in the field wrote to a friend: 'C'est incompréhensible, mon cher collègue, mais on ne trouve jamais de murs.') Yet the work was leisured and methodical, and Budge's allegation[163] that he 'attacked mound after mound, but excavated none of them completely' is an unfair one, if only because no mound in the history of archaeology has ever been *completely* excavated – least of all those where Budge himself worked.

Little has yet been said of the nature of the finds which de Sarzec brought to the Louvre from Telloh, and this must now be remedied, since by 1901 they had earned for the site the doubtful distinction of being characterized 'the Pompeii of early Babylonian antiquity'. The finds are divided into many different categories, but first and foremost among these comes the archaic sculpture of the late third millennium: portrait-statues in diorite or other hard stones of the *ishakku* governors of the city. Today more than a score of them adorn the Louvre, while others found their way to England and America after de Sarzec's final departure from Telloh. The cuneiform inscriptions with which they were usually covered show at least six of those in the Louvre to represent Gudea, the seventh and most famous governor of Lagash.

These statues were the first examples of pre-Babylonian art to reach Europe, and they brought sharply into focus an archaic culture whose existence had till now been hardly more than suspected. Even the art of the Assyrians, separated in time from these new finds by a matter of 1,500 years, began to appear by comparison stereotyped or over-representational. And herein lay the importance of the new exhibits at the Louvre, for they drew the attention not only of antiquarians and scholars but of art-critics and the great contemporary artists of the French school. For here at last, resurrected from the remote past, were masterpieces of art which could be assessed on their own merits 'independently of any question of their age or school, of the sources from which they sprang, of the conditions which helped to shape them and of the traditions which they embody'.[164] Since those days much criticism has been lavished upon them, as also upon the work of even earlier Sumerian sculptures. It must suffice here to say that in aesthetic expression alone they rival the work of almost any period in the history of art.

One of the earlier carvings from Telloh, which go back another 500 years before the time of Gudea, is the fragmentary 'Stela of the Vultures', whose subject is as important as its style. It represents, as H. G. Wells pointed out, the birth of military discipline; the earliest record of a force of armed men marching in step and led by a commander. Wells says:

The natural man is a spasmodic and untrustworthy fighter, very violent when he is roused, but very difficult to keep roused. The men who fight in cave paintings are loose scrappers, not warriors. There have only been warriors since the dawn of the early city-states. The warrior appears in

57 A surviving fragment of the so-called 'Stela of the Vultures', a Sumerian relief (c.2600 BC) showing Eannatum, 'Divine Bailiff of Lagash', at the head of his army in phalanx formation and (below) driving his chariot. Discovered by French excavators at Telloh.

formation in early Sumerian carvings. There you see him in a sort of phalanx, advancing with his shield locked with that of the next man and their spears at a level making an invincible line. All down the changing historical record that body of disciplined infantrymen appears and reappears. . . .[165]

The Sumerian texts from Telloh are no less interesting. Among the records of the early governors is the story of one such armed expedition against the neighbouring state of Umma (Tell Jokha), which may be said to be the first military campaign in the known history of the world. The 'Stela of the Vultures' was set up by a prince called Eannatum to mark the boundary between the two states. Umma was situated higher up on the same branch of the Euphrates as Girsu, and quarrels between them were usually on the subject of irrigation water. There is an equally interesting record of a later governor, Entemena, who decided to remove the cause of such disputes by building a canal to bring water directly to Lagash from the Tigris. This canal still survives in the form of the Gharraf, which leaves the Tigris at the Kut barrage and flows southwards towards Telloh.

Unhappily a great proportion of the tablets obtained from Telloh do not derive from de Sarzec's legitimate excavations, for it was about this time that the illicit trade in antiquities started in real earnest. It is not impossible that the whole trouble may be traced to de Sarzec's own indiscretion in letting it be known that he had sold his first group of finds to the Louvre for £5,000. Added to this, Rassam's semi-commercial rapacity over removable antiquities was sufficiently obvious to make them equally fair game for rival speculators. In any case the early 1880s saw the first recognized dealers in antiquities established in the Baghdad bazaar. The hand which they took in the excavation of Telloh makes a story sufficiently characteristic to tell in full, and for this purpose it will be most convenient to quote at some length from Wallis Budge, who himself extracted it from various sources on a visit to Iraq some years later:

After 1881 the intervals between de Sarzec's periods of work on the mounds grew longer and longer; and as he took no steps to safeguard his interest in them, the local Arabs, working hand-in-hand with the men who had been with Rassam in 1879–82, and supplied with money by the dealers in Baghdad, began to excavate the mounds on their own account. Their object was not to find large antiquities, which could not be easily smuggled out of the country, but inscribed clay tablets, which could be carried on the person in the folds of the cloak, or packed in small boxes....

The ruins of Tall Loh were clearly those of a great mercantile community and of a royal residence; and this being so, the records of the business transacted there, the tax accounts and the temple library must be there somewhere. The search for the record office and clearing-house of Lagash could not be successfully carried on by clandestine excavations at night; so by arrangement with local officials the work was carried on openly by day.... At length the unauthorized diggers found what they were looking for in a small compact mound, in which was a series of little chambers containing baked clay inscribed tablets. The news of their discovery spread, as such things will, with extraordinary rapidity; and before they had made arrangements to remove the tablets, de Sarzec appeared at Al-Basrah. The diggers hurriedly shovelled back sand and earth over the chambers and began to dig in another mound, one which de Sarzac had partially excavated.[166]

On his arrival at Telloh they denied all knowledge of any discovery of tablets, and by one excuse or another prevented him from digging in the mound where they actually were. After de Sarzec's departure the tablet chambers were once more opened up and, in a comparatively short period, between 35,000 and 40,000 tablets found their way into the hands of the Baghdad dealers. Budge says:

Every buyer exported his purchases as soon as possible; and so the great collection of Tall Loh tablets was very soon scattered all over the civilized world.

Even in more recent years Telloh has been a difficult site to protect from illicit digging. During the interval between de Sarzec's death in 1901 and the resumption of the French excavation in 1903, and again after the First World War, spasmodic looting continued, not only of tablets but of larger antiquities. Further diorite statues came to light and, after changing hands many times, found their way into various museums. A magnificent life-size 'Governor of Lagash' was bought by the British Museum from a London dealer; the head and body of one small but very fine 'Gudea' came to rest some thousands of miles apart, in the University Museum of

Pennsylvania and the Iraq Museum respectively; others have since been recovered. The Louvre authorities closed their excavations at Telloh with some appearance of finality in 1931, but there can be no pretence that the site is in the scientific or any other sense completely explored.

AMERICAN EXCAVATORS IN IRAQ

The first American excavations in Mesopotamia began in 1887 at the site of Nippur, which lies on the old easternmost course of the Euphrates, not far from the squalid little modern settlement called Suq al Afaq. From the very start the members of the expedition, including the field-director, Peters, found themselves completely out of their element in dealing with the tribal people in whose territory they were to work, and considerably overawed by the magnitude of the task which they had accepted with so much enthusiasm in the comfortable but now remote committee room of Pennsylvania University. Hilprecht at least, who was one of the party which set out from Hillah across the *chol* on a February morning, was sufficiently impressed by his first sight of the great ziggurat mound which was their destination. In a style at that time prescribed for narratives of exploration he relates:

Finally on the third morning Bint-al-Amir majestically towering above the wide-stretched mounds of Nuffar, rose clear on the horizon. More than 2,000 years ago the huge terraces and walls of the most renowned Babylonian sanctuary had crumbled to a formless mass. But even in their utter desolation they still seemed to testify to the lofty aspirations of a bygone race. . . .

He adds more prosaically:

What would our committee at home have said at the sight of this enormous ruin, resembling more a picturesque mountain range than the last impressive remains of human constructions.

Peters neglected every precaution which could have contributed towards the quiet progress of his work, and since the Afaq tribes were and are a poor and thieving people, not always within control of the local authorities, trouble was bound to follow. Instead of placing himself and his party under the protection of an appropriate sheikh, and paying him a small subsidy in return for supplying labour and protecting his interests, he established his camp on the summit of the ziggurat mound and allowed his Turkish commissar to dictate terms. A gang of 100 to 250 Arab workmen under no Arabic-speaking authority would at any time prove something of a handful, and the exaggerated ferocity bred in Peters himself by nervous anxiety and inadequate knowledge of local manners of course proved fatal. Early in April thieving began at night and a tribesman was shot dead by one of the camp-guards. Fearing some mass retaliation, Peters sent for a section of gendarmes from Diwani-yah, and on their arrival the mound was surrounded and besieged by the Afaq. The rest is related by Hilprecht:

On Thursday, 18 April, long before the sun rose, the whole expedition was in readiness to vacate the mounds and to force their way to Hilla, when upon the treacherous order of Mukota, an Arab secretly set fire to our huts of reeds and mats and laid the whole camp in ashes in the short space of five minutes. For a while the utmost confusion prevailed; the *zabtiye* got demoralized, and occupied a neighbouring hill; and while we were trying to save our effects, many of the Arabs commenced plundering. Half the horses perished in the flames, firearms and saddlebags and $1000 in gold fell into the hands of the marauders, but all the antiquities were saved. Under the war-dance and yells of the frantic Arabs the expedition finally withdrew. . . .[167]

So Peters' first season at Nippur ended in chaos and disaster.

Surprisingly enough the group of antiquarian enthusiasts in the United States who had financed this venture seemed comparatively undeterred by its initial misfire, and determined to persevere. In the new year of 1890 the expedition returned to Nippur to try its luck once more. Circumstances were now more favourable, for the Afaq marshes had in the interval been afflicted by a cholera epidemic which had left the tribes dispirited and impoverished, and though the Americans persisted in the curious policy of attempting to intimidate them with firework displays and other 'big magics' considered effective with 'savage' peoples, the good wages they offered proved an irresistible attraction. The new and improved excavating camp at the foot of the mound, with its roomy compound enclosed by a bastion of camel-thorn, became a permanent installation, and three long seasons' work were accomplished before the end of the century.

As was the case with so many other Babylonian sites, by far the most important result of the Nippur excavations was the great mass of inscribed material found there. In all, about 30,000 tablets were collected, mostly texts written in the Sumerian language and dating over a period of a thousand years, starting with the mid-third millennium BC. Most significant of all was the group devoted to Sumerian literature. For it must be remembered that, out of the quarter of a million or so cuneiform Sumerian texts which have in the past come to light in Babylonia, over ninety-five per cent are economic in character, that is to say, bills, receipts, contracts of sale and exchange and other business documents, conforming to a set of conventional formulae and consequently fairly easy to read. The Sumerian literary tablets from Nippur number in all about 2,100 and constitute a major proportion of those at present known to exist. The contribution which their publication has already made to the study of Sumerian culture is of course immense.[168]

Judging from the publications of Peters, Hilprecht and others and the present appearance of the site, method in the Nippur excavations had reached about the same standard of efficiency as under the directorship of de Sarzec at Telloh. It is perhaps an indication of the birth of some sort of professional conscience in this respect that it should now have become a subject of mutual criticism among archaeologists of different nationalities. Budge, for instance, who was in Iraq on a British Museum mission while excavations both at Nippur and Telloh were in progress, formed an equally poor opinion of the pretensions of either to call themselves 'scientific', and was not beyond opposing this opinion to French and American criticism of his colleagues and predecessors who had excavated for the British Museum. Of de Sarzec, for instance, he writes:

A French archaeologist, in describing Rassam's excavations in 1879–1882, remarks, '*En Chaldée comme en Assyrie ses travaux ressemblent plus à un pillage qu'à une fouille scientifique*' (Fossey, *Manuel*, p. 52); and the excavations of de Sarzec may be rightly described by the same words.[169]

In another paragraph, replying to criticism by Breasted of British excavating methods at Kuyunjik, which he called 'unscientific', Budge is equally disparaging about the work at Nippur: 'More travellers than one who have seen the site of the American excavations at Nippur have failed to see there any exhibition of scientific digging.'

WALLIS BUDGE

Wallis Budge was at this time an assistant in the Department of Oriental Antiquities at the British Museum. His first mission to Mesopotamia took place in 1888, and resulted from a most peculiar and unfortunate situation which had arisen in regard to ancient sites in Assyria and Babylonia previously excavated by the Trustees' agents.

When Rassam finally left Iraq for good in 1882 he had appointed workmen to guard such important sites as Kuyunjik in the north and Abu Habbah in the south, where the museum considered itself to have proprietory rights, and to prevent any excavation by un-authorized parties. Since that time large consignments of tablets had begun to be dispatched to various European museums by Baghdad dealers, and evidence provided by the character and text of some of them suggested that they originated in the very sites which the Trustees were paying guardians to protect. It was sufficiently dis-concerting to find that in some cases the dealers from whom the tablets were bought seemed likely to be the guardians themselves; but what was even worse, owing to Rassam's habit of leaving his excavations unsupervised, certain tablets now on the market seemed likely to have been found during excavations paid for by the British Museum. This was a situation which plainly required investigation, and Budge was selected as the most suitable person to undertake this difficult task, having gained some experience of such negotia-tions while purchasing antiquities for the museum in Egypt during the previous year.

Partly in order to place his mission on a more outwardly com-prehensible footing, the Trustees at the same time decided to request a renewal of their *firman* for the excavations in Mesopotamia. The problem as to which site should be chosen must have been con-

58 Wallis Budge, who, as agent of the British Museum, recovered many thousands of cuneiform tablets illicitly sold to dealers in Baghdad by Rassam's workmen and guards. He had previously recovered the famous Tell el Amarna tablets from the antiquities market in Egypt.

siderable, since work in the past had been started and abandoned on such a very large number of mounds, and none could in any sense be considered completed. Budge, in fact, makes the entirely true and very significant admission that, in his search for antiquities, 'No British excavator had yet laid bare the ruins of the buildings of any Assyrian or Babylonian town'.[170] Facts such as these did not facilitate the negotiation of a *firman*, especially as the Turks themselves had recently shown signs of becoming archaeologically minded. An Imperial Ottoman Museum had been founded and placed in charge of a cultured and enterprising Ottoman official, while plans were being made for excavations subsidized by the Porte. In the end Kuyunjik was provisionally selected for the renewed attentions of British excavators.

Budge, who was ready to leave London by December 1887, now paid a second visit to Egypt on his way to Baghdad, and it was on this occasion that he succeeded in purchasing part of the famous Tell el Amarna tablets, which give so poignant a picture of the decaying Egyptian Empire in the time of the Apostate Pharaoh, Akhenaten. Owing to the difficulties involved in sending them to England, they were still in his possession when he reached Basra by boat from Suez.

From Basra, Budge travelled by river-steamer up the Tigris. On reaching Baghdad he had an invitation to stay on board the small

Indian mail steamer *Comet*, which was temporarily moored in mid-stream near the centre of the town, and thither he betook himself in one of the circular coracles, called *gufas*, which are as characteristic of the Iraq waterways as camels are in the desert. There was an alarming tussle with customs officials, who mistook the box containing the Amarna tablets for smuggled whisky; but thanks to the intervention of Butterworth, the captain of the *Comet*, both Budge and his box were in the end safely admitted to 'British territory'.

The next step was to call at the British Residency and present to Colonel Tweedie, then Consul-General in Baghdad, the letters of introduction with which he had been provided by Lord Salisbury, Rawlinson and others. He was, of course, fascinated to see the milieu which had provided a setting for so many distinguished pioneers of Mesopotamian archaeology, and his excellent account of it is enhanced by a photograph[171] of the central courtyard showing Tweedie in diplomatic uniform supported by his staff and Sikh guard. It is easily recognizable as the same building which appears in the clumsy engravings made by Felix Jones thirty years earlier.[172]

Tweedie impressed his visitor very much in the same way as Stratford Canning had Layard on his first visit to the Istanbul Embassy. He embarked at once on a lengthy discussion of the Arab horse, quoting just sufficient opinions of Arab and Persian writers in the original tongue to acquaint Budge with his mastery of oriental languages Then, turning to the letters of introduction, he first professed himself unable to comprehend why such distinguished scholars and diplomats should favour with personal communications 'a humble Indian officer sent to Baghdad to qualify for a pension'. Though unable to offer Budge accommodation in the Residency, he invited him, whenever he cared, to eat at his table, adding: 'And I can promise to give you a new kind of curry every night for a month at a stretch, so good a cook has God given me.' Finally, he expressed himself in no uncertain terms on the subject of the Trustees and their tablets. In effect, he informed Budge that (*a*) only Britons should from the first have been employed as supervisors of excavations, (*b*) the Museum had no legal right at all to appoint watchmen after leaving a site, (*c*) the Museum should have selected certain sites and excavated them completely because it would now be out of the question to prevent illicit digging at the many sites to which they had drawn the attention of local dealers. Tweedie next informed him that the local Turkish Inspector of Antiquities was aware of the purpose for which he had come to Baghdad and would do everything possible to prevent him from purchasing tablets himself. He warned him that if he got into trouble on this account he could not expect any official help. Ending characteristically with the usual rather pointless Arab proverb about a fox and a camel, he rose and invited Budge to lunch among the carpets, hangings and fretted panelling collected in the past by Rawlinson, Taylor, Rich and many others.

Knowing the character of most provincial Turkish officials, and having by this time probably summed up Wallis Budge, Tweedie cannot have anticipated that his official advice would be taken as more than a formal admonition. Budge, in fact, went straight from the Residency to call on Badri Beg, the Antiquities Inspector, from whom he received every courtesy. He says:

He described the difficulties which attended the purchase of tablets and their export from Baghdad, and proposed that I should commission him to act as buyer for the Museum. When I explained that this was impossible he showed no ill-feeling, but promptly said that he would do his utmost to persuade Hamdi Bey and the Porte to renew our permit to make excavations. In return he begged me to propose that the appointment as Delegate to watch our excavations on behalf of the Porte, if the permit were obtained, should be given to him, and I thanked him and agreed to do so.

Budge made arrangements with Badri Beg to be taken to the houses of the dealers who had tablets in their possession and was impressed with the size of their collections, which in some cases amounted to 'many hundreds'. He also noted that the majority of them came from sites excavated by the British Museum. He then took particulars of the dealers' names and returned to the *Comet*. On comparing the names with those on the letters of introduction given him by Rassam to the guardians employed by the Trustees, he was hardly surprised to find that they were identical. During the following days he set to work purchasing tablets for the museum on a large scale, and found the dealers most anxious to sell. This was easily explained when he discovered from a reliable source that Badri Beg had arranged for his purchases to be confiscated from him on his departure from Baghdad and sold back to the dealers for a fraction of the price which he had paid. To ensure the success of this plan the inspector had customs officials posted in a boat to watch his movements to and from the *Comet*. Budge, however, had arranged that the boxes containing the tablets should be brought out by *gufa* at night, and the whole of his purchases were thus safely shipped on the side of the steamer facing away from the shore. Soon afterwards the *Comet* left for Basra carrying a Persian nobleman bound for India on a state visit. Budge's Babylonian tablets, together with those from Tell el Amarna, were transferred to an Indian mail steamer with the Khan's baggage. Badri Beg was under the impression that Budge had not yet taken delivery of the tablets and, in order to reassure him, Budge let it be known that he was about to pay a lengthy visit to Babylon and Abu Habbah.

Budge excuses himself for this very blatant piece of sharp practice on the grounds of the Turkish Government's inability to enforce its own laws and acquire the tablets for the Imperial Ottoman Museum:

I had to decide whether the tablets should go to Berlin, or France, or America or the British Museum, for there was not the remotest chance of their going to Constantinople, and I determined that they should go to the British Museum, and so I bought them. It was exactly the same in Egypt, although the Trustees had no claim at all on the Tall-al-Amarnah tablets. Had I not come to a decision at once, and taken the eighty-two tablets when I had the chance of getting them, they would certainly have gone to the Berlin Museum, or into the possession of some private collector, or anywhere except the Government Museum of Egyptian Antiquities, Cairo. When the Directors of Museums in the East make it worth the while of natives to bring their 'finds' to them, nothing of importance will find its way to Europe or America.[173]

Budge now visited Babylon, Birs Nimrod and Abu Habbah, and everywhere found traces of a brisk trade in Babylonian tablets. He was considerably shocked by the evidence which he saw not only of havoc wrought on the sites by unskilled diggers, but by stories of the clumsy attempts to export the tablets when found. One man had sent several loosely packed cases on camel-back to Damascus, and was surprised when they arrived full of powdered clay. Another had smuggled his tablets in bales of cotton, which went through the machine before they could be extracted. Generally speaking it seemed surprising that any had reached the dealers intact. One might suppose that all this would have convinced Budge of the soundness of Colonel Tweedie's judgment in the matter. His reaction, on the contrary, was to make a mental note of the site called Der, a few miles from Abu Habbah, as being another which might be subjected to the same treatment (see below).

After a brief visit to the ruins of 'Aqar Quf, he left Baghdad by river steamer for Basra. When a strict customs examination of his baggage failed to produce any tablets, the Baghdad authorities drafted a telegram to Istanbul asking for authority to prevent him leaving the country. In return for a small service, a friendly post office official arranged an accident to the wires just outside the city, and by the time the reply arrived, Budge had embarked for England.

It is hardly surprising that Budge's findings in connection with the 'leakages' of tablets from sites excavated by Rassam should have led to some unpleasantness on his return to London. Evidence of their having both expressed themselves energetically on the subject is provided by a repercussion some years later in the form of an action for slander brought by Rassam against Budge in 1893. A contemporary number of the *Daily News* gives the following slightly facetious account of it:

Mr Rassam has obtained a verdict for fifty pounds in his action against Mr Budge of the British Museum. It is enough. Mr Rassam was the gentleman who took out the famous letter to King Theodore of Abyssinia, and was imprisoned, and afterwards handsomely indemnified for his pains. Subsequently he conducted Assyrian excavations at Abu Habbah, in the interest of the British Museum, but, greatly to the disgust of the Museum, the best things discovered did not find their way to the national collection. Other Museums obtained them off the private brokers into whose hands they passed. Mr Budge, a British Museum official, expressed himself too freely on the subject in regard to the conduct and responsibility of Mr Rassam. He said that we only got the rubbish, and that the foreigners got the good things, and moreover, that they got them through the negligence of Mr Rassam, or with his connivance. He went so far as to say that the overseers were the relations of Mr Rassam, and that they furthered his private breaches of trust. This was not true, they were not Mr Rassam's relations; and the Eastern imagination is so luxuriant. Mr Rassam maintained that all he found he sent home, and it was not his fault if precious things were afterwards found by others and sold at a good profit. It was his misfortune, beyond question, for as the mound was excavated at the expense of his employers, all the plums should have gone to them. Mr Budge made what most persons would have considered an ample apology, but this was not enough for Mr Rassam or for his counsellors. Sir Henry Layard and Mr Renouf gave evidence on behalf of Mr Rassam, and the trial was in some respects a sort of antiquarian festival. These distinguished persons have not been in the intimacy of Ashur-bani-pal for nothing. Their measures of time are not as our measures. Otherwise the better part of a week would hardly have been devoted to such a case.[174]

One would have supposed that, in view of what had happened, Budge would have had some misgivings as to his official reception on any future visit to Baghdad. Yet stories such as the discomfiture of Badri Beg have a tendency to be remembered only as long as their entertainment value lasts. As it proved, he returned twice more to Iraq; and spent two further winter seasons excavating and buying antiquities. In the summer of 1888 the Trustees, who were considering the compilation of a private catalogue of the tablets from Nineveh, decided that the trenches and debris of Kuyunjik should be given one more 'going over' in order to give the published list a definitive character. The Turkish authorities insisted that the person to be in charge of the excavations should make application in person for the *firman*. So Budge was dispatched to Istanbul to enlist the help of the Ambassador, Sir William White. He gives the most interesting account of his first visit to Hamdi Bey, Director of the Imperial Ottoman Museum, and of his beautiful house, 'Cool Fountain', overlooking the Bosphorus, with its elaborate garden and priceless collection of art treasures. He found this aristocratic and cultivated Turk 'provoked almost beyond endurance' by a vulgar and abusive article about himself just published in the *Contemporary Review* by an English archaeologist called J. T. Bent, whom he had been compelled to prevent from exporting certain antiquities from Turkish territory. The passages from this article, which Budge re-quotes, with their bad-mannered references to the 'ladies of his house', give one an impression of how very few Englishmen at that time were capable of sensibility or discrimination in dealing with Eastern peoples. It is to Hamdi's credit that he nevertheless received Budge with the greatest courtesy, and, though it was now contrary to the Turkish law, agreed to the Trustees' continued search for tablets at Kuyunjik, provided only that they would in return present the Ottoman Museum with archaeological publications and castes of Assyrian reliefs to the equivalent value. This arrangement Budge of course eagerly accepted. The granting of the actual *firman*, however, depended in the end on a direct appeal to the Sultan by the Ambassador, and this White agreed to effect only on the basis of a curious private bargain. He stipulated that when Budge left for Mosul he should take with him White's young son, who was at a loose end in Istanbul and anxious for some experience of Eastern travel.

Budge and young White travelled by boat to Alexandretta, where a member of the well-known Catani family set them on their way by the old Aleppo-Mardin road to Mosul. Budge's excavations at Kuyunjik on this occasion consisted in hardly more than sifting through the earth thrown out by previous excavators, and the fact that he found about 200 tablets in this way testifies to the crudeness of earlier digging methods. A great deal of his time in Mosul was spent in the purchase of ancient Greek, Syriac and Arabic manuscripts from the various religious communities. He also, as we have seen, visited Balawat with Hormuzd Rassam's nephew, Nimrud (see p. 153). In the spring of 1889 he returned to London.

Budge's third season's work in Iraq was mainly concerned with the site called Der, near Abu Habbah, which he had taken note of on his first visit to Babylonia. During the summer of 1889 the Trustees applied for a new permit to excavate Der 'and a number of other sites in the neighbourhood'. The Porte preferred that this should limit their work to Der itself, but otherwise agreed to arranging a *firman*. This involved applying to the government of Baghdad for particulars of the situation, ownership, etc., of the site, and it became generally known that Budge was about to excavate it. When Budge reached Baghdad in the winter of 1890 he had hardly been an hour in the town before he heard of the effect which this had had. In point of fact the Vâli of Baghdad had decided, apparently with the connivance of the Istanbul authorities, to make a preliminary 'examination' of the site before the *firman* was granted, and this examination had been astonishingly productive. Nearly 10,000 tablets had been sold to the dealers in Baghdad and he had then been able conscientiously to inform the Porte that Der had no great possibilities and there should be no objection to giving Budge his *firman*.

Budge's informant was able to give him a first-hand account of the discovery. He said that

there were many thousands of contract-tablets and business documents in clay cases, stamped with the impressions of the seals of witnesses. The biggest of these were deposited in large unbaked earthenware jars, which stood in the ground, and the small were stacked in heaps on slabs of stone laid flat on the earth. They tried to move the jars without emptying them, but the jars collapsed under the weight of their contents, and many tablets were broken by falling on the ground. . . . In one chamber they found rows of tablets lying on slabs, as if they had been arranged there in some special order.[175]

Fallen from these were small triangular inscribed labels which had been attached to them by fibrous cords. A very considerable number of carved cylinder-seals had been found among the tablets.

The informant was also greatly surprised to find Budge a little put out on hearing his story. He said:

Be not sad of heart for such a thing has never happened to any seeker for antikat before. We have all the tablets in Baghdad, we are all your friends, and we have kept the tablets for you. You will buy them and they shall go out of the country quickly, and you will be able to live with your English friends in Baghdad and not be obliged to sit in the desert with the jackals and the vultures, and burn by day and freeze by night. Besides, there are now many oranges in Baghdad.[176]

In comparison with the Vâli's spectacular success as an archaeologist, Budge's own modest excavations at Der were necessarily something of an anti-climax. In any case, when he left Iraq for the last time a few weeks later the two groups of Der tablets, numbering 2,500 and 7,000 respectively, which he had purchased in Baghdad were by far the most formidable result of his third season.

The site of Der has once more received the attention of the local government in recent years under remarkably different circumstances. In 1941 it was one of the sites selected by the writer for the training of Arab personnel attached to the Antiquities Department. The exact stratification of the mounds was worked out from the surface to the original virgin soil and correlated with such dating material as the tablets offered. At the same time a corpus of pottery and cylinder seals was compiled ranging over a period of 2,000 years. The site appears to represent a suburb of Sippar founded in the time of King Sargon of Akkad. Most recently, in 1975, an archive of almost 2,000 tablets was found by a Belgian expedition.[177]

CHAPTER THIRTEEN

Ethics and method

In reading the foregoing chapters it would be possible to conclude that the entire preoccupation of western archaeologists in Meso-potamia in the last century consisted in looting valuable antiquities from the country and indigenous people to whom they rightfully belonged, by methods as damaging to the antiquities themselves as to the ancient monuments constituting the sources from which they were derived. Yet on closer examination this inference appears plainly ridiculous. It involves one in an argument by no means restricted to the sphere of antiquities, but embracing the immensely more extensive subject of colonial exploitation; a subject whose every aspect has in the past been so distorted by propaganda that it is scarcely any longer susceptible of judicial logic. It is a milieu where the simplest ethics have become so obscured by growth and change that a static judgment may provide a *casus belli*; where a son's guiding principles may be the antithesis of his father's most sacred convictions, without detriment to the regard of one for the other. To every ingenuous question there is a dusty answer. Did John Company interfere with the autonomous development of India? Did the Americans pay a fair price to the Indian who owned Manhattan? Were the Arab wars of conquest really wars of liberation? Did Balfour know there were any Arabs in Palestine? If the answers to these most poignant questions leave us still hot for certainties, the ground will be no safer in the straiter sphere of archaeology.

Mesopotamia in the nineteenth century was a neglected province of a decaying empire, for the most part shamefully administered by corrupt Ottoman officials. The Arab peoples of the country had reached so low an ebb that their rights were in abeyance and their traditions almost forgotten. For all the manly virtues which they inherited from their imperial ancestors, six centuries of oppression had left them backward and ignorant. In the realm of antiquities, derived, after all, from what they had been taught to consider a heretical age, it would have been absurd to expect them to under-stand the value, intrinsic or otherwise, of these monuments which chance had located within their territory, let alone the necessity for their preservation. The Westerner, therefore, who considered the stones of Assyria a world-heritage could hardly be blamed for preferring to see them installed in a museum within reach of an epigraphist, rather than rotting in a mound where a chance rainstorm might leave them at the mercy of Arab gypsum-burners.

Up to the last years of the century and the appearance of individuals such as Hamdi Bey, the Turks also had been equally indifferent to the fate of pre-Islamic monuments. Indeed, they had often enough opposed and obstructed the activities of western excavators, but for the wrong reasons. Their opposition was almost always actuated by religious prejudice, personal spite or ordinary malice. Furthermore, this very opposition itself proved as great a detriment to the efficiency of the excavations as shortage of funds. The disabilities created by both circumstances were regrettable, but they inevitably serve to augment our admiration for the men whose patience and ingenuity rose superior to them. One would hardly have expected Layard to abandon his work at Nimrud on the assumption that some future generation of archaeologists would be better equipped; nor would one have wished Botta to entrust the Khorsabad sculptures to the Pasha of Mosul in trust for an Iraq nation of the future. No logic or ethics of an age which they could not foresee must be allowed to detract from the human endeavour of these great explorers. Nevertheless, it is in some sense with a feeling of relief that one turns at this point to an entirely new phase in the history of archeology. The end of the century in fact marked such a conspicuous epoch in the evolution of historical research that it must here be dwelt upon at some length.

THE FIRST GERMAN EXCAVATORS

In the first place, then, it should be unreservedly affirmed that the new development resulted from the appearance in the field of the first German archaeologists. Like their colleagues of other nationalities these newcomers were by no means averse to the discovery of removable antiquities for their museums or the acquisition of texts for the benefit of the many German scholars who had followed Grotefend in the realm of Assyriology. Yet their main purpose was a new one, namely, the careful examination of the architectural and social setting from which such antiquities had hitherto been so heedlessly removed. We have already quoted Budge's significant admission (p. 166 above) that no excavation had yet laid bare the *buildings* of a Babylonian town. To repair this omission was the Germans' first aim; their second was to elucidate for the first time the historical significance of stratification in Mesopotamian mounds. In the first thirteen years of the new century both aims were accomplished with a patience and methodical ingenuity which set an entirely new standard for the conduct of archaeological excavations in all parts of the world.

The success of this great enterprise owed much to the leadership of Robert Koldewey, an individual universally regarded with

59 Robert Koldewey, who conducted the excavation of Babylon from 1899 to 1913. A pioneer in the field of systematic digging, he learnt and taught new methods of tracing mud-brick walls, universally employed from that time onwards. Working through-out the year, his team set a high standard of patience and austere living.

respect and affection. By far the greatest task which he and his colleagues set themselves was the final and definitive excavation of the ruins of Babylon, a work with which his expedition was pre-occupied from March 1899 until a few months before the First World War. As we have seen, the Germans were by no means the first in the field at Babylon, and Koldewey himself modestly remarks:

It involves no depreciation of the labours of our predecessors when we say that they are superseded in almost every detail by the results of our many years of excavations, so far as the knowledge of the city ruins are concerned, and thus it would be hardly worth while to controvert expressly their numerous errors.[178]

The same fact will also perhaps help to excuse the rather brief reference in the preceding pages to these same earlier attempts on the site.

There is little to suggest that excavating technique among the Germans was not born fully-fledged. Presumably the following of baked-brick walls, which presents little difficulty, led impercept-ibly to a mastery of the far more difficult task of tracing sun-dried brickwork. It is, in any case, certain that by the end of their second season they had equipped themselves with a gang of skilled Arab wall-tracers whose descendants and successors have formed the nucleus of the workmen employed on almost every excavation from that day to this. Little difficulty was here presented by stratification, since buildings belonging to different occupational levels could usually be identified by the bricks inscribed with the names of their builders; but the recovery of architectural detail soon became a fine art, with the result that, by the time the work at Babylon was interrupted by the first rumours of war in Europe, the whole layout of the imperial city, with its complicated fortifications, monumental gateways, procession street and almost every one of its principal buildings, had been excavated or otherwise traced sufficiently to make a convincing and reliable reconstruction. Thus, in Budge's sense, the 'buildings were laid bare'; and yet to those who visit the site today the result is somewhat disappointing. Here are no tidy and comprehensible ruins, such as one sees in Greece or Egypt; for it is in the nature of mud-brick walls that their remains, once exposed, are difficult to preserve. As a result, save for the dominating outline of the more massive structures, and some recent reconstructions, the site presents for the modern visitor a scene of devastation almost as complete as when first discovered by European travellers.

The city which the Germans excavated dates largely from the time of the Neo-Babylonian Empire (seventh to sixth centuries BC), and a great many of its monuments were the work of Nebuchadnezzar. Most of these fall within the area of the Inner City, which was traversed north to south by the *Via Sacra* of Babylonian ceremonial. This street was elevated twelve-and-a-half metres above plain-level and paved with slabs of red and white marble nearly a metre square. The walls which flanked it on either side, and whose foundations penetrated deep into the ruins of earlier cities, were faced with bricks glazed in bright colours and ornamented with a triple frieze of heraldic animals in relief (bulls, lions and dragons). In the centre of the town the street skirted the east wall of the great temple-enclosure, Etemenanki, and, turning westwards beyond it, spanned the Euphrates on a fine arched bridge, passing on into the

60 The Ishtar Gate at the entrance to the Inner City of Babylon in the time of Nebuchadnezzar II (605–562 BC); reconstructed in Berlin from the fallen remains of glazed brickwork which the Germans collected during their excavations.

western quarter of the city. Etemenanki, with its high ziggurat, shares with Birs Nimrod the honour of possibly representing the biblical tower of Babel. The tower itself was seventy-five metres high, with a triple staircase, and receded in a succession of stages or storeys. According to an almost contemporary inscription, the uppermost storey was adorned with six sanctuaries consecrated to various gods, though this did not accord with the dimensions assumed by the excavators. Almost every brick of its structure was quarried away by the builders of Hillah after the Germans departed, and nothing is now left but a reedy lake of water in a deep depression.

At its north end, where the procession street passed through the double fortification of the Inner City, was the famous Ishtar Gate, with its double portals flanked by gigantic towers. This too was faced in shining glazed brickwork, with bulls and dragons in relief (which were repeated, unglazed, on its deep foundations). The greater part of its structure above ground had been demolished and the glazed bricks scattered; but these, and the small part which remained standing, proved sufficient to reveal the original appearance of the building. The Germans therefore took it upon themselves to remove the surviving ornament, and incorporated it in a full-size reconstruction of the gate in the Berlin Museum. Since the number of conspicuous *objets d'art* produced by the whole of their thirteen years' excavations could practically be counted on the fingers of one hand, this decision was perfectly understandable.

The subsequent fate of these Ishtar Gate decorations is in itself symptomatic of the new ethic in the realm of excavation. When Koldewey left for home in 1917 the 649 cases containing the bricks were left stored in the German expedition-house at Hillah, and, on the establishment by the British of a post-war government in Iraq, came under the charge of Miss Gertrude Bell, who, as Oriental Secretary to the High Commissioner, Sir Percy Cox, had assumed responsibility for constituting an antiquities service. There they remained intact until 1926, when, in conformity with the newly-established Antiquities Law, their release to the German Government was sanctioned, in exchange for representative examples of the restored panels and two magnificent models of the city of Babylon which now adorn the Iraq and Babylon museums. The remainder of the cases reached Berlin in 1927.

Babylon was not the only site where the success of the German excavators made the efforts of their predecessors appear ineffectual. The Assyrian site of Ashur was also excavated almost continuously from 1902 to 1914, mainly under the direction of Walter Andrae.[179] This first capital of the embryo nation, dating from the time when it was no more than a city-state, was in those days most picturesquely set on a spur of rock surrounded on two sides by the waters of the Tigris. It was heavily fortified and crowned by at least three ziggurats, including E-harsag-kurkurra ('The Great Mountain and House of all Lands'). Here, also, the Germans traced out the walls of houses and temples of the city; but they also made a new and extremely important experiment. Selecting a major building, the Temple of Ishtar, consort of the city's patron-god, Ashur, they carried down its excavation through the ruins of half-a-dozen earlier temples to an original archaic shrine dating from the days when Assyria was a tiny province on the borders of prosperous Sumer.

It was a brilliant feat of excavating, and the prototype of all stratigraphical investigations in later times. It involved the tracing, clearing, photographing and planning of every building in turn, before clearing away its ruins and attending to its predecessor. Its reward and justification was the discovery of the archaic temple buried beneath the deeply accumulated evidence of its great antiquity, and providing for the first time detailed evidence of Sumerian religious rites and the paraphernalia connected with them in its original setting.

During the years the Germans worked at Babylon and Ashur, expeditions were still being sponsored by institutions of other nationalities. Americans at Bismayah, the 'Lost City of Adab', were intelligently emulating German methods.[180] The French at Kish[181] and elsewhere had yet made little concession to progressive tendencies. King, representing the British Museum at Kuyunjik, may at least be given credit for being the first to suspect a pre-Assyrian settlement there. But all this work was secondary in importance compared with the strong line of scientific development apparent in the activities of the Deutsch-Orient Gesellschaft. If any reservation is to be made in praising the Germans, it is in connection with the public presentation of their results. Total preoccupation with scientific minutiae robbed their writings of all but academic appeal, and the educative potential of their work suffered accordingly. Any layman who has attempted to interest himself in the German reports is likely to agree with Koldewey when he himself admits: 'The gradual progress of the excavations, important and stimulating as it is for the explorers, appears of less interest to those who take little share in it.'[182]

EXPANSION OF RESEARCH

About the end of the first decade of the twentieth century it seemed to occur simultaneously to individuals and institutions of several nationalities that the ruins and monuments of the pre-Islamic age in Mesopotamia were by no means the only ones which merited the attention of scholars and antiquarians. In the years 1907–8 the French[183] took the initiative in making a serious examination of early Moslem and medieval remains, and by 1909 no less than four separate parties might have been found travelling around the country exploring and carefully recording the ruins and ancient buildings of these later periods. Conrad Preusser, a member of the Babylon expedition, was busy photographing and planning Christian churches and lesser-known Moslem shrines.[184] Sarre and

61 Gertrude Bell photographed outside her tent at Babylon in 1909.

Herzfeld[185] were making an even more productive journey of exploration down the Euphrates and up the Tigris, visiting among other famous Islamic sites the ruins of Samarra, where Herzfeld later excavated. The Czech geographer, Alois Musil, was making an elaborate topographical study of the Middle Euphrates and Al Jazirah.[186] And finally, Gertrude Bell had embarked on the journey of exploration referred to in an earlier chapter, and afterwards described in *Amurath to Amurath*. (It was on this journey that Miss Bell made the study of Al 'Ukhaidir later published separately.)

It is greatly to Gertrude Bell's credit that during her travels in 1909 her sensitive understanding of the peoples with whom she was associated enabled her to recognize the first stirrings of what has later come to be known as the 'Arab Awakening'. All through their centuries of repression, the Arabs had preserved at lease a sense of their own unity. They remained a community, speaking one language, descended – partly, at least – from the same ancestors and living a traditional life inherited from a common civilization. The advent of missionaries with printing presses and the improvement of education had in the end something to do with the revival of their national consciousness, and political nationalism was an early symptom of their cultural renaissance.

The early impression which Gertrude Bell received of the great change which was taking place in the Arab world is well described by her in a letter to Lord Cromer:

And yet there was a new note. For the first time in all the turbulent centuries to which those desolate regions bear witness, a potent word had gone forth, and those who had caught it listened in amazement, asking one another for an explanation of its meaning. Liberty – what is liberty? I think the question which ran so perpetually through the black tents would have received no better a solution in the royal pavilions which had once spread their glories over the plain. Idly though it fell from the lips of the Bedouin, it foretold change. That sense of change, uneasy and bewildered, hung over the whole of the Ottoman Empire; it was rarely unalloyed with anxiety; there was, it must be admitted, little to encourage an unqualified confidence in the immediate future. But one thing was certain; the moving Finger had inscribed a fresh title upon the page.[187]

Writing in 1910 Gertrude Bell could not have foreseen the form which the first step in the Arab *risorgimento* would take five years later, nor the considerable part which she was to play in it herself. When in 1917 a British-Indian army occupied Baghdad and General Maude's famous speech announced to the people Great Britain's support for the 'aspirations of their Race', she was still serving on the 'Arab Bureau' in Cairo, which contributed so much to the corresponding liberation of the Levant states. A few years later she herself returned to Iraq as Oriental Secretary to the first British High Commissioner.

The situation in regard to the proper preservation of antiquities under the new regime had become a matter of discussion within a few months of the occupation, and on Miss Bell's arrival it was at once clear that no one could be better equipped than she to assume the responsibility of creating an Antiquities Service based on the inauguration of a national collection, and to advise on the legislation required for the purpose. The newly-formed department was accordingly placed in her charge, and both it and the embryo museum were temporarily accommodated in a single modest room in the Sarai. Miss Bell thus became Iraq's first Director of Antiquities and simultaneously the founder of the Iraq Museum.

The decision to regularize and exactly prescribe the conduct of archaeological excavations came by no means too soon. Even before the signing of the 1918 armistice the British Museum already had a representative in the field. This was R. Campbell Thompson, who had worked at Nineveh before the war and now once more found himself serving in Iraq as a Captain in the Intelligence Corps. During 1918 he made some not very effectual soundings both at Ur (Tell Muqayyar) and twenty miles further south at Abu Shahrein, the biblical Eridu and site of a famous Sumerian shrine, both of which had last received the attentions of Taylor in 1853–4 (see Chapter Eleven).[188] Thompson used Indian troops to do the actual digging, whereas H. R. Hall, who succeeded him at Ur the following year, obtained for this purpose the services of seventy Turkish war-prisoners. Hall's rather tentative work at Ur was much less important than his discovery some miles away at Al 'Ubaid of a

62 R. Cambell-Thompson excavated with Woolley and T. E. Lawrence at Carchemish (1914), at Ur and Eridu (1918) and, with M. E. L. Mallowan, was the last archaeologist to dig in the Kuyunjik mound at Nineveh.

small temple platform – clearly the Sumerian prototype of the later ziggurats and contemporary with the archaic Ishtar Temple at Ashur. The fine architectural embellishments fallen from the façade of the now vanished shrine included the great copper lintel ornamented with stags heads and the lion–bird, Im–dugud. In the absence as yet of any definite regulation, they were divided between the British Museum and Gertrude Bell's new national collection. Funds grew short after this, and it was not until 1922 that an expedition, now representing the combined resources of the British Museum and the University Museum of Pennsylvania, returned to Ur under the directorship of C. L. (later Sir Leonard) Woolley. This may be said to have inaugurated the great archaeological revival of the 1920s and early 1930s.

The law which from now onwards governed the affairs of excavators, though it owed something to Turkish regulations conceived twenty-five years earlier by Hamdi Bey, was entirely in keeping with the new political identity of the state. Foreign expeditions were not permitted to operate in the country unless constituted on prescribed lines and including certain experts such as an epigraphist, an architect and a competent photographer. A party thus constituted might obtain an excavating permit for a single site whose exact limits were previously determined, and which could then be excavated only in a manner judged by the Director of Antiquities to be in keeping with the most improved and up–to–date methods. All movable finds were to be numbered and registered, and although all antiquities, movable or otherwise, were in the first place the property of the state, at the end of a season's work a representative collection of objects would be assigned to the excavator in recompense for his pains and expense. The remainder would be added to the national collection.

63 The excavation team at Ur in 1926, in front of the expedition house: Woolley himself stands on Mrs Woolley's right, with the foreman Hamoudi (half in shadow) and M. E. L. Mallowan, while on Mrs Woolley's left is Father Eric Burrows, the epigraphist.

The administration of this law presented few difficulties and it remained in force a dozen years without serious criticism except from the most irresponsible quarters. True, an equitable division of finds at the end of a season called for the most uncompromising integrity on the part of the director and corresponding forbearance among the excavators. Gertrude Bell in fact describes in one of her letters with what reluctance she found herself often compelled in the 'divisions' to relieve an excavator of some of his most cherished discoveries. Yet on the whole the archaeologists were satisfied and the size and wealth of the national collection increased at a prodigious speed without effort or expenditure on the part of the nation.

By 1932, when the British mandate ended, there were eleven expeditions of five different nationalities operating in the country simultaneously. The museum was now housed in a fairly large building, and the Department of Antiquities, now under the care of Sidney Smith (later Keeper of the Department of Egyptian and Babylonian Antiquities in the British Museum), had been augmented by the addition of several new services, such as a library, photographic section and laboratory to cope with the care and preservation of the now considerable stream of antiquities arriving from the field.

Any attempt here to summarize the work of the various institutions and individuals who contributed to the total of archaeological discovery between the wars would risk deteriorating into a mere catalogue. It will therefore be more interesting to consider the period as a whole, and observe the shifting trend in historical interest, as well as some striking new steps in the evolution of method and practice.

If one exception should be made to this ruling it is in the case of Sir Leonard Woolley's discovery of the 'Royal Cemetery' at Ur, which captured the public imagination more than any similar event since Howard Carter unearthed Tutankhamun's tomb in 1922.

THE ROYAL CEMETERY OF UR

Arriving for the first time at Tell Muqayyar in 1922, Woolley's party found their nearest point of contact with civilization to be a small station known as Ur-Junction on the Baghdad–Basra railway, having a branch line leading to Nasiriyah, some miles to the east. Both the ruined ziggurat at Ur and the tiny temple-platform at Al 'Ubaid are in fact visible from the train window. The site today is separated from the Arabian Gulf by more than 100 miles of desert and marshes, and it is difficult to imagine it in Sumerian times as a prosperous harbour-town. Yet this was what Woolley found it to have been. His early investigations revealed a fortified city covering about four square miles of country, with quays for shipping running far in among the buildings. For the rest it was occupied by streets and the houses of ordinary Sumerian citizens, except for a great walled enclosure in the centre, which contained most of its temples and other public buildings. The houses themselves were so exactly like those of a small town in Iraq today – say, for instance, Najaf – that if one could see air photographs of both they would be almost indistinguishable, except, of course, for the character of the religious buildings in the centre. Possibly one of the only differences was that, at Ur, doorways were usually arched owing to the shortage of wood for making lintels, and the rooms were narrower owing to having no steel beams. The Sumerians often buried their dead beneath the floors of their houses, and Woolley found several houses which had evidently become so full of graves that the living inhabitants had had to move.

There is also no need to say much about the daily life of the Sumerians at home, as illustrated by their private possessions which remained in the ruined houses – again because almost every domestic detail exactly resembled those which characterize the life of modern Iraqi peasants. They had the same domestic animals, ate the same food cooked in the same way, slept on the same bedding and bought their provisions in the same sort of market.

Woolley excavated almost the whole of the temple-enclosure, and the evidence which it provided of Sumerian public life was most remarkable. By far the most conspicuous building was, of course, the ziggurat. Many times rebuilt and improved, its triple staircase was still sufficiently well preserved to be partially restored, and the artificial-mountain theory was here confirmed by evidence which Woolley found suggesting that its upper terraces had been adorned with quite large trees.

64 The ziggurat at Ur immediately after excavation.

In fact the whole ritual purpose of the ziggurat was by that time beginning to become much more clear owing to the light thrown upon it by newly-deciphered Sumerian religious texts, as well as scenes represented on cylinder-seals and carved reliefs. It appeared that the small shrine at the summit of the tower was used mostly at the great New Year Festival connected with the irrigation of the land and the fertility of the crops. One imagines a long procession of priests and notables winding its way up the ziggurat, from the summit of which one could see the smoke of sacrifices rising from other shrines just visible across the wide expanse of cultivated plain, where the same ceremony was being performed. Each year a new priest and priestess were chosen to symbolize the principles of fertility in a *hieros gamos* which was the climax of the ceremony. After it was over they were perhaps considered to have no further part in ordinary human life and were themselves consequently sacrificed. It has been suggested, and is by no means improbable, that it was the graves of these unfortunate people which Woolley discovered in the neighbouring cemetery 5,000 years later. At the time they were provisionally referred to as 'kings' and 'queens', though royal titles were rare among the inscribed finds.

The cemetery was first excavated in the winter season of 1926. It lay just outside the walls of the inner city, and the graves were dug down into the accumulated rubbish heaps of previous generations. The more important tombs were rectangular chambers built of stone rubble, either vaulted or, in some cases, covered with genuine domes, which in themselves were a remarkable thing to find at such an early date. It is also interesting that out of the scores of these which appeared, only a few had escaped the attention of tomb-robbers in ancient times, and the first one which came to light was one of many which contained nothing but a few broken fragments of gold leaf littered about the floor. The first undisturbed tomb was that of some great lady whose name will never be known. A square shaft led to it from the surface, and about half-way down in the filling Woolley found the magnificent gold dagger and gold cylinder-seal of a prince (*lugal*) called Meskalamdug, who had evidently flung them into the shaft as it was being filled, in a gesture of farewell. When the tomb itself was reached, the diggers experienced one of those thrills which the archaeologist of today shares with the tomb-robbers of other times. Woolley says:

The vault had been built over a centring of stout wooden beams which ran right through the stonework, and their decay had left half a dozen holes, through which one could glimpse parts of the dim interior and by the light of electric torches, could even see on the floor below the shapes of green copper vessels and catch an occasional gleam of gold.[189]

There proved to be five bodies within, four of which were those of male servants sacrificed as part of the ritual of burial. The fifth was that of the lady herself, wearing a gold headdress and holding a fluted gold tumbler to her lips. But it remained for an adjoining pair of tombs to give the first real impression of the grim ceremony which accompanied this kind of funeral. This next pair were identified by inscribed cylinder-seals, which they contained, as a man and woman called Abargi and Pu-abi, who, as we have said, were at the time presumed to be a king and queen. First Abargi had been buried in a single vaulted chamber. In front of its door was a rectangular open shaft with a ramp leading down to it, and this was filled with the bodies of guards and attendants sacrificed so that they might accompany Abargi into the afterlife. Some of the soldiers wore copper helmets and carried spears or daggers. One had a bundle of spears with gold heads and another, silver ones. The women attendants seem to have been more nearly court ladies than servants. Nine of them wore elaborate headdresses of lapis lazuli and carnelian beads, 'Spanish combs' in silver and gold, necklaces and bracelets. There were also two four-wheeled wagons with the bones of the oxen which drew them still between the shafts and those of the drivers beside them. Amongst the other bodies lay many striking objects, such as two enormous harps heavily inlaid and decorated with bulls' heads in gold and lapis. Inside the actual vaulted tomb there was very little left, since it had been plundered in antiquity. How this had happened was explained when Woolley investigated the neighbouring tomb of Pu-abi.

65 Part of a decorated lyre from the Royal Cemetery at Ur. The bull's head is in gold and the wooden sounding-box is ornamented with a mosaic of carnelian and lapis lazuli.

Pu-abi's vault was built beside that of Abargi, but in this case the 'death-pit' with its human sacrifices was situated above and extended over the vault of the tomb next door. The workmen digging the shaft had encountered the stonework of Abargi's tomb and evidently could not resist breaking into it and rifling its contents. Afterwards the hole in the floor of the 'death pit' was concealed by placing over it a great wooden chest containing all Pu-abi's clothes.

The array of skeletons in Pu-abi's tomb was very impressive indeed. There were five soldiers, ten court ladies and a beautifully decorated chariot. There were even traces of the harness and a copper rein-ring through which the reins had passed surmounted by a charming little figure of a donkey in gold alloy. Here also there were interesting objects evidently in everyday use at the time – inlaid gaming boards, tools such as chisels and saws and a long gold tube of the sort used for drinking out of a deep jar. There was a great pile of offerings – mostly consisting of eating and drinking vessels made of gold, silver, copper or coloured stone. In this case the vault itself was undisturbed and more valuable objects lay about inside it. A list of them really reads very much like the catalogue in an auction at Christie's:

A set of silver vessels consisting of a shallow platter, a jug with tall neck and long spout and a number of slender silver tumblers nested one inside the other.
A similar tumbler in gold, fluted and chased, with a fluted feeding bowl, a chalice and a plain oval bowl.
Two magnificent lions' heads in silver.
The head of a cow in silver.
Two silver tables for offerings.
Silver lamps and two pairs of imitation cockle-shells in gold, each containing different cosmetics,

and so on. Two female attendants were beside the bier on which the queen herself lay in all her finery, holding the gold cup to her lips. In addition to the elaborate headdress reconstructed in the British Museum, she had with her a spare diadem made of white leather covered with lapis beads and supporting a row of little gold animals – gazelles, bulls, goats, etc., and a fringe of gold leaves.

In the third and largest 'death pit' the ritual sacrifices had assumed the proportions of a massacre. The bodies of six men-servants and no less than sixty-eight women were laid in regular rows across the floor – the heads of one row lying on the legs of the next. Out of this shambles one little human detail emerged. One of the maids-in-waiting had been late for her own funeral. Having no time to put on her silver hair-ribbon like the rest, she pushed it still rolled up into her pocket, where Woolley found it 5,000 years later.

THE SUMERIANS AND THEIR ORIGINS

Most of the other expeditions which came to Iraq during these early years after the First World War were equally preoccupied with Sumerian remains. The Deutsch-Orient Gesellschaft had obtained a concession for the final excavation of Warka and were meticulously planning Sumerian and pre-Sumerian temples. The French at Kish had a Sumerian palace and cemetery, and Americans at Farah (ancient Shuruppak), buildings of the same period. In 1929 James Henry Breasted's Oriental Institute of Chicago, which owed its creation to the generosity of J. D. Rockefeller, Jnr, extended its new field activities to Iraq. A concession was first obtained for the completion of Botta and Place's work at Khorsabad, but in 1931 this was extended to a group of Sumerian cities in the Diyala area east of Baghdad. Under the very able direction of Henri Frankfort, Sumerian shrines at Tell Asmar, Khafajah and Tell Agrab were soon yielding a great volume of sculptures, nothing like which had been seen since the Gudea statues from Lagash astonished the art world half a century before.

But while all this excavating was in progress, archaeologists were again occupied with the problem of origins. Who were these Sumerians, and what was the background of their precocious ingenuity? Was their culture evolved in southern Iraq from the beginning, or was it imported from elsewhere during some early migration. Following the German example at Ashur, it therefore became the fashion, when a Sumerian building had been excavated, planned and properly recorded, to sink a shaft beneath it, penetrating stage by stage through the accumulated debris of earlier occupations, until eventually the original clean soil of the delta was reached. Each stage produced characteristic pottery and other evidence to distinguish it from that above and below, and when the soundings of this sort at Ur, Warka, Kish and elsewhere were compared, they showed a most striking similarity. In every case three distinct phases could be recognized among the relics of the pre- or proto-Sumerians. All three phases had sufficient features in common to suggest a continuous and almost uninterrupted evolution, but they were conveniently distinguishable, particularly owing to their contemporary fashions of decorating pottery.

In the first phase a greenish pottery was used with rather beautiful designs in black paint. In the second, all painted decoration, disappeared and shiny burnished vessels were used, while in the third, paint returned with elaborate geometric designs in two colours.

But, meanwhile, these simple shaft-soundings were not enough to teach one more than a very little about the people who used the pottery. So the next logical stage in the investigation was to take each phase in turn and look for the site of a village or town dating from that period and never again occupied afterwards. This proved to be possible.

First of all Sir Leonard Woolley discovered that the site of Al 'Ubaid, where Hall had unearthed his Sumerian temple, actually represented a settlement or village corresponding to phase one. Here the first arrivals in southern Iraq had built themselves reed-huts on the fertile islands which were beginning to appear in the marshes of the drying delta. Everywhere among their huts he found the greenish pottery with the black designs, which had sufficiently close parallels with pottery found at sites like Susa, in the Persian mountains, tentatively to suggest that the people who made it had descended into Iraq from the Iranian highlands. So phase one, for want of a better name, came to be called after the little mound – Al 'Ubaid.

Meanwhile, the Germans, who were working at Warka on the other side of the Euphrates, had found a part of their site where phase two was represented by buildings on the surface. So phase two came to be known as the Uruk period (Uruk being the more correct spelling of the biblical Erech). The culture which these buildings represented showed a most definite advance on Woolley's marsh-dwellers of phase one, who seemed now to be enriched by an influx of new people from elsewhere. For one thing, fine temples were now built of mud-brick and decorated with a peculiar kind of mosaic. Writing appears for the first time, and primitive pictographs are inscribed with a stylus on clay tablets and signed with a carved cylinder-seal. Also there is the beginnings of relief-sculpture in which the fully-fledged Sumerians afterwards excelled.

Finally Steven Langdon of Oxford found a site near Kish called Jamdat Nasr, where phase three was represented on the surface by a temple and graves containing painted jars with distinctive geometrical designs in two colours, which again seemed to suggest a second immigration from elsewhere. Here the arts of building, sculpture, and writing were yet further advanced, and the stage was almost completely set for the beginnings of the Sumerian dynasties.

There appeared to be no definite point in the sequence described above at which it could be said that characteristically Sumerian culture first arrived. The elements of it were in fact already to be detected among the marsh-dwellers of the Al 'Ubaid phase, and it seemed likely that it was among them that it had first begun to crystallize.

And so in the 1930s the search for origins continued – no longer in southern Iraq, because its possibilities seemed to have been exhausted, but now in the Mosul area. One of the first fruits of the renewed investigation was the discovery of a new and brilliant painted-pottery culture, which extended from the Tigris westwards to the Mediterranean long before 4000 BC. This was called Tell Halaf, because it was first found by Baron Max von Oppenheim in a mound of that name near the source of the Khabur river. The beautiful polychrome vessels which were made at this period were now found by the British Museum at Arpachiyah near Nineveh and by the University Museum of Pennsylvania at Tepe Gawra beyond Khorsabad. And still it was clear, from the very advanced degree of civilization which went with it, that one was nowhere near the beginning.

In 1931 M. E. L. Mallowan, who was now working for the British Museum at Nineveh, decided to make a determined effort to find something earlier. Starting beneath the foundations of an Assyrian temple in the centre of the Kuyunjik mound, he proceeded to dig a deep shaft from the surface down to virgin soil. From this shaft, as he descended stage by stage, came pottery, cylinder-seals, beads, and even sculpture, representing all the successive phases of Iraq's history. Passing through the Assyrian, Babylonian, Akkadian and Sumerian periods he reached the phases three, two, and one of the south, and beneath it the brilliantly decorated jars of Tell Halaf. By this time he was twenty-one metres beneath the surface, and the shaft, which had started fairly large, had gradually been reduced by the spiral staircase round it to an inadequate little pit about two metres square. So that all he was able to recover from the two or three metres remaining above virgin soil was a handful of potsherds decorated with peculiar scratched designs never before seen, and from 1931 until 1943 these eleven sherds remained the only clue to the culture of the earliest-known villagers of Iraq.

THE DEVELOPMENT OF SCIENTIFIC METHOD

As has already been explained, the above is no more than a brief summary of the trend of archaeological research in Iraq between the wars. No reference has been made to those expeditions whose investigations were concerned with periods outside the main stream of historical research – Americans, for instance, at Khorsabad under Gordon Loud, exploring a great walled area of temples and public buildings, undetected by Botta and Place; André Parrot's French expedition at Tell Hariri, just over the border in Syria, revealing the ancient city of Mari, with its great archive of tablets – these and others have been most adequately recorded elsewhere and would over-complicate the theme of this narrative. One must turn rather to examine a most striking characteristic now at last observable in the work of all these expeditions, namely, the great improvement in scientific method.

A good example of the conscientious respect with which ancient sites were now treated by the new generation of archaeologists is afforded by Sir Leonard Woolley's approach to the excavation of Ur. It is a little known fact that he first discovered the famous Royal Cemetery within a few weeks of starting to dig in 1922. That it was not actually excavated until four years later was due entirely to his professional scruples. As he says himself:

In the first place our diggers were raw and clumsy, and for the clearing of a cemetery skilled labour is essential; again we were ourselves new to the country and had not had time to secure proper influence over the men, for whom the temptation of small gold objects was irresistible. . . . But the decisive argument for postponing work on the graves was this: very little indeed was known of Mesopotamian archaeology, so little that the objects from these graves were vaguely dated by such authorities as I could consult to the Neo-Babylonian, or, as more probable, to the Persian period, and though I could form no alternative theory I felt that this was doubtful in the extreme. . . . The more rich the cemetery promised to be, the more necessary was it to leave it alone until external evidence had given us a more or less definite chronology.[190]

By 1926, when the excavation of the Sumerian graves was finally undertaken, all this had changed. Woolley had by that time adapted his already considerable knowledge of excavating technique to the peculiar conditions of Mesopotamia, and was able to treat the fragile contents of the graves with the extreme delicacy and ingenuity which they called for. His skilled workmen, with the remarkable versatility characteristic of some Arabs, had quickly mastered the intricate processes of preservation with wax and plaster, and under the supervision of Woolley himself and his brilliantly competent Syrian foreman, were equal to the almost unbelievable feats of craftsmanship which were required of them. A complete and elaborate female headdress of gold and precious stones could be removed from the crushed skull which it covered, without disturbing the arrangement of the gold ornaments or the order of the beads. Alternatively the whole head with its adornment still in place could be removed intact on a bed of plaster and subsequently exhibited in a museum. A gigantic harp, whose skeleton and sounding-box had completely perished, leaving only the thousands of fragments of coloured mosaic with which it was ornamented, could be preserved without losing the shape or pattern, and if necessary reconstructed. In one case such a harp, ornamented only with a copper bull's head and one mosaic panel, had completely perished; yet the impression which it had left in the ground could be filled with liquid plaster and the exact shape thus recovered.

These random examples are perhaps enough to suggest the skill required in the new-style excavating. The dating of the graves had already largely been established by an equally ingenious process of linking archaeological data and inscriptions.

Woolley's painstaking research and methodical recording were all the more creditable in view of the somewhat inadequate financial backing which such expeditions sometimes received. Unfortunately, it was still a characteristic of most European institutions that they appeared to grudge every penny beyond the absolute minimum necessary to keep their expeditions in the field. Even this was sometimes only made possible by an additional vote from some generous private individual. The result was a tradition, particularly in English camps, of personal austerity and discomfort, as the only alternative to over-economy and improvisation in the actual field-work. In the early 1930s this circumstance was sharply emphasized by the arrival in the field of better-equipped and more heavily subsidized expeditions sponsored by the richer American universities. Notable among these was Chicago's Oriental Institute, which was now engaged in establishing a chain of elaborate research stations throughout the Near and Middle East. In a changing world, James Henry Breasted's conception for the institute of which he had become director was, to say the least of it, abreast of the times. It accorded with and even anticipated improvements in communications and security which were then beginning to appear and have since more completely materialized. These excavating establishments need no longer be envisaged as groups of intrepid explorers braving the perils and hardships of a savage country in the cause of science. They were to be research centres of western character, established in these countries with the collaboration and protection of the local government. There seemed no reason to suppose that their efficiency would be impaired by provision of the equipment and amenities enjoyed by similar institutions in America. Chicago House at Luxor in Egypt, with its quiet library and gardens, became

66 *The Chicago Oriental Institute Expedition at Tell Asmar in 1934. Left to right: Seton Lloyd, J. E. Lloyd, Leslie Grant, Mary Chubb, Rigmor Jacobsen, Rachel Levy, Harold Hill, Henri Frankfort (Director), Thorkild Jacobsen, Pinhas Delougaz and Hamilton Darby.*

a pleasant outpost of the academic world, as well as an ideal setting for deliberate research. At Megiddo in Palestine, a kite balloon was used for accurate vertical photography, while at Tell Asmar, forty miles east of Baghdad, a desert station with fully-equipped photographic studio and laboratory provided a centre for the excavation of a whole group of most productive Sumerian sites, a score of miles from the nearest modern settlement.

It may well be imagined that such new-fangled developments in the field caused some raising of eyebrows in circles where vocational austerity was still the order of the day. This was matched among the Americans by a sort of diffident incomprehension. In fact, the lean and bearded figure of the traditional archaeologist with his field-boots and solar topee, was, to the new generation, no less incongruous a figure than that which the hatless and bare-kneed American presented to the elderly French or German professor. There is little doubt, however, that each generation in the end came to learn something from the other, and that the archaeologist of the future will benefit from the experience of both.

Certainly no one could have accused the Chicago excavators in Iraq of failing in patience or neglecting any device, however intricate, for recovering scientific information. At Khafajah, one of the Diyala sites, a flat area of ground rising only a metre or so above the plain was found to represent the remnants of an important Sumerian temple. It was built of the small, irregular mud-bricks associated with the early dynasties, but its ruins had been so eroded by wind and water that the greater part of the buildings remained standing only two brick-courses high. Pinhas Delougaz, who was in charge of this section of the Tell Asmar excavations, decided that in order to recover the plan, it would be necessary to articulate every single brick, in a manner which the Germans had found effective at Warka. This great labour was cheerfully undertaken with no prospect of compensation in the form of removable objects. In itself, however, it was entirely successful. A group of Arab craftsmen were employed in the very delicate process of chipping away the dried-mud surface covering the bricks. The chips themselves had to be removed by blowing; and for this purpose Delougaz installed portable cylinders of compressed air. Gradually the pattern of the bricks gave the outline of walls, and the walls formed themselves into buildings. By the end of the second season's work, a complete and remarkable plan had been recovered.[191]

Approached by a staircase on one side was a square platform upon whose summit the principal shrine must have stood. Before it was a wide courtyard filled with pedestals for offerings and curious ritual water-basins. Grouped around this was accommodation of various sorts for the priests, and the whole precinct was enclosed and protected by a double fortification of buttressed walls, arranged in a perfect oval. As has already been said, no single part of these buildings remained standing more than a few inches above the ground; yet, save in one point where the trial trench of an earlier excavator had cut through the brickwork without detecting them, every scrap of information which they were able to afford was successfully recovered. In the end the process of cleaning had become so skilful and meticulous that, in the courtyard before the shrine, Delougaz was able to reveal and photograph footmarks of men and animals. At one point, even, one could detect the imprint left in the mud 5,000 years ago by the hoofs of a large ram, and the slipping feet of a herdsman trying to restrain him.

A more practical result of this investigation was to follow. Noticing the close similarity between the remnants of the square platform inside the Khafajah Oval and that of the contemporary Nin-Harsag Temple, which Hall found at Al 'Ubaid in 1918, Delougaz undertook a short re-examination of the latter site. After a few days' work, with his team of skilled men, he was able to trace out an oval enclosure-wall almost exactly resembling his own at Khafajah.[192] Clearly such work as this would be impossible without ample time and sufficient funds, nor would it be practical for an excavator seeking a maximum of portable antiquities. It is quoted here as a justification, if any be needed, of contemporary standards of research.

The decade which ended with the outbreak of war in 1939 brought to a conclusion a distinctive phase in the archaeological exploration of Mesopotamia by western institutions and scholars. If much of the initiative behind these activities may seem till then to have been British, a reason can be found in the close political relationships with Iraq which Britain succeeded in maintaining until comparatively recent times.

Many visitors to Baghdad during the second quarter of the present century may remember a fine building on the west bank

67 *The walls of the 'Oval Temple' enclosure at Khafajah (c.2600 BC). Surviving to a height of only a few inches, they were traced by articulating individual mud bricks.*

of the Tigris, which had served first as a British Residency and later – until its destruction by fire in 1959 – as the British Embassy's headquarters. Near its main entrance, in a vestibule which served as a miniature portrait gallery, one might see at a glance the whole saga of British representation in the country once called 'Turkish Arabia'. Here was Rich, the first great orientalist, with his look of sober responsibility; Taylor, the recluse, in his library of Arabic books and manuscripts; Rawlinson, the soldier-scholar, absorbed in the enigma of cuneiform writing; Tweedie, whose interest was divided between the men and the horses of Arabia; and others whose names have been omitted from these pages. Their faces appeared, summoned from the past: a company of witnesses to Britain's century-long association with Iraq in the realm of culture. Facing them in striking counterpoint were the High Commissioners and Ambassadors of more recent years: men whose concern was for the welfare of the modern state and whose preoccupation with its future transcended their interest in its past. And, always in one's imagination, between the two groups stood the figure of Gertrude Bell, who alone watched the transition from bondage and retrospection to the promise of political freedom, and to whose clear vision the tradition of Mesopotamian research owed its perpetuation in a new era.

CHAPTER FOURTEEN

The modern era

Soon after the admission of Iraq to the League of Nations as an independent state, significant changes took place in the Department of Antiquities. In 1932 the British Assyriologist Sidney Smith, under whose directorship it had prospered for a number of years, was recalled by the Trustees of the British Museum to fill the vacancy left by the death of H. R. Hall. In Baghdad, the newly appointed director was Sati al-Husri, already a well-known personality in the Arab world. Born at Sana'a in the Yemen, but educated at Istanbul, he had shown unusual ability as a teacher in the Imperial Ottoman Service and eventually, as an associate of the Committee of Union and Progress, had come to be considered one of the most influential educators in Turkey. Nevertheless, he emerged from the war as a fervent Arab nationalist, and had been offered by King Feisal I the task of reorganizing education in Iraq. Finding his own ideas on this subject more radical than those of his Iraqi colleagues,

68 H.R.H. Princess Alice of Athlone, received at the Iraq Museum in 1939 by the Director (Sati al-Husri) and the author.

69 *The vaulted Han Ortmah or 'Han Marjan' in Baghdad, dating from the fourteenth century. It was restored as a museum by the Iraq Antiquities Department in 1939.*

he accepted instead the less conspicuous post we have already mentioned.

In Iraq during these early days of independence, the attention of the young was already being directed to the nation's unique historical heritage, partly as a corrective to indiscriminate westernization. It was not, therefore, surprising that in the Antiquities Department new interest should now be taken in Islamic relics, with emphasis on such scanty remains as were still to be found testifying to the greatness of the 'Abbasid Caliphate. To this purpose Sati applied the full force of his personal energy and administrative ability. A large part of the Department's funds were now devoted to the restoration of Islamic monuments in Baghdad; precious architectural relics were rescued from shrines in remoter parts of the country, whose ruinous state was beyond repair, and exhibited in the old ''Abbasid Palace'. Other buildings which received attention at this time included the 'Abbasid Minaret in the Suq al-Ghasil and the huge fourteenth century caravanserai, known as the Han Ortmah or 'Han Marjan', which was by then filled with rubble almost to the springing of its vaults. One of the city gates, dating from the last days of the Caliphate in the thirteenth century, was nicely rebuilt to make a Museum of Arms and Weapons.

A less welcome aspect of Sati's patriotic reformation (soundly based, as one must admit, on the records of earlier times) was expressed in his thinly-disguised distaste for the activities of foreign archaeologists. Soon after his appointment, this led him to revise the terms of the old Antiquities Law, conscientiously devised by

Gertrude Bell ten years earlier. In the new version a clause was introduced, greatly limiting the rights of foreign excavators to a share of their removable finds. There were at that time half-a-dozen major expeditions well established in the Mesopotamian field, and Sati had perhaps underestimated the reaction of their directors to these new and crippling restrictions. Already, in 1932, Woolley had withdrawn from Ur, to dig under more lenient regulations in Syria. Two years later, Parrot's party from the Louvre, on the point of transferring their activities from Telloh to ancient Larsa, were diverted instead to the site of Mari, also beyond the Syrian frontier. Their example was then followed by Mallowan's team from Arpachiyah, who were soon to be found breaking new ground on the banks of the Syrian Khabur river. By 1939, American excavators too had left the country and only the Germans remained at Warka.

It was in this same year, shortly before the outbreak of war, that the present writer accepted the post of Technical Adviser to the newly-styled Directorate General of Antiquities: a fact which may perhaps be taken to excuse the occasional use of the first person singular in the paragraphs which follow.

Returning to Baghdad in the spring of 1939, after two seasons' excavation in Turkey, I found Gertrude Bell's museum and its dependent offices still housed in the old building at the eastern end of the Shuhada Bridge, which she had appropriated for the purpose in 1926. I was installed in a room which still contained her 'roll-top' desk and her portrait hung on the wall behind my chair. For the rest, the first thing that became apparent was that both the growth of the Department and the development of the museum were greatly hampered by lack of space, and that the Director was considering ambitious plans for a new and magnificent building to accommodate them. A design had been prepared by German architects and although, for the present at least, its funding appeared to be totally impracticable, he had already selected a fine site on the west bank of the river. Faced, however, with the imminent danger of its appropriation by some other ministry, he seemed anxious to stake his claim by some form of preparatory building activity. The solution which had occurred to him was that of constructing some sort of impressive portico at the entrance to the (still empty) site. He wanted something 'in the Assyrian Style' and already had his eye on the fine pair of *lamassu* winged bulls which Gordon Loud had discovered some years before at Khorsabad, afterwards reburying them for protection. Their transport to Baghdad and installation in a mock-Assyrian gateway became my first assignment and has been referred to in Chapter Nine. Today, forty years later, the gateway is still there, harmonizing curiously with the modern museum building behind it.

Another matter of great interest to Sati al-Husri in those days was the inauguration of excavations by the Department itself. At

70 The excavated foundations of the mosque and Dar-al-'Imara Palace at Wasit, near Kut, built by the 'Umayyad governor of Iraq, Hajjaj ibn Yusuf, in about AD 703. The site was investigated by the Iraq Antiquities Department between 1936 and 1942.

first it had been clear to him that his staff were as yet inadequately qualified in archaeological method. But when in 1936 two young Iraqi students returned from the United States after obtaining archaeological degrees at the University of Chicago, his intention became more practicable. Whatever motive had prompted his choice of America (a country for which he had little affection) for their specialized training, the decision now seemed to have been well advised. Of the two, Taha Baqir was primarily a cuneiformist and likely to be of greater use at a later stage; but Fuad Safar, after some preliminary experience in the field, proved perfectly competent to conduct an uncomplicated excavation, with the support of a locally-trained architect-surveyor, Mohammed-Ali Mustafa.

Under these circumstances, Sati's first experiments were wisely confined to Islamic sites, with substantial architectural remains easily accessible. When therefore I arrived in 1939, I found two excavations intermittently in progress without the benefit of foreign assistance. One of these was at Samarra, the short-lived capital of the Caliphs in the ninth century AD, already very thoroughly explored by Herzfeld from 1912 onwards. Great quantities of gypsum wall-ornament had been collected from the ruins of luxurious private houses, some of whose plans had been recorded. Unfortunately neither the translator nor the Government Press had done justice to the report on this subject which had already been published. The second excavation, by that time in the hands of Fuad Safar, was at the site of Wasit, the briefly prosperous Islamic city, founded in about AD 703 on the old Dujaila Canal, near Kut. Here, one of the three most celebrated 'Umayyad mosques, with its adjacent 'Dar-al-'Imara' Palace, had been admirably excavated, and I was shown Fuad's draft of a most professional report in English, complete with good plans and

71 The excavation team at Tell 'Uqair in 1941. Standing (left to right): Sa'id Jafar (photographer), Fuad Safar and Seton Lloyd (joint directors), and Mohammed-Ali Mustafa (architect). Seated: the drivers Mahmud, Peter and Suheil.

drawings of pottery.[193] Rather than entrust this to local printers, I took the typescript to Cairo, where I obtained help in printing it, both from the French Institute and from H. E. Taha Hussain, the blind Minister of Education, whose remarkable autobiography (*Al Ayyam*, published in English as *The Stream of Days*) eventually appeared almost simultaneously with Fuad's report in 1945.

By 1941 the time finally seemed ripe to organize the first Iraqi excavation at a pre-Islamic site. Nor was it difficult to find a suitable one, since we now had our own inspectors working with the Land Settlement Officers and bringing in piles of surface finds from unexcavated sites claimed as Crown Property. Our choice was Tell 'Uqair, near the much bigger mound called Tell Ibrahim (ancient Kutha). And here, as is now widely known, we came upon a well-preserved proto-Sumerian temple, decorated internally with the earliest coloured murals at that time known, dating from *c.*3000 BC. This was a remarkable and curious excavation. The walls of the temple on its mud-brick platform remained standing, in part several metres high, so that our wall-tracers were able, for once, actually to enter the building through its own main entrance. When it became clear that the interior was decorated with 'pictures', there was justifiably some excitement and the Sherqati workmen gathered in a bunch to inspect. This scene has remained in one's mind, because at that moment a local employee, working higher up the hill, dug into a nest of young scorpions and, wishing to join in the fun, took up a shovel-full and slung them over the heads of the crowd below.

The directorship and subsequent publication of the excavation at 'Uqair was shared between myself and Fuad Safar.[194] It marked the beginning of a partnership between us which lasted for eight years and developed into a very close friendship. In later times, as Inspector-General, he became the *eminence grise* of the Department. His tragic death on duty in 1978 was a serious loss to Mesopotamian archaeology and a great blow to his many friends.

The 'Uqair excavation was interrupted in May 1941 by the pro-German insurrection in Iraq, led by Rashid Ali al-Gailani, during which the Baghdad British were confined to the Embassy compound. But we returned to 'Uqair in June to finish our second season's work, finding that damage to the site was restricted to a hole in the temple platform where an anti-aircraft battery had been installed. By then, Sati al-Husri and the Museum Curator, Abdul-Razzaq Lutfi, had left the country, but the work of the Department proceeded normally under my temporary guidance. By 1942 we had started another dig, nearer to Baghdad at 'Aqar Quf (ancient Dur Kurigalzu), where the Kassite kings had built their own capital city in the mid-second millennium BC. This time it was Taha Baqir who took charge of the enterprise, once more assisted by the architect Mohammed-Ali Mustafa. It was carried out on a very large scale. The façades of the colossal ziggurat, with the temples surrounding it, were exposed, and the adjoining royal palace provided much inscribed material, from which Taha could resolve some of the enigmas of Kassite history. My two Iraqi colleagues showed remarkable ability in conducting this major excavation, my own help being limited to weekly visits. I was at that time partly occupied in furnishing the fine old house at South Gate, which I shared with a number of batchelor friends until my marriage. Also, a new Director-General had been appointed to the Antiquities Department, which seemed galvanized into sudden activity.

The waning influence of Sati al-Husri's vigorous nationalism was now renewed in a more acceptable form by the urbane

72 Staff of the Iraq Antiquities Department and guests in front of the eroded ziggurat of 'Aqar Quf in 1944. Standing, left to right: Fuad Safar (4th), Taha Baqir, Director (6th), Antran (8th), Selim Lewi (9th), Mohammed-Ali Mustafa, architect (12th). Seated, left to right: Seton Lloyd (3rd), Dr Naji al-Asil (7th), Ulrica Lloyd (8th), Christopher Scaife (9th), Rita Maxwell (10th), Dr R. S. Stacey (11th).

diplomacy of Dr Naji al-Asil. The status and dignity which our establishment began to attain under his direction owed something to the personal image which he himself succeeded deservedly in acquiring. In earlier days, Dr Naji had been an eye-specialist in the service of the Hashemite ruler, King Hussein of the Hejaz, to whom his literary and linguistic gifts proved invaluable. Loyalty to the king led to his appointment as Arab plenipotentiary in London: a post which he retained until the overthrow of Hussein by Abdul-Aziz ibn as-Sa'ud. Returning to Baghdad in 1925, he first devoted his energies to the teaching of Islamic history and philosophy, but the end of the British mandate in 1932 served to revive his interest in foreign affairs, and he became Foreign Minister for a brief time under the precociously liberal premiership of Hikmet Suleiman. A change of government left him for some years at odds with the ruling majority; his eventual appointment to our Department resulted partly from a belated reconciliation with his political rivals. He was thus enabled to devote his remaining years to the pragmatic advancement of Mesopotamian archaeology, in a milieu unhampered by xenophobia.

While Naji was reorganizing the Department in 1943, my partnership with Fuad was renewed in an excavation which caused something of a stir when reported in *The Times* and elsewhere.[194] Pottery identical with that discovered by Mallowan, almost thirty metres beneath the surface of the palace mound at Nineveh, had attracted us to a small site called Hassuna, on the fringe of the cultivation south of Mosul. And it was here, during two seasons' digging, that we were able to find evidence dating from the sixth millennium BC of a people in transition from a nomadic life to settled agriculture. The camp-fires of the earliest arrivals were

73 (Opposite) Excavations at Hassuna in 1944.

74 Re-discovery of the black lion sculpture at Eridu (probably c.2000 BC); shown by Dr Naji al-Asil to the British Ambassador (right), Mr Stewart Perowne and Lady Stonehewer-Bird.

there, surrounded by their primitive belongings. Their tall 'milk-jars' temporarily interested us, because they were usually half filled with the tiny bones of tailless amphibians. This was explained one morning when we returned to the dig after two days of rain, for the jars, which had been emptied for photographic purposes, each contained a party of toads, this time ~~~~~~~~~~~~~~

Our little tent camp at Hassuna tended to attract the nightly attention of Jabur tribesmen from the open Jazirah desert. During the frequent exchanges of fire, our guards were instructed to shoot over their heads; but a young Kurd, enlisted after the briefing, next morning collected a punctured tobacco pouch and a broken pipe, with which he seemed better satisfied. This was the situation when my wife joined me at Hassuna after our marriage in 1944. Our relations with the Jabur improved greatly when she set up a miniature medical clinic for their families.

Back in Baghdad, Naji had conceived the extremely sensible idea that the Department should publish annually its own archaeological journal. It was to be called *Sumer* and, for the cover, my wife designed an appropriate monogram, which has since become the Department's symbol. To correspond with the first issue of *Sumer*. Naji also had a prestigious plan to start excavations at the site of ancient Eridu: reputedly the earliest Sumerian shrine, dedicated to Enki, God of Wisdom. Abu Shahrein, as it is now called, occupies a very isolated situation in the southern desert, about ten miles from Ur, and it was from the ruins of Woolley's old expedition-house there that we were compelled to bring building materials for our own, including bricks stamped with the names of Babylonian kings. The flat-topped mound, twenty metres high, with the scanty remains of a ziggurat at one end, seemed partly obscured by long curtains of drifting sand trailing far out into the plain on the sides away from the prevailing wind. We had no illusions about the climatic difficulties in store for us: endemic duststorms alternating with spells of heavy rain. Our new building was strengthened accordingly and survived four seasons' work, though requiring to be re-excavated at the start of each season.

Attempts to excavate Tell Abu Shahrein had been made in the past by no less than three British archaeologists; but clearly none of them could make head or tail of the ruins. This now seems hardly surprising, to judge by the complicated history of the city which gradually became clear in the course of our own excavations. The first settlers there in about 5000 BC built a tiny chapel, perhaps already dedicated to the god Enki. This was rebuilt on an increasingly pretentious scale throughout the four phases of the so-called ''Ubaidian period'. Raised now on its own platform, the temple increased in grandeur from 3500 BC onwards, when an enclosed precinct of subsidiary buildings was annexed to it, protected by a stone retaining-wall. Later, in the 'Uruk period', these minor buildings were demolished and sealed in, to form an emplacement for a final manifestation of contemporary architecture and ornament. Soon after 3000 BC the whole complex seems to have been abandoned and remained almost deserted until, nearly a thousand years later, a pious king of Ur revived the cult and built a clumsy ziggurat at the highest point of the ruins.

Outside the sacred enclosure, we found the graves of the 'Ubaidian people, often buried in pairs with their beautiful painted pottery and personal belongings. Sometimes a man even had the bones of his dog laid across his chest, with a meatbone near its mouth. The first of these burials were found at a time when I had gone to spend Christmas in Baghdad. When I returned I described the scene in a letter to my wife:

When I got to the dig, there they all were, lying neatly and quietly with their feet all pointing one way: the people who painted the pottery and brought their fish as offerings to that little temple: brittle and rather chilly, but with their comforting household things laid beside them. I can never get over that feeling of being suddenly *among them* when you find the graves. . . .

While Fuad and I were excavating Eridu, Taha Baqir had the advantage of attending to an attractive little site called Tell Harmal, discovered on the Baquba road hardly five miles from the centre of Baghdad, where a new suburb was about to be built. This proved to have been an administrative post on the fringes of the second-millennium city-state of Eshnunna, which had made its first appearance on the historical map during the excavation of its capital at Tell Asmar during the 1930s. The ancient name of the new site proved to be Shaduppum, which could be translated as 'The Treasury' or 'Accountants' Office'; and this helped to explain the abundance of cuneiform tablets which came to light, including among them Eshnunna's Code of Laws.

75 Excavated ruins of the principal temple at Tell Harmal (Shaduppum), near Baghdad, where the tablets were found, including the Eshnunna Code of Laws, written in Akkadian.

An irregular rectangle of defensive walls enclosed one major temple and a complex of clerical buildings: the latter a goldmine of inscribed material. The entrance to the temple was guarded by a magnificent pair of terracotta lions, the innumerable fragments of which could be pieced together in the Iraq Museum's increasingly efficient laboratory. Also, with a maximum dimension of only 150 metres, it proved possible, between 1945 and 1949, to excavate and partially restore the entire fortress, while its written documents compensated us in part for the lack of inscribed material at Eridu.[195]

It was at the time when these two excavations were practically finished that I myself was offered and accepted the Directorship of the British Institute of Archaeology at Ankara, which necessitated my final departure from Baghdad. My obvious regrets on this score were to some extent mitigated by a simultaneous event which was a source of great satisfaction. In 1949, my close friend and colleague, Max Mallowan returned, to renew the field activities of the British School of Archaeology in Iraq, founded by Gertrude Bell.

THE POST-WAR YEARS

During the 1950s archaeological activity in Iraq seemed to acquire a new lease of life. Foreign expeditions, now often staffed by specialists from new faculties in western universities, found themselves plentifully endowed. Prominent among these were Americans, who returned to the country, either to resume excavations or to plan useful forms of topographical survey. Once more there was a team from Pennsylvania at the site of Nippur; another from Chicago renewed the exploration of the Diyala region east of Baghdad – the once-populous province revealed a century earlier by Felix Jones' survey of the old Nahr Awan Canal.[196] In the sphere of prehistory, a pointer to future developments in archaeology was R. J. Braidwood's Jarmo Project: an excavation of an early village site shared with environmental specialists on an inter-disciplinary basis.[197] In 1950 the Germans had returned to Warka under the leadership of H. J. Lenzen, a veteran of pre-war seasons, whose fabulous discoveries of proto-Sumerian architecture were to continue without interruption for a further two decades. Beyond the Syrian frontier in the north, the French too resumed work at Mari, still under the leadership of André Parrot, with a prospect of many new and striking finds. With all this activity in progress among non-Arab archaeologists, Naji al-Asil and his staff most willingly added their own quota of exploration and reconstruction.

The Eridu excavations had come to an end in 1949, when it began to appear that the remainder of the original temple complex lay beneath the immovable bulk of the later ziggurat ruins. Fuad Safar had indeed found the remnants of two modest Sumerian palaces outside the perimeter of the main mound; but their excavation had added little to our knowledge of the period to which they belonged. The sensation caused by our finds in previous seasons had greatly enhanced the reputation of the Department and its Director; but it also became clear that professional colleagues were anxiously awaiting a fuller publication than the preliminary reports in *Sumer* and elsewhere could provide. Before leaving Iraq, I had completed some chapters and drawings for such a book, but had been com-pelled to rely on others for the remainder, since it depended on field-notes kept in Arabic. Knowing the pressure of work to which Fuad was continually submitted, I had privately doubted whether the book would ever see the light of day. Its appearance thirty years later will now be a posthumous tribute to his work and integrity.

By 1951, Professor Safar had already taken charge of another major operation, which was destined to absorb much of the Department's funds and energies during the following quarter-century. This time it was the excavation of Hatra: the strange, isolated ruins of a walled city in the centre of the Jazirah desert, west of Ashur. Naji and his advisers could hardly have chosen a site of greater interest to Arab historians, or more abundantly rewarding for the study of art in Parthian times.[198] A single example of the many Aramaic and other inscriptions discovered in or near Hatra's great central palace may serve to support this contention. Dated to approximately AD 78, it reads: 'SANATRUQ, KING OF THE ARABS, SON OF NASRU MY LORD BUILT IT.' At the time when this Arab dynasty was ruling, Hatra had long been a dependency of the Parthian Empire. Strategically placed between the two rivers, it served as a centre for the enlistment and training of Jazirah tribes-men and, from now onwards, with fortress walls enclosing an area of almost 800 acres, it repeatedly resisted the attacks made by Roman armies under the emperors Trajan and Severus.* When however, the conquests of the Sassanian kings threatened the existence of the Parthian Dynasty, it was to the Romans that Hatra turned for protection against its new enemy: a step which eventually led to its capture and destruction by Shapur I in AD 232. Passing by its ruins in AD 363, the Latin historian Ammianus Marcellinus described it as 'an old city lying in the midst of the desert and long abandoned'.

Successive phases in the history of Hatra as a city are interestingly reflected in the stylistically hybrid character of its surviving architecture and sculpture. Columned buildings of Hellenistic times contrast strangely with the ponderous ruins of a great Parthian palace-temple, whose arched façade and open-fronted *iwans* face a broad parade-ground. The main sanctuary is dedicated to Shamash, the old Babylonian sun-god; but a dozen minor shrines in its vicinity have proved to be associated by their contents with a wide variety of other deities. Among the many sculptures derived from this source, one fine statue is identified by a Latin inscription as 'Nergal-Hercules'; another, combining both Assyrian and classical attributes, as 'Ashur-Bel'.

To reach Hatra from the east, one crosses a perennial stream called Wadi Tharthar. When planning my first visit there with Fuad in 1941, we had first to ensure that the rickety bridge over the wadi was passable by car. Hatra itself was (and still is) a meeting-place for the great Shammar tribe; so, in the end, we were escorted there by the paramount sheikh, Ajil Yarwah – a patriarchal figure of great stature, heading an impressive convoy of dusty touring-cars. He had insisted that the Tharthar stream was in any case 'fordable' and now, finding it in spate, would not be persuaded to the contrary until he had sent in his negro servant on the end of a rope. Swept away by the tide, he was quickly retrieved, uttering tremendous curses; but the bridge proved usable and, coming over a low hill Hatra duly appeared, confronting us with an 'Old Testament' scene whose every detail must have remained unchanged for a thousand years. Within the ruined walls, a section of the Shammar were encamped, exactly as Layard must have seen them on a previous occasion (Chapter Eight): family groups of black tents, each with its fine horses, saluki dogs and grazing camels. Returning there as an official guest in 1966, I was unprepared for its appearance as a 'tourist centre'. Horses and dogs were gone; a single camel in gaudy trappings was paraded before clicking cameras, and beside the car-park there was at least one helicopter. Compensation for these changes was to be found only in the painstaking and effective restoration of ancient buildings, which do credit to Iraqi craftsmanship.

It has been tempting to dwell on the work at Hatra, if only

76 A finely preserved royal statue from Hatra of the first century BC. Ht c. 2.30 m.

* The city's contemporary history is recorded by the Latin writers, Herodian and Dio Cassius.

because the architecture which it has revealed and the great collection of sculpture now shared between the museums of Baghdad and Mosul, have till now been made available for study exclusively in publications with very limited circulation. If we return now to the contemporary activities of foreign archaeologists over the past three decades, a different picture presents itself. First then, the British School of Archaeology in Iraq. Mallowan, after his return to Baghdad in 1949, had little difficulty in choosing a site for prolonged excavation. For him, certain Assyrian mounds were still permeated with the memory of British explorers in the last century, whose names have appeared earlier in this book. After brief preliminary soundings therefore, his thoughts were drawn inexorably back to the site of Nimrud and to the unlimited potentialities which Layard's work there had revealed. His proposal to act on this impulse proved agreeable to Naji al-Asil and he was soon installed on the mound with a small party of helpers.

The dig at Nimrud lasted for twelve years, with two short intervals caused by political events. Mallowan himself continued to act as director until 1957, when his leadership of the expedition was taken over by a younger excavator, David Oates, about whom more will presently be said. The workforce during the first season consisted of seventy men, about all that a party of four people could manage; but Mallowan's own account of a later year, when his staff had increased to twelve, speaks of 200 workmen, with wages at the equivalent of three shillings (15p) per day. By the time the operation came to an end in 1963, the accumulated results in the form of art treasures, inscribed texts and recorded architecture were of course prodigious. But since in the present context, references to them must necessarily be restricted, attention should be drawn to Mallowan's own magnificent publication.[199] This book, in two

77 Excavations by Mallowan in progress on the palace mound at Nimrud in 1956, seen from the ziggurat.

volumes with plans composing a third, can only be considered something of a masterpiece. The similarity of its title to Layard's 1849 publication alone serves to emphasize the writer's strong sense of continuity in British archaeological tradition. The style of the text also, as he himself explains, is modelled to some extent on that of his predecessor.

Starting in the unexcavated chambers of Layard's North-west Palace, one of Mallowan's earliest finds was the great inscribed stela, bearing Ashur-nasirpal's account of how the city was rebuilt and of the great feast at which he claims to have entertained 69,574 people in celebration of his accomplishment. But several of his most striking finds in this area came from brick-lined water wells, which Layard had no time fully to explore. From one of these, at a depth of twenty-four metres, came first the pair of carved ivory plaques, jewels of craftsmanship depicting a 'negro mauled by a lioness', one of which is in the British Museum; secondly, the beautiful female head now popularly known as the 'Mona Lisa'. Phoenician ivories such as these were a class of object plentifully represented among the finds in other parts of the site. Over the following years, excavations proceeded from one section of the citadel to another, with finds notably concentrated in such buildings as the 'Burnt Palace' and the 'Nabu Temple'. But private houses were excavated too, while the stone retaining walls and quays along the waterfront were also investigated.

78 *Ivory head of a woman, perhaps from a piece of ornamental furniture, found by Mallowan in a well beneath the 'Northwest Palace' at Nimrud, and known to the excavators as the 'Mona Lisa'. Late eighth century BC. Ht 16 cm.*

In 1957, a new discovery shifted the centre of operations at Nimrud to a mound in the extreme south-east corner of the Lower City. Here, in an area marked on Felix Jones' map[200] as 'Eastern Suburbs', David Oates had discovered the enormous Royal Arsenal of the Assyrian kings, later to be called 'Fort Shalmaneser'. Built around three wide courtyards were chambers and galleries providing accommodation for every kind of military ordnance, and, annexed to these, a residential palace facing an impressive parade ground. A secondary purpose for which these buildings had been used was to store the rich booty brought back by the kings' foreign campaigns – predominantly finely-carved ivory ornament, once applied to furniture or other objects. One gallery alone, with a length of 30 metres, was filled to a depth of 1·50 metres with riches of this sort, lying in disorder. The delicate task of removing them proved so formidable that, when the Nimrud expedition came to an end in 1963, other such galleries had to be left unexcavated.

We have been speaking till now about isolated excavations; but in these same years, much was also undertaken in the realm of surface exploration, relating to historical environment. In southern Iraq, American studies of this sort, combining the physical evidence with that of the written texts, have already been mentioned. Their usefulness has long been apparent, and was recently once more emphasized in a passage from the work of a younger writer:

79 *A fine ivory carving from Mallowan's excavations in 'Fort Shalmaneser' at Nimrud, showing Egyptian influence. Ht 13.2 cm.*

The technique of archaeological survey has taken its place alongside excavation and the use of written sources as a third avenue by which we may approach the Mesopotamian world. It can throw light on subjects beyond the reach of the other techniques, and its potential value is evident to anyone concerned with a subject such as the agricultural structure which underpinned the military expansion of the Assyrian empire, or the exact nature of the urban revolution in early Sumer.[201]

So, in the northern provinces also, during the 1950s, travelling scholars set out to create a more orderly picture of the country which, for a thousand years had been regarded as the homeland of the Assyrians. Already, in pre-war days, land surveys had contributed something to the recognition of settlement patterns and communications; but their findings needed to be integrated by study in greater depth. Meanwhile, the whole subject had been given new interest and urgency by Parrot's discovery of a great archive in the palace at Mari, whose contents were at that time being gradually elucidated. Here, among the administrative records and state documents of two different kings, geographical references appeared in bewildering numbers among their day-to-day correspondence. The territory of the Assyrian Shamsi-Adad I, who had temporarily annexed Mari in about 1800 BC, covered the whole of Assyria southward to the Eshnunna frontier; that of Zimrilim, a more northerly province; so, apart from other matters, a wealth of topographical information seemed suddenly available for correlation with the more scanty findings of archaeology.

Among the first to accept this challenge was David Oates, a British archaeologist already mentioned, who was later to direct the excavations at 'Fort Shalmaneser'. The findings from his survey (1954–8) were incorporated in 'a profoundly interesting book' (Mallowan),[202] dealing largely with the subject just envisaged. Nor had his interests been confined chronologically to the 'Assyrian millennium'. Dedicated in part as a tribute to the work of Poidebard and Stein on the *limes* frontiers of Rome, its coverage was extended to remains of the Hellenistic, Parthian and Byzantine periods, all well represented in his chosen area. Where earlier epochs were concerned, his attention was attracted in particular to the much-neglected Sinjar province, west of Mosul; and it was there that he selected a site for further investigation when his work at Nimrud came to an end.[203]

Tell al-Rimah, excavated in due course by the British School between 1964 and 1971, entirely fulfilled Oates' expectations. With its unique architecture and well-documented history as a state capital, it has provided us with an illuminating vignette of political and domestic life in the second and first millennia BC.

Meanwhile, throughout the 1960s and 1970s studies of Neolithic man and the origins of agriculture had by no means been neglected. Within a few miles of Rimah, Soviet archaeologists at Yarim Tepe had been industriously elaborating our knowledge of the 'Hassuna phase' in prehistory, while east of Sinjar, Japanese excavators were studying its sequel. On the east bank of the Tigris, near Samarra, an Iraqi scholar named Behnam Abu-al-Soof found a fortified village of the mid-fifth millennium BC, with mud-brick houses built to a uniform plan and a congregation of cult-figures sculptured in stone. On the British side, two prehistorians who had in their time assisted Mallowan at Nimrud, themselves conducted successful excavations at sites selected during regional surveys. Joan Oates at Choga Mami, on the eastern limits of the alluvial plain, traced the remains of embryo irrigation canals, already serving agricultural purposes in the fifth millennium BC. Diana Helbaek, working in the Jazirah desert near Hatra, made an even more striking discovery. In a tiny mound called Umm Dabaghiyah, in a level of occupation perhaps contemporary with the camp-sites at Hassuna, regular ranges of small storage compartments had been built, apparently for the purpose of drying skins. Near them quantities of animal bones were found, among which the great majority were those of the onager (wild ass). The excavator boldly postulated the existence in this desert outpost of a commerce in onager skins; and, during her final season of digging, this theory was (almost miraculously) substantiated. The hunters themselves lived in clay houses ('with hooded chimney-breasts and plastered cupboards'). On their walls were found graffiti, clearly depicting the capture of these animals with the aid of nets.[204]

And so, the prolonged enquiry into the history of Mesopotamian man still continues, among the mounds which his activities have created. If in recent years some preference may have been shown for new forms of research which amplify our knowledge of his social and technological development, the reasons are not far to seek. Most greatly prized by excavators in earlier times were relics of his art and architecture, or inscriptions proving his capacity for abstract thought. The main source of such finds were of course sites which could be identified by one means or another as ancient centres of wealth and culture. To suggest today that all of these have now been located – let alone exhaustively explored – would plainly be ridiculous, and we must accept the fact that the total evidence accumulated during over a century of excavation amounts to no more than a small fraction of what remains to be found. Nevertheless, in a changing world new factors have now to be considered in planning an archaeological operation, and excavators are faced with unfamiliar problems. First, in the realm of economy, they may find that, since the days of the 'great excavations', the cost of labour has increased by as much as 1,000 per cent, making the purely mechanical task of removing unstratified debris prohibitive. They will find that modern systems of excavation are 'labour-intensive' and accordingly feel compelled to choose sites where the occupation-level of major relevance occurs near the surface. Alternatively, operations in the form of 'surveys', about which much has already been said, may recommend themselves on economic grounds. To these the term 'superficial' can only be applied in the most literal sense.

Notes

Chapter One (pp. 7–21) 1 Eldred 1583. 2 Beauchamp 1791. 3 Tudela 1575. 4 Ratisbon 1871. 5 Tavernier 1678. 6 Otter 1748. 7 D'Anville 1779. 8 Sienna 1683. 9 Haukal 1938–9. 10 Della Valle 1663. 11 Tudela 1575. 12 Rauwolff 1693, p. 204. 13 Shirley 1613. 14 Niebuhr 1776. 15 Alexander 1928. 16 Harris 1944. Also *Barclay Fox's Journals* (ed. Britt), London 1979. 17 Rawlinson 1898. 18 'Coronation'. 19 Layard 1887. 20 Described much later in Mitford 1884. 21 Rich 1836, vol. 1, p. 22.

Chapter Two (pp. 22–31) 22 Buckingham 1827. 23 Soane 1912. 24 Bell 1924. 25 See also Hasankeyf (*sic*) in Hachette 1960, p. 445. Gertrude Bell (1924, footnote on p. 229) apparently missed the place.

Chapter Three (pp. 32–42) 26 Longrigg 1925, p. 252. 27 Alexander 1928, p. 33. 28 Buckingham 1827, vol. 2, p. 214. 29 Buckingham 1827, vol. 2, p. 192. 30 Alexander 1928, p. 68. 31 Alexander 1928, pp. 65–6. 32 Alexander 1928, p. 41. 33 Alexander 1928, p. 58. 34 Alexander 1928, p. 61. 35 Alexander 1928, p. 82. 36 Rich 1839, p. 1.

Chapter Four (pp. 43–56) 37 Buckingham 1827. 38 Buckingham 1827, p. 508. 39 For a full and up-to-date description of Urfa, see Segal 1970. 40 Buckingham 1827, p. 104. 41 Tavernier 1678, p. 69. 42 Cf. map in Oates 1968, Fig. 2.

Chapter Five (pp. 57–72) 43 Alexander 1928, p. 130. 44 See Barnett 1974. 45 Buckingham 1827, vol. 2, pp. 160 ff. 46 Alexander 1928, p. 324. 47 Buckingham 1827, vol. 2, p. 490. 48 Buckingham 1827, vol. 2, p. 211. 49 Hilprecht 1904, p. 44. See also Barnett 1972. 50 Porter 1822. 51 See Baqir 1944–6. 52 Porter 1822, vol. 2, p. 245. 53 Rich 1836, vol. 1, p. 326. 54 Barnett 1974, pp. 24 ff, has an account of Bellino's death. 55 Bell 1924, p. 282. 56 Rich 1836, vol. 2, p. 51. 57 Alexander 1928, p. 298. 58 Rich 1836, vol. 1, p. xxx.

Chapter Six (pp. 73–86) 59 Gadd 1936, p. 12. 60 Budge 1925, p. 26. 61 Cf. Rawlinson 1898, p. 67. 62 Budge 1925, p. 33. 63 Filmer 1937. 64 Rawlinson 1898, p. 146; but see also Cameron. 65 Budge 1925, p. 35. 66 Budge 1925, p. 36. 67 Baillie-Fraser 1840. 68 Grove 1831. 69 Grove 1831, p. 198. 70 Coke 1927, p. 259. 71 Hilprecht 1904. 72 Baillie-Fraser 1840, vol. 2, pp. 1–165. 73 Budge 1920, vol. 2, p. 292. The tablet is now reinstated in the wall of the British Consulate-General in Basra. 74 Ainsworth 1888, vol. 1, p. vi. 75 Principal titles: Chesney 1850, Chesney 1868 and Ainsworth 1830. 76 Richardson 1840. 77 Ainsworth 1888. 78 Rawlinson 1898, p. 142.

Chapter Seven (pp. 87–100) 79 Layard 1849a. 80 Layard 1887, p. 17. 81 Gadd 1936, p. 14. 82 Layard 1849a. For other titles by Layard, see Bibliography. 83 Layard 1893, vol. 1, p. 327. 84 Layard 1893, vol. 1, p. 329. 85 See Botta 1849–50. 86 Layard 1803, vol. 1, p. 339. 87 Wigram 1914, Ch. 5. 88 Sykes 1915.

Chapter Eight (pp. 101–114) 89 Layard 1849a, vol. 2, p. 191. 90 Ross 1902, p. x. 91 Layard 1849a. 92 Rawlinson 1898, p. 152. 93 Layard 1849a, vol. 1, pp. 79–80. 94 Hilprecht 1903, p. 102. 95 Gadd 1936. 96 Layard 1849a, vol. 1, p. 83. 97 Layard 1849a, vol. 1, p. 310. 98 Cf. Oates 1968, Fig. 2, p. 14; also Lloyd 1978, pp. 123 ff.

Chapter Nine (pp. 115–129) 99 Layard 1849a, vol. 1, p. 353. 100 Layard 1849a, vol. 1, p. 341. 101 Layard 1849a, vol. 1, p. 351. 102 Layard 1849a, vol. 1, p. 341. 103 Layard 1849a, vol. 2, p. 9. 104 *Morning Post*, 3 March 1847. 105 Place 1867, vol. 3, pl. 44. 106 Layard 1849a, vol. 2, p. 81. 107 Layard 1849a, vol. 1, frontispiece. 108 Baqir 1946. 109 Botta 1849–50. 110 Gadd 1936, p. 48. 111 Gadd 1936, p. 48. 112 Campbell-Thompson 1928, p. 41. 113 Layard 1853a, p. 589. 114 Campbell-Thompson 1929, p. 38. 115 Campbell-Thompson 1929, p. 39. 116 Campbell-Thompson 1929, p. 133. 117 Campbell-Thompson 1929, pp. 135–6. 118 See Bache and Speiser 1930–3. 119 Layard 1853a, p. 278. 120 Mentioned in Mallowan 1936. 121 Budge 1925, p. 79. 122 *Journal Asiatique*, vol. VI, p. 548. 123 See Waterfield 1963, pt 3, p. 227ff.

Chapter Ten (pp. 130–143) 124 Budge 1920, p. 232. 125 Loftus 1857/1971. 126 Hilprecht 1903, p. 152. 127 Loftus 1857, p. 260. 128 See Moorey 1971. 129 Place 1867. 130 Loud and Altman 1938. 131 Waterfield 1963, pt 3, pp. 227 ff. 132 Rassam 1897. 133 Mallowan 1956, p. 79. 134 Rassam 1897, p. 24. 135 Gadd 1936, pp. 99–100. 136 Place 1867, p. 101. 137 This is what occurred according to Place's own account. Budge's version in *By Nile and Tigris*, vol. I, p. 170, is apparently erroneous, as is also the date. 138 Place 1867. 139 Gadd 1936, p. 101. 140 Jones 1857. 141 Cf. Ya'qûbi, Ya'qût, Ibn Serapion, etc. 142 Appended to Jones 1857. 143 Chesney 1850.

Chapter Eleven (pp. 144–157) 144 Taylor 1855. 145 Campbell-Thompson 1929, p. 49. 146 Campbell-Thompson 1929, p. 52. 147 Rassam 1897, preface. 148 Layard 1903, vol. 2, p. 238. 149 Waterfield 1963, facing p. 267. 150 Rassam 1897, p. 200. 151 Hilprecht 1903, p. 205. 152 Cf. Budge's castigation of James Henry Breasted (Budge 1925, pp. 143–4). 153 Rassam 1897, pp. 207–8. 154 See also Mallowan 1956, p. 79. 155 Rassam 1897, p. 210, a folio ref. 156 Budge 1925, p. 132. 157 Again see Mallowan 1956, p. 79. 158 Rassam 1897, p. 313. These antiquities were doubtless Neo-Hittite. 159 Rassam 1897, p. 407. 160 Hilprecht 1903, p. 279.

Chapter Twelve (pp. 158–172) 161 Hilprecht 1903, p. 216. 162 Budge 1925, p. 198. 163 Budge 1925, p. 198. 164 Woolley 1935, p. 29. 165 Wells 1942, p. 31. 166 Budge 1925, p. 198. 167 Hilprecht 1903, p. 317. 168 Cf. an early study in Kramer 1944/1961. 169 Budge 1925, p. 202. 170 Budge 1920, vol. 1, p. 126. 171 Budge 1920, vol. 1, facing p. 230. 172 Jones 1857, facing p. 310. 173 Budge 1920, vol. 1, p. 241. 174 Budge 1920, vol. 2, p. 303. 175 Budge 1920, vol. 2, p. 268. 176 Budge 1920, vol. 2, p. 258. 177 Postgate 1977, p. 62.

Chapter Thirteen (pp. 173–193) 178 Koldewey 1914, p. ix. 179 Andrae 1902, *et seq.* 180 Banks 1912. 181 Genouillac 1924–5. 182 Koldewey 1914, preface. 183 Massignon 1910–12. 184 Preusser 1911. 185 Sarre and Herzfeld 1911–20. 186 Musil's publication (1927) is only marred by a grotesque system of transliterating Arabic names. His collection of classical and Arabic references, etc., is immensely useful. 187 Bell 1924, preface. 188 Thompson's soundings were published in the *Journal of the Royal Asiatic Society*, XV, and *Archaeologia*, 70. 189 Woolley 1929, p. 70. 190 Woolley 1934, p. 6. 191 Delougaz 1940, frontispiece. 192 Delougaz 1938.

Chapter Fourteen (pp. 194–209) 193 Safar 1945. 194 *The Times*, 15 June 1944. Lloyd and Safar 1945. 195 Baqir 1959. 196 Jones 1857. 197 Braidwood 1960. 198 Al-Salihi 1973. 199 Mallowan 1966. 200 This plan is reproduced in Postgate 1977, p. 110, top left. 201 Postgate 1977, p. 66. 202 Oates 1968. 203 For the discovery of Tell Rimah see Lloyd 1938. 204 Further details of all these excavations are to be found in a recent work by the present writer (Lloyd 1978).

AINSWORTH, W. F. *Researches in Assyria, Babylonia and Chaldea*, London 1838.
— *A Personal Narrative of the Euphrates Expedition*, 2 vols., London 1888.
ALEXANDER, C. M. *Baghdad in Bygone Days*, London 1928.
ANDRAE, W. *Mitteilungen der Deutsch-Orient-Gesellschaft*, no. 20, Berlin 1902 *et seq.* and *Wissenschaftliche Veröffentlichungen der D.O.G.*, Leipzig and Berlin, nos. 23, 34 and 39.
AL-SALIHI, W. I. 'Hatra', in *Historical Monuments in Iraq*, no. 2, Iraq Directorate-General of Antiquities, Baghdad 1973.
BACHE, C. and SPEISER, E. A. 'Tell Billa', in *Bulletin of the American Schools of Oriental Research*, 1930–33.
BADGER, A. P. *The Nestorians and their Rituals*, 2 vols., London 1852.
BAILLIE-FRASER, J. *Travels in Koordistan, Mesopotamia, etc.*, 2 vols., London 1840.
BANKS, E. J. *Bismaya or the Lost City of Adab*, New York and London 1912.
BAQIR, TAHA 'Aqar Quf', *Iraq*, supplements 1944–5 and vol. 8 (1946).
— *Tell Harmal*, Iraq Directorate-General of Antiquities, Baghdad 1959.
BARNETT, R. D. 'Sir Robert Ker Porter: Regency Artist and Traveller', *Iran*, 10 (1972).
— 'Charles Bellino and the Beginnings of Assyriology', *Iraq*, 36 (1974).
BEAUCHAMP, L'ABBÉ DE *Journal des Sçavarr*, Paris 1791.
BELL, GERTRUDE *Amurath to Amurath*, London 1924.
BRAIDWOOD, R. J. *Prehistoric Investigations in Iraqi Kurdistan*, Studies in Ancient Oriental Civilization, no. 31, Chicago 1960.
BOTTA, P. E. *Monument de Ninive*, Paris 1849–50.
BUCKINGHAM, J. S. *Travels in Mesopotamia*, 2 vols., London 1827.
BUDGE, WALLIS *By Nile and Tigris*, London 1920.
— *The Rise and Progress of Assyriology*, London 1925.
CAMPBELL-THOMPSON, R. *A Century of Exploration at Nineveh*, London 1929.
CHESNEY, F. R. *Expedition for the Survey of the Rivers Euphrates and Tigris*, 2 vols., London 1850.
— *Narrative of the Euphrates Expedition*, London 1868.
COKE, R. *Baghdad City of Peace*, London 1927.
D'ANVILLE *L'Euphrate et le Tigre*, Paris 1779.
DELLA VALLE, PIETRO *Suite des Fameux Voyages de Pietro Della Valle*, 4 vols., Paris 1663.
DELOUGAZ, P. 'A Short Investigation of the Temple at Al'Ubaid', *Iraq*, 5, pt 1 (1938).
— *The Temple Oval at Khafaje*, Oriental Institute Publications, no. 53, Chicago 1940.
ELDRED, J. *The Voyage of Mr John Eldred to Trypolis in Syria by Sea, and from Thence by Land to Babylon and Balsara*, London 1583 (Hakluyt, vol. 6, Glasgow 1904).
FILMER, H. *The Pageant of Persia*, London 1937.
GADD, C. J. *Stones of Assyria*, London 1936.
GENOUILLAC, H. DE *Fouilles Françaises d'El-'Akhymer*, nos. 1 & 2, Paris 1924–25.
GROVES, A. N. *Journal of Mr Anthony N. Groves, Missionary*, London 1831.
HACHETTE (World Guides) *Turkey*, Paris 1960.
HASLIP, J. *Lady Hester Stanhope*, London 1934.
HARRIS, WILSON *Caroline Fox*, London 1944.
HAUKAL, IBN *Liber Imaginis Terrae*, Arabic text edited by J. H. Kramers, 2 vols., Leiden 1938–9.
HILPRECHT, H. V. *Exploration in Bible Lands*, Edinburgh 1903.
— *The Excavations in Assyria and Babylonia*, Philadelphia 1904.

JONES, FELIX *Memoirs of Commander James Felix Jones, I.N.*, 1848 (reprinted in the form of *Selections from the Records of the Bombay Government*, new series, no. 43, Bombay 1857).
KOLDEWEY, R. *The Excavations at Babylon*, London 1914.
KRAMER, S. N. *Sumerian Mythology*, Philadelphia 1944 (rev. edn, 1961).
LAYARD, A. H. *Nineveh and its Remains*, 2 vols., London 1849a.
— *The Monuments of Nineveh*, 5 vols., 1849b.
— *Discoveries in the Ruins of Nineveh and Babylon*, London 1853a.
— *The Monuments of Nineveh*, second series, London 1853b.
— *Early Adventures in Persia, Susiana and Babylonia*, London 1887.
— *Autobiography and Letters*, 2 vols., London 1903.
LLOYD, SETON *Mesopotamia: Excavations on Sumerian Sites*, London 1936.
— 'Some Ancient Sites in the Sinjar District', *Iraq*, 5 (1938).
— *The Archaeology of Mesopotamia*, London 1978.
LLOYD, S. AND SAFAR, F. 'Tell 'Uqair: Excavations by the Iraq Directorate-General of Antiquities in 1940–41', *Journal of Near Eastern Studies*, 2 (1943).
— 'Tell Hassuna: Excavations by the Iraq Directorate-General of Antiquities, 1943–44', *Journal of Near Eastern Studies*, 4 (1945).
LOFTUS, W. K. *Travels and Researches in Chaldaea and Susiana*, London 1857 (reprinted 1971).
LONGRIGG, S. H. *Four Centuries of Modern Iraq*, Oxford 1925.
LOUD, GORDON *Khorsabad*, vol. 1, Oriental Institute Publications no. 38, Chicago 1936.
LOUD, G. AND ALTMAN, C. B. *Khorsabad*, vol. 2, Oriental Institute Publications no. 40, Chicago 1938.
MALLOWAN, M. E. L. 'Archaeological Survey of the Habur Region of North Syria', *Iraq*, 3 (1936).
— *Twenty-five Years of Mesopotamian Discovery*, London 1956.
— *Nimrud and its Remains*, 3 vols., Aberdeen 1966.
MASSIGNON, L. *Mission en Mesopotamie*, 2 vols., Cairo 1910–12.
MITFORD, E. L. *A Land-March from England to Ceylon*, London 1884.
MOOREY, P. R. S. 'Babylonian Tools from Tell Sifr', *Iraq*, 33, pt 2 (1971).
MUSIL, A. *The Middle Euphrates*, New York 1927.
NIEBUHR, K. *Voyage en Arabie*, Amsterdam 1776.
OATES, D. *Studies in the Ancient History of Northern Iraq*, London 1968.
OATES, D. AND J. *The Rise of Civilization*, Oxford and New York 1976.
OTTER, JEAN *Voyage en Turquie et en Perse*, Paris 1748.
PLACE, V. *Ninive et l'Assyrie*, 3 vols., Paris 1867.
PORTER, R. KER *Travels in Georgia, Persia, Armenia, Ancient Babylonia etc.*, 2 vols., London 1822.
POSTGATE, N. *The First Empires*, Oxford and New York 1977.
PREUSSER, C. *Nordmesopotamische Baukenmäler Altchristlischer und Islamischer Zeit*, Leipzig 1911.
RASSAM, H. *Asshur and the Land of Nimrod*, New York 1897.
RATISBON, PETHAHIAH OF *Travels*, translated by Benisch, London 1861.
RAUWOLFF, LEONHART in *A Collection of Curious Voyages and Travels*, 12 vols., by John Ray, London 1693.
RAWLINSON, GEORGE *Memoir of Major-General Sir Henry Creswicke Rawlinson*, London 1898.
RICH, C. J. *Narrative of a Residence in Koordistan by the Late Claudius James Rich Esquire*, edited by his widow, 2 vols., London 1836.
— *Narrative of a Journey to the Site of Babylon*, London 1839.

RICHARDSON, HENRY *The Loss of the Tigris: A Poem*, London 1840.

ROSS, H. J. *Letters from the East 1837–1857*, London 1902.

SAFAR, FUAD *Wasit: the Sixth Season's Excavations*, Iraq Directorate-General of Antiquities, Baghdad 1945.

SARRE, F. AND HERZFELD, E. *Archäologische Reise im Euphrat- und Tigris-Gebiet*, 4 vols., Berlin 1911–20.

SEGAL, J. B. *Edessa: 'The Blessed City'*, Oxford 1970.

SHIRLEY, SIR ANTHONY *Narrative of Travels in Persia*, London 1613.

SIENNA, VINCENZO MARIA DI S. CATERINA DI *Il Viaggi all Indie Orientali*, Venice 1683.

SOANE, E. B. *To Mesopotamia and Kurdistan in Disguise*, London 1912.

SYKES, SIR MARK *The Caliph's Last Heritage*, London 1915.

TUDELA, BENJAMIN OF *The Itinerary of Benjamin of Tudela* (translated by M. N. Adler, London 1907).

TAVERNIER *The Six Voyages of Tavernier through Turkey into Asia*, London 1678.

TAYLOR, J. E. 'Notes on Abu Shahrein and Tell-el-Lahm', *Journal of the Royal Asiatic Soc.* (1855), pp. 404–12.

WATERFIELD, GORDON *Layard of Nineveh*, London 1963.

WELLS, H. G. *Phoenix*, London 1942.

WIGRAM, W. A. AND T. A. *The Cradle of Mankind*, London 1914.

WOOLLEY, C. L. *Ur of the Chaldees*, London 1929.

— *Ur Excavations*, vol. 2, *The Royal Cemetery*, London and Philadelphia 1934.

— *The Development of Sumerian Art*, London 1935.

Index